Stuck Moving

OR, HOW I LEARNED TO LOVE
(AND LAMENT) ANTHROPOLOGY

ATELIER: ETHNOGRAPHIC INQUIRY IN THE TWENTY-FIRST CENTURY

Kevin Lewis O'Neill, Series Editor

Stuck Moving

OR, HOW I LEARNED TO LOVE
(AND LAMENT) ANTHROPOLOGY

Peter Benson

UNIVERSITY OF CALIFORNIA PRESS

University of California Press
Oakland, California

Detailed copyright information for rights holders who provided
permission for use can be found in this book's Credits section.

Library of Congress Cataloging-in-Publication Data

Names: Benson, Peter, 1979- author.
Title: Stuck moving : or, how I learned to love (and lament) anthropology /
    Peter Benson.
Other titles: Atelier (Oakland, Calif.) ; 9.
Description: Oakland,California : University of California Press, [2023] |
    Includes bibliographical references and index.
Identifiers: LCCN 2022030883 (print) | LCCN 2022030884 (ebook) |
    ISBN 9780520388734 (cloth) | ISBN 9780520388741 (paperback) |
    ISBN 9780520388758 (ebook)
Subjects: LCSH: Benson, Peter, 1979- | Anthropologists—Biography. |
    Emotions—Anthropological aspects. | Conduct of life.
Classification: LCC GN21.B458 A3 2023 (print) | LCC GN21.B458
    (ebook) | DDC 301.092—dc23/eng/20220804
LC record available at https://lccn.loc.gov/2022030883
LC ebook record available at https://lccn.loc.gov/2022030884

32   31   30   29   28   27   26   25   24   23
10   9   8   7   6   5   4   3   2   1

For Kedron

Contents

List of Figures

Acknowledgments

Thanks to Mom and Dad for raising and shaping me, filling my life with culture and history, and, most recently, trashing an early draft of this book—a healthy airing. A dispute about this book's depiction of my childhood and our life together. In writing this book, I thought I was getting away from anthropology. But it turns out I was learning the back-and-forth of sharing viewpoints and perspectives with people I am writing about. Something I didn't do in my previous work. Thanks for always being there and for being such loving, committed parents and grandparents. I love you guys.

Thanks to the tobacco farmers whose criticism of my earlier work pushed me to reassess my relationship to anthropology and develop a different approach.

Thanks to Sherri Harris and Mary DuParri, the therapists with whom I worked over the course of this project.

Thanks to the Shalvah community for helping me switch gears and become a different person.

Thanks to the support of many undergraduate students at Washington University in St. Louis who worked as research assistants on this project.

Thanks to my colleagues at the University of Delaware for their intellectual support and engagement.

Thanks to Carolyn Barnes for valuable comments on early drafts and for providing meaningful social and moral support throughout the writing process.

Thanks to other friends and colleagues who gave me encouragement and support, offered feedback on the project, and/or commented on parts of the manuscript, including Chloe Ahmann, Jean Allman, Fred Appel, Ruth Behar, Lindsay Bell, Shefali Chandra, Talia Dan-Cohen, Jason De León, Kate Dudley, Andrea Friedman, Ted Fischer, Lisa Gezon, Danielle Giffort, Ann Kingsolver, Stuart Kirsch, Arthur Kleinman, Kate Mariner, Jeffrey McCune Jr., Jason Pine, Court Rosen, and Katrina Daly Thompson.

Thanks to Kate Marshall, acquisitions editor at University of California Press, and Kevin O'Neill, the series editor, for affirming and supporting this experiment and, over many stages, sharing crucial insights on method and framing. Thanks to Enrique Ochoa-Kaup, Chad Attenborough, and Francisco Reinking, also at University of California Press. Thanks to other authors in the Atelier book series who critically and constructively engaged this work in the mode of peer review, namely Darcie DeAngelo, Anthony Fontes, Erica James, and Emrah Yildiz. Thanks to Susan Lepselter and John Modern, the book's peer reviewers, as well as one anonymous reviewer.

Thanks to the many people who assisted me in the manic process of acquiring the rights to reproduce copyrighted material. Apart from the permissions noted on the credits page, I received permissions from Sara Ahmed, Homi Bhabha, Ted Conover, and Kirk West as well as the American Anthropological Association, Berghahn Books, Bloomsbury Publishing, Broadway Video, Detour Filmproduction, Duke University Press, Duquesne University Press, Éditions Fata Morgana, Éditions Gallimard, Indiana University Press, HarperCollins Publishers, Macmillan Publishers, Metro-Goldwyn-Mayer Studios, *Mosaic: An Interdisciplinary Critical Journal*, Paramount Pictures, Penguin Random House, Princeton University Press, Reservoir Media Management, Simon & Schuster, State University of New York Press, University of Chicago Press, University of Minnesota Press, Verso Books, W. W. Norton & Company, and *Yankee Magazine*.

Thanks to Katie Zdybel for editorial work across several drafts. Thanks to Heather Tekavec for proofreading and assistance with the bibliography. Thanks to Mary Reid and Kara Aisenbrey for additional proofreading.

Thanks to Erica Olsen for copyediting. Thanks to Do Mi Stauber for indexing. I'm grateful to each of these individuals for amazing and supportive work that improved the quality of this book.

Thanks to Beto for hospitality and friendship in North Carolina.

Thanks to the love of family on Kedron's side and my side and in Guatemala.

Thanks to Manny and Henry for being a part of this cheddar project and making the little life so vital and compelling. Thanks to Kedron Thomas. Thanks for being such a wonderful person. Thanks for loving and taking care of me and our family in so many ways. And thanks for reading multiple drafts of this manuscript, providing extensive comments and analysis, and supporting the publication of a deeply personal book about our life.

Author's Note

This book is unconventional. A self-conscious experiment in form that draws together two vernaculars: anthropological thought and the pop culture of my youth. It is a fraught exercise. I write as a white guy about angst and alienation in the privileged spaces of anthropology and higher education. I appreciate the irony. I hope, nonetheless, that my experiences with and critical perspectives on the culture of academia might be useful. I seek to expand possibilities of anthropological representation while challenging epistemological, aesthetic, and professional norms in my discipline. It bothers me that anthropology can be so sanctimonious. I take aim at the ableist conceit that anthropologists are noncharacters or outside observers studying a messy world—professionals with no backstage or blooper reel. We write other people as contextual and cultural characters, often in close-ups. But we are disciplined to construct and position ourselves as analytical, authoritative, diagnostic, and rational. Much of my life has been a mess. My work has been undertaken amid struggles with pregnancy loss, bipolar disorder, and drug addiction. I have deep regrets about my participation in an exploitative field. I have deep regrets about many things. I have hurt people and been hurt by people. I hope my stories and reflections add to what others have already written about a more open, honest, and self-deprecating anthropology.

I am currently a professor at the University of Delaware. I wrote this book when I was an associate professor at Washington University in St. Louis. That environment—living in the middle of the country and working at an elite, private research university—is the book's setting.

1 Sixteen Candles

Stoned, sitting on the couch, glass pipe and a bag of weed on the wooden coffee table in the cozy, second-floor living room where an original Italian marketing poster for *Vertigo* hangs on the wall ("nel capolavoro di Alfred Hitchcock"),[1] an orange poster with the film's iconic hermeneutical spiral advertisement image,[2] a shabby, graduate-school-days table brought from Boston, which is very much unlike our glorious, half-million-dollar, three-story, five-bedroom house of three thousand square feet (plus the plot) of the St. Louis metropolitan area, land that used to be part of the Louisiana Territory and before that the Mississippian culture, and that is now ours, purchased with the salaries of two professors, college sweethearts caught committed in a relationship that at so many junctures spiraled, the haunting and sentimental Jeff Buckley song "Last Goodbye" playing for years in the background.[3] Two people bonded by some glue—if only the experience of having weathered so much shit together—who, like everyone, get stuck and keep moving, stuck moving, working life in fits and starts, keeping

---

1. Hitchcock, *Vertigo*.
2. Belton, *Alfred Hitchcock's* Vertigo *and the Hermeneutic Spiral*.
3. Buckley, "Last Goodbye."

things from crumbling in a nowhere-near-crumbling 1910s house paid for by financial aid recipients from families where there are few college degrees. Two people who met in the underneath of Vanderbilt Hall in the late nineties and smoked cigarettes on the dorm's patio, looking across West End Avenue, where there used to be a Tower Records, when CDs were a thing, when this conjugation became a thing, two people with different geographical and cultural backgrounds who have a biblical upbringing in common and who, upon arrival at move-in-goodbye-go weekend, wanted bodies bad and felt shame and necessity,[4] freedom and shame, and who, through patches, stuck it out, marrying one year after reaching the legal drinking age, probably just to sanctify the situation, and who have a framed print of a drawing by a popular American artist hanging on a wall downstairs, a wedding gift from a classmate, one of the bridesmaids, with the epigram "I saw them standing there pretending to be just friends, when all the time in the world could not pry them apart." Two people who are not the offspring of academic or otherwise knowledge-economy families, who went to graduate school at the world's greatest university and went through hell there, and the hell didn't end there ("Forever, forever ever? Forever, ever"),[5] two people who joined the professoriate and, unlike most of their colleagues, were repaying student loans decades beyond the dorm room nights. I'm stoned, on the couch, home alone,[6] stuck in the upstairs playroom of adolescence, kicking and screaming,[7] rapturously, exhaustingly snatched in fun and games, obsessed with endless war and film art, war movies, all kinds of movies, an embarrassment of shelves, everything in its right place,[8] staying up "very, very, very, very late,"[9] more than a decade beyond the dorm, tenured, cushioned, having made a career writing hypercritical, ventilating scholarly publications about societal hypocrisies and industrial harms and winning professional awards, all the while amassing heaping personal wreckage in my own life and hurting people, assholing my way through graduate school and after-

4. Williams, *Shame and Necessity.*
5. Outkast, "Ms. Jackson."
6. Columbus, *Home Alone.*
7. Baumbach, *Kicking and Screaming.*
8. Radiohead, "Everything in Its Right Place."
9. Counting Crows, "Round Here."

ward, hurting my sweetheart of the rodeo,[10] who had a poster in her dorm room that read, "Buck Mills Berry Me," and a sweet refrain, saying, "I have a tender heart and a gentle spirit," and hurting a good man, wielding ethnography in ways that hurt a really good man who felt like a father to me, shitting all over affections and relationships. I sink into the leather, lagging and lost, failing at a version of life, reaching fort-da, back and forth for my pipe, blazing on repeat, flat looping, going nowhere, a not-contributing slouch of a schlub, not seen for years in the lobbies of the Hyatts and Hiltons, absent from the scene conversation hubbub buzz of the anthropological voice, professionally, sociologically, and biochemically stuck.[11]

The Sitch

It was on that couch, and in those days, that I checked out an experimental film made at the height of the war.[12] Its lack of direction and abrasive, improvisational violences and appalling brutishness were challenging and hard to appreciate. No coherent or compelling plot, except a vague theme of breakdown. Widely acclaimed as "an essential piece of the canon of 1960s American independent cinema," it is revered for innovative cinema verité methods, postmodern blurrings of fiction and documentary, and maniacal obsessions with conspiracy and revolution.[13] The director characterized the filmmaking process as a blended experience of "a circus, a military campaign, a nightmare, an orgy, and a high."[14] And, well, these nouns happened to fit my own sitch. Purposeless pot plot. Problematic lack of structure and agency. Penchant for polemics.

And now. No longer drinking or doing drugs, one might or might not say sober, contending with past and persistent wrongdoings and deficiencies, undertaking artistries and productivities after ethnography, I have put that dreadful movie in my desert island trunk, and I want to make my own.

---

10. The Byrds, *Sweetheart of the Rodeo*.
11. Fischer, *Emergent Forms of Life and the Anthropological Voice*.
12. Mailer, *Maidstone*.
13. Guest, "Norman Mailer Collection."
14. Norman Mailer, quoted in Goodell, *Independent Feature Film Production*, 389.

I am inspired by its use of fragments and fleeting images, its embrace of an aesthetics of incompleteness, failure, and the unvarnished okayness of being not great, and how these features might lend themselves to an anthropology that unhides the illiberal real lives of anthropologist selves. Approaches that further trouble the construction of the anthropologist as an exemplary professional with indubitable knowledge, territory, and psyche.[15] Approaches that continue to challenge genre conventions in materials and styles of self-experience, self-expression, and writerly personality as much as the aboutness of population- and field-based projects that inevitably take on the terms of "the them, the there."

But let's be honest. Mine is not the navel that everyone wants to be gazing at. (Mostly) straight. Male. Tenured. At an elite institution. Here I am at the fountain. Periodic trips from the swivel to the Student Center for the salad bar and soda machine. Large screens beam. Ethos of exploration. Mission statements. My mission is to go out there and get them. It's been like this since North Carolina. Every year for a decade, my editor has called me to check in. I've fabled hypothetical field sites and project framings. A new one each year, it seems. The shame of the second book. And a self—stuck in the first one.

"Sure thing, shooters out in Chesterfield and suburban settler identity."

"Or, um, I like sports. I can write about what's happening in sports."

"No?"

"Yes, right, of course, I'm an anthropologist. The field. The voices. Vignettes."

"Okay, then. I'm gonna interview parents about concussions. Get the gritty perspectives. I'll land a big grant and fly around the country for peewee games. How does that sound?"

Because the normal trajectory is to move on to the second book. To steadily keep researching and publishing. But I didn't do that. Mental breakdown and substance abuse stalled my career. And now. In contending with an ethnography hangover and ill health, I'm writing about those very topics.

Because let's be honest. Everybody's dealing with shit, and it's difficult to talk about. Academia is replete with mental illness, unhappiness, and

15. Durban, "Anthropology and Ableism."

anguish: graduate school, funding and grants, writing all the time, having a life, the job market . . . And everybody must write in the constraining "an ethnography of" genre for access to jobs and promotion. And those books take forever to write. And they are not pleasurable to read or write. We cannibalize other people's lives in producing insular and technical knowledge products for a paywall purgatory, and we cannibalize each other in a constricted job market.[16] We're stuck forever reasserting the indispensability of a curious thing that—it's at the same time acknowledged—should burn.[17] It's comical to want to destroy your livelihood; it's also a veritable, genuine moment. I can't let anthropology burn . . . because I fell in love with it a long time ago. And because salary, health care, commitments, relationships, and retirement savings. I'm attached to "it." I suspect all anthropologists have stories of love and lament that make this endeavor a monument, a work of mourning, and a marriage of plain old dirty laundry.[18]

I'm in the privileged position of being able to tarry with nonrespectability more easily than others. I feel able to say these things and experiment with form and conception. I came out of grad school before the economic crises and pandemic. I benefited from a market of abundant jobs. I wrote in the abiding colonial genre for my tenure book. I've made a living according to an absurd premise of higher-education hoping: that further empowering and credentialing relatively privileged people within a system designed to unequally deliver advantages could undo foundational social structures.[19] A discipline dedicated to making suffering, the abject, and cultural otherness available for upstanding liberal future citizens to consume.[20] The reproduction of a profession, a class hierarchy, and society.

tl;dr

This is a book about a recovering drug addict and recovering anthropologist who feels jammed, stuck in the middle (Middle America, middle age,

---

16. Jobson, "The Case for Letting Anthropology Burn."
17. Ibid.
18. Derrida, *The Work of Mourning*.
19. Bourdieu and Passeron, *Reproduction in Education, Society and Culture*.
20. Robbins, "Beyond the Suffering Subject"; Trouillot, *Global Transformations*.

midcareer, mediocrity, meaninglessness). The lens of analysis is reversed to expose the backstage of a life in anthropology, the messy, unbecoming self behind scholarship, the fraught dynamics of being professional and institutional. The resulting untidy, grunge anthropology—raw, emotional, ironical, introspective, angry, jaded, distorted—turns out to be a source of both critical engagement with the discipline and personal catharsis for a despondent main character.

Spheres of personal formation—anthropology, higher education, family, religion, the military, sports, popular culture—have fed into and supported pleasures, fulfillments, definition, and belonging for straight man. They have also been sources of confusion, disheartenment, indignation, and alienation. In the mode of "affect-inflected" anthropology,[21] this saga about straight man as unfinishedness roams around sites of experience, metamorphosis, and writing.[22] Love and lament in life—and specifically in anthropology. A kind of real-life campus novel that takes on anthropology's function as a culture resource for global health and the neoliberal university and unsettles the discipline's hopeful claims about its own role in social change. A long-form curriculum vitae chronicling hopelessness not as epic narrative, but in the disarray and fraying of the little life, in stuckness and minor moves. What Donna Haraway calls "modest possibilities of partial recuperation."[23] The "little narrative."[24] Wild strawberries.[25] ("The deep, satisfied smile of a man who just now understands the punchline of a joke he heard long ago.")[26]

about a boy[27]

fits and starts since the semester's start. here i am in my swivel with the old radiator. i turn the room's heat on and off on the hour to keep the temp right there, right there. right where it's a dance with the antiquated interior of the old dorm in a swivel chair. two computer monitors for bragging

---

21. Stewart, "In the World That Affect Proposed," 195.
22. Biehl and Locke, *Unfinished.*
23. Haraway, *Staying with the Trouble*, 10.
24. Lyotard, *The Postmodern Condition*, 60.
25. Bergman, *Wild Strawberries.*
26. Ball, *American Beauty*, 96.
27. Hornby, *About a Boy.*

purposes. my treasured matted and framed print of the famous portrait of composer philip glass by the painter chuck close from an early eighties whitney museum exhibition hangs above the nonfunctioning fireplace. textiles on all sides of my office. two table runners. one on top of the other. both from sololá. and here i am in my swivel. this is meaningful and vulnerable for me. intimates. hurts. illness. hardships. making do. coming thru. man, this boy's beautiful.

the playlist i made this morning for writing. i call it "sixteen candles."[28]

1. "these are days"—10,000 maniacs
2. "fast car"—tracy chapman
3. "the only living boy in new york"—simon & garfunkel
4. "you only live once"—the strokes
5. "given to fly"—pearl jam
6. "gloria"—patti smith
7. "pocahontas"—neil young & crazy horse
8. "don't let me down"—the beatles
9. "corduroy"—pearl jam
10. "orange crush"—r.e.m.
11. "the scientist"—coldplay
12. "new york, new york"—ryan adams
13. "story of my life"—one direction
14. "all night"—beyoncé
15. "lovehappy"—the carters
16. "bitter sweet symphony"—the verve[29]

just turned the knob on the radiator. i'm looking at phil. years ago, when i wrote, i listened to him a lot. the score for *the fog of war*.[30] if i had not been stoned the whole time, that mind-numbing classical music minimalism would have been unbearable.

---

28. Hughes, *Sixteen Candles*.
29. See the bibliography for references for the songs in this playlist.
30. Glass, *The Fog of War (A Film by Errol Morris)*; Morris, *The Fog of War*.

1. Peter at Lake Atitlán, Guatemala, 2004. Photograph by Kedron Thomas.

who knew that not a single word of this movie would be written under the influence of a substance other than oat milk? and who knew it would be a mixtape about—what else—love?

deep adores. oh, i pour. sometimes like never before. feels so swell. falling into a pile of autumn leaves. trusting and carefree. like a good hug. a warm bundle stroll. a meander back to where i more moved into me-ness. me before the damns and declension and disease and debilities. me before the profit-driven enrollments and celebrity and all the stupid anthropology. a boy undone and remade at the lake and on bus rides and around hearths and in palabras and over chiltepe. my love-tumble into an angry anthropology of guatemala.

a book about a boy. vulnerabilities. irregularities. indiscretions. honest indignation. expansive mood spectrum. uncomfortable in the university club. they don't know anything about me. i'm a lithium script. i have a humoral system, and i admit it. read all about it.

what's it like to be a scholar marked by brilliance and acumen and clinical disorder and disease? what's it like to be a first-generation college graduate and achieve acclaim in institutional and professional environments that feel alienating and exploitative? and despite discomforts about mundanity and the ordinary, to find respite from the estrangement of work life in the safety and affection of a nucleated family paradigm?

two pells going to hell. felt free. bees. omg. clicked. fitting. grooves. keys. practically lived together. practically married. pearl jam. r.e.m. alternative everything. lisa loeb. counting crows. can't even mention 'em now without eye rolls. she doc martens. flannels. grunge, esta chica. and que bonita. accessories. cigarettes. clinton the president. indie movies. gender studies. gramsci. more and more theory. flirtations. cd collections. kinship connection. me bridesmaid. never the bride. sometimes she cried. hanging out. getting to know everything about. lying on far sides. twin bed. i liked her name. never encountered one before. or again.

that spring semester. she returned from a weekend trip with friends. rushed to my room. stood me up from my chair. (always there.) my swivel where i was reading and listening to music. (my two things.) we didn't know what was going on because this was finally true. we both knew.

and then. from the dorm to the corner where the b, c, and d lines connect. bush bombing "the them, the there." butler putting out a book a year. we marched against the war. guatemala summers. ezln poster. couple. anti-couple. academic scenesters. sartre and de beauvoir. les deux magots. more and more foucault. complete mess. we didn't know. how to inhabit marriage and be against it. it's complicated. the mess wasn't pure recklessness. infelicitous. going steady, not ready.[31] difficult conjuncture, however in love with each other.

i want to be known better. who i am. fries. hard cries. not knowing that grandpa died. how to reside. how to be me. hurting she. the weathering and the storms. the fucking norms. pain and regret. damns and connects. the best friendship on the planet.

food: french fries (by far)
next: pete eats beets

31. Jay-Z, "4:44."

drink: diet coke

liar!: laphroaig 10 year and a bud light

car: manny's hand-me-down

song, her and him: "harvest moon," neil young

song, just him: "stardust," hoagy carmichael

version: nat king cole (omg)

foreign: godard

domestic: van sant (maybe)

crush: river phoenix

best friend: eddie vedder

day: 5-14-96

month: october

why?: baseball playoffs + birthday + connecticut colors

sport, to play: none

sport, to watch: whatever the kids want (maybe)

exercise: none

wow, so cool!: okay. the elliptical. half an hour per day

place: my couch

seriously: the coffee shop on campus

no, seriously: the couch at the coffee shop on campus

dude, for reals: preschool parking lot, 3-2-15 (birthday)

moment: standing with my overweight mom atop the hard climb of temple iv at tikal

space-time: guate, pre-9/11 summer, coldplay's album debut[32]

thesis: man, this boy's beautiful

it's a statement. that i could be gay. i'm not. but that i could be, and it'd be okay. i grew up believing it wasn't okay. i think about my sons. it makes me: upset. tired. pissed. write. protective and supportive. thinking about that whole affirmation. ("whatever the mess you are, you're mine, okay")[33]

32. See the bibliography for references for the songs and album in this list.
33. The New Pornographers, "Challengers."

that. how i've felt overwritten and underdescribed. convoluted inside. alienated in what i'm called and supposed to be. not like i've got some grand alternative identity. but believe you me, maybe like everybody. deficiency. irresolution. blurred genres. a boy who is like his writing. an art project.

(¡córrase canchito!)

okay, the moral of the story.

boyish boy meets boyish girl. relates. dates. soulmates. innates. they went and fell in love, and there's an end of peace and fun, and cozy times together.[34]

methods

("m-c-m, the transformation of money into commodities, and the change of commodities back again into money; or buying in order to sell.")[35]

research funds + amazon.com + travelocity.com + (literal, not personal) baggage + food/lodging + fuel + ~~deep hanging out~~ fieldwork + ~~information from other people's lives~~ data = #culturalcommodity #knowledgeeconomy #anthropology @amazon.com.

there's this group of people who have it all figured out. compared to earlier generations of civilization custodians, these humanity shepherds, they're finally on the right track. watch 'em trait affiliate. a yay culture of celebratory extractivism. ethics aboveness. apartness admirability. buzzword burnishings. and it's funny because this discipline about the historical and social contexts, life conditions, subjective lives, and inner worlds of other people—i mean, tbh—it's a lot lodged in assumptions about the superiority of a certain kind of society. advanced seriousness. rigidifying self-nutshelling (i'm thinking deleuze). secularized spiritual reformations and the role of schools and institutions. and the better-than belief in a rational knowing and conforming sapient homo. none of that shit-stinking complicity, deviance realism, and conditional messiness of monkeying around. because where would anthropology be— etymologically, alphabetically, institutionally, and self-importantly—with

34. Alcott, *Little Women*, 183.
35. Marx, *Capital*, 146.

the plain acknowledgment that we have never been human?[36] admitting is the first step.

this discipline about the historical and social contexts, life conditions, subjective lives, and inner worlds of other people—i mean, tbh—it a lot upholds a model of a coherent, reasoned, and procreative liberal self.[37] the colonial view of overdetermining structures and contexts of the cultures over nyah and isolations of agency over hyah. scholars of superior intelligence and morality, made so by anthropology, who have transcended culture and society, the determinants that explain and attest to everyone else's peculiarity. such abnormality obsessions among the normals and morals. it's as if . . . as if the purpose of fieldwork fort-da-ing ("i did it!")[38] and difference them-there diagramming is a productive ableist selving practice. this homo erectus thing of being presumptively toward, developmentally mored. membering in a compassion enterprise where everything is rigorous but way vaguely scored and all about hitting the right chords and having a travel itinerary and being onboard without infelicitously deploying the word "explored" and hauling information and analysis for vitae lines, for more.

man, my book is throwing shade. but hey, we're all made. let's talk about it. just not at the hyatts and hiltons. or a bar.

a book about man. so said straight man. white man. unbearably white.[39] i'm wondering if it's okay for him to, say, get into issues of adolescence, masculinity, and intimacy without delving into gender studies. to talk about race and class without much critical theory. to make all sorts of assumptions. no profound reflection on structured eases. this book of lyricism and bad poetry, clang associations of bipolar disease and rampant cultural appropriation and wild citation. no problematizing lits or interrogating anything about any of this dumb shit. because i'm not crazy about how academic books distance and depersonalize. marshal so-called "literatures" to establish sexy-smart signification for selves that supposedly aren't falling apart and literary works in themselves. how books hide an offstage of afraid. pretensions and public secrets. difficulty and despair

36. Latour, *We Have Never Been Modern*.
37. Durban, "Anthropology and Ableism."
38. Baudrillard, *America*, 20.
39. Vampire Weekend, "Unbearably White."

that even a tenured professor, in the ivory tower, feels up here. not fitting in and wanting to stand out. i wanna be somebody else. a more angular face. feeling like this is all a marketplace. and so. this is a story about how the neoliberal university's goal to credential and entertain has crushed my soul and driven me insane. a book about a professor who complains and invites you into his brain.

oh, for the love of anthropology! such a weird practice. strangelove.[40] livelihoods based on intimately entering and exploiting the raw lives of strangers for academic production and lifestyle consumption. ethnography as predation perhaps.[41] and even though intimacy is the basis of the expropriation activities, apart from talk of reflexivity and positioning as part of a knowing process, there isn't much personal about the anthropologists themselves in the annals (their favorite foods, the music that soundtracks their writing, or the messy personal relationships that background and shape it). all kinds of shit about the field and the field and social fields. the stuff of juicy diaries and the underneath of rugs. the non-manual laborers scholars accumulate alterity capital on recording devices and word processors for liveness enframings "an ethnography of." an uptight and debilitating argumentation mode on which careers and a science depend. local contexts. thumbtacks on maps. a contest, and way way about judgment. the at-all-costs avoidance of anything (scare quotes) problematic. the refrains of "decolonize" amid continuous field site extractions for more emancipatory inscriptions and canonizations of modernity contradictions. diagnoses. the graph-ing of ethnos-es. overseas (e.g., the balinese).[42] or even down the street. analyses. validation of scientific expertise. become a player in the anthropology of this or that disease. a boon for the board of trustees. ("damn y'all really finna turn 'decolonize' into the next 'intersectional,' huh? how tf you decolonize something that is inherently driven by and thrives off of colonialism?")[43]

ik, right? poor me. here i am at the fountain. diet coke. the pressure of beaming television screens. the pressure from my editor. the pressure from my discipline.

40. Kubrick, *Dr. Strangelove or: How I Learned to Stop Worrying and Love the Bomb.*
41. O'Neill, *Hunted.*
42. Geertz, *The Interpretation of Cultures.*
43. @Satirony, Twitter, October 26, 2019, 11:49 a.m., 12:50 p.m.

maybe i'll do to myself what i did to them—the tobacco growers in north carolina. make a portrait and put myself in a frame. on the books. lots of behind-the-scenes footage! an intensely personal, art anthropology. my living room. my museum.[44]

peter benson, despite himself, is bigger than ever.[45]

i'm saying things that anthropologists talk about when we're off script. not in manuscripts. maybe on some fellowship. hyatts and hiltons. but i'm saying things out in the open.[46] all kinds of shit about the field and the field and social fields. because in the relativism discipline, there are strong opinions about norms and superior forms that we carry and hold. ambivalence and complicity stories need to be told. something else for artistries that don't fit the "an ethnography of" mold.

he never knew he'd be an anthropologist someday. wanted an excuse to get away. and, like, he's arrived, and got this good alive, and yet, so much feels like a bunch of lies—like a pained sales pitch for pretext purposes and institutional revenues, and a way to get health care while talking class warfare and measuring reputations in airfare.

ik, right? poor me. in a brick house, still throwing brickbats.[47] this square. look at these eyes and look at this hair. look how fair. i speak suburban and have a dimple. this baby face is shorn, and this cut is simple. but hey, i'm a lot like the kids. the students have ambitions just like this.[48] i went to the schools and took the vows and ended up hospitalized and addicted to drugs, and i'm angry about how life and work is. arrays of privilege, yes. but i would be remiss. the "complex darkness" . . . the "terrible reserves of repressed fears and angers" related to mental illness.[49] the inability to disclose disability—even or especially in the university. the fear of stigma about a supposedly compromised mentality. the specters of madness, of foolishness, of "a less than fully rational person,"[50] someone with "cracks or flaws" who is "out of the ordinary, distracted with desire

44. Taussig, *My Cocaine Museum.*
45. Holmes, "Kanye West, despite Himself, Is Bigger than Ever."
46. Eminem, "The Real Slim Shady."
47. The Carters, "LoveHappy."
48. Eminem, "White America."
49. Martin, *Bipolar Expeditions,* xvii.
50. Ibid.

and excitement, and passionately preoccupied," which is to say, "crazy."[51] the air of preening collegiality. you've got spunk, creativity, oddness, and sensations, and wherever you go, you're shunned for destabilizing the norms of social formations. despite pedigree and accumulated wealth, and happiness and health, every week you've got a seat at a table at a meeting where they're talking about step twelve. and maybe we have little in common. we come from different places and have different lives. but maybe it's in vulnerability that we're nearest. i have more than a few, like everyone else, too, warts and all, and fatal flaws, and i hold them dear as some sort of "ness." i'm scared that myself, in sickness and susceptibility, is never gonna be okay. i'm scared of what other people might say. i want to do a good job. i want to be worth, and i'm feeling all the time stuckness in forever setting forth.[52] so little has gone as planned. it doesn't feel like a journey. it feels like me. an authenticity of hards and knots and a lot, despite privileges of identities and money and an anthropology-building key.

Letters and Lyrics

A book that is not a simple question of fiction or nonfiction. Experimental anthropology composed as a stylized construct "like novels [. . . that] stick to reality,"[53] a reality-based book that reflects a blend of documentary and imaginative forms.[54] There are sixteen candles. Sixteen letters, "a litter," about a "plurality of subjects," an "inmixing of subjects," to quote Jacques Lacan.[55] A professor grapples with drug addiction, mental illness, fraught intimacies and domesticities, professional conflicts and concerns, meanings of failure and success, and the regrets of a life. This is also a book about nothing, like the classic sitcom *Seinfeld,* looking at frustrations, annoyances, and idiocies of American life and, especially, the domain of higher education.[56]

---

51. Ibid., xix.
52. Vedder, "Setting Forth."
53. Fischer, *Anthropology in the Meantime,* 7.
54. Wolfe and Johnson, *The New Journalism.*
55. Lacan, "Seminar on 'The Purloined Letter,'" 10, 18.
56. Pierson, "A Show about Nothing."

This book, this spiel, abounds with escapisms and nostalgias of popular culture from my decade, "the low I love,"[57] some spectrum of mass culture and pastiche society, a particularizing situatedness. This book is also permeated with references and resonances from other wartimes. Jerry (Garcia, not Seinfeld) died in '95. I'm rummaging thru heaps and hoards collected and consumed during decades. (Cue "Mr. Jones" by Counting Crows.)[58] A run-on yearbook entry of glimpses, insides, codes, clasps, ratchets, delicates, acknowledgments. Scouring stores, boxes, box stores, embarrassment shelves, footage, square footage. Getting lost in tangents, detours, cul-de-sacs, and rabbit holes. This book casts a sentimental wannabe who came of age consuming jam-band eccentricities and whimsicalities, grunge apathies and antipathies, and otherwise alternative stuff as, um, let's see, "genre flailing," "throwing language and gesture and policy and interpretations at a thing," at something like a world, "to make it slow or make it stop."[59]

A book that is a retelling of the story of Rip Van Winkle. A boy stuck in the 1990s observes the world ending on the tube and falls asleep. He wakes up with X tunes and tudes and it's the 2020s and the world is ending.

"It's all good."

But the chance that it's all good is the exact same as the likelihood that someone can tell the whole truth.[60]

"No worries. You're fine."

No, actually, I'm not fine. And worries? How much time is there? I brought some home movies, a flash drive. Can we dim the lights? A time capsule called "heart-shaped box."[61] Immersions of my life. Mellon collie and the infinite sadness.[62] Sincerity longing. Irreverence. Cynicism. Slackerism. Disillusionment. Reality bites.[63] Ugly feelings.[64] There's no centering or overarching intellectual or theoretical argument or agenda

---

57. Dumm, *A Politics of the Ordinary*, 8.
58. Counting Crows, "Mr. Jones."
59. Berlant, "Genre Flailing," 157.
60. Derrida, *On the Name*, 29.
61. Nirvana, "Heart-Shaped Box."
62. Smashing Pumpkins, *Mellon Collie and the Infinite Sadness*.
63. Stiller, *Reality Bites*.
64. Ngai, *Ugly Feelings*.

here. I work with half-baked curiosities about how depressive modes are interesting and provocative alternatives for curbing the enthusiasm.[65] For considering, heeding encumbrances, hindrances, inheritances, responsibilities—the overwhelm. For carrying that weight.[66]

My decision to avoid a golden thread or linear arc involves the fact that I already did something like that in my tobacco book. That approach now seems totalizing and inflexible. And it's a source of hard feelings. I have come to question the morality of deriving knowledge-class livelihoods from penetrating ethnography. I have become interested in why anthropologists are obsessed with extreme close-ups of other people and why there is perpetual pushback against exposing and disclosing not only more about our own subjective interiors and messy lives but also the possibility that anthropology is not so exceptional or essential. That anthropology is promotional and proselytizing. A culture of exclusivity and elitism. A manifestation of a will to power, our own hunger that is masked in our stories about that of other people, our interest in professing for a living.[67]

I do not engage in or contribute to scholarly conversations about mental illness, addiction, or recovery. Or anything. But my use of experimental form lends itself to a story, blurring genres to mimic the instability and morphology of the main character's life—and to discuss sensitive, controversial, and difficult material.[68] I do not put forth claims about what it means to be stuck, jammed, or moving. The only mention of negative dialectics is this one.[69] I have built a career on critical analyses of the lives of others and impersonal polemics about society. This "diary-study" feels like a moral and responsible redirection given the alienating aftermath of my earlier research: a nonprescriptive redirection for me after ethnography.[70]

65. Ahmed, *The Promise of Happiness*; Halberstam, *The Queer Art of Failure*; Love, *Feeling Backward*.
66. The Beatles, "Carry That Weight."
67. Nietzsche, *Thus Spoke Zarathustra*, 88–90.
68. Pine, *The Alchemy of Meth*, xx.
69. Buck-Morss, *The Origin of Negative Dialectics*.
70. Reber, *Coming to Our Senses*, 7.

Time Life

A story of myself might unfold as, oh, a chronicle of young love, deviations, and evolutions. Or a tour of the house, the family photos. Or the pop
culture wing of my shelf life. Or an account of good and bad behavior. Or
a map of stretched highs and lows, ebbs and flows, committals, close calls,
and deep lulls. Or "critical events" hanging as alibis and benchmarks.[71] Or
a "self-generalization" embedded within a narrative of a "national public
sphere,"[72] referencing points in a procession of presidents, recessions,
crimes/fights of the century, natural/social disasters, this and that
World Series or dynasty, decades of war before, during, and after the
Cold War.

Toddling when the Gipper passed his first major tax cut, I was playing
war and eating cereal with *SportsCenter* by the second slash. In the '96
Yanks, I saw black-and-white stills of the old-time greats. Neil Young in
Pearl Jam. The Who in just about everything. Just about everything in
Beck and Radiohead. In R.E.M. . . . . Cue "Turn! Turn! Turn! (To Everything
There Is a Season)" by the Byrds.[73]

Fieldwork in North Carolina wound down with a catastrophic
happening happening on TV. The calendar marks anniversary dates for
hospitalization and sobriety. And everything is going fine.[74] Everything is
splendid. Whitening toothpaste, organic good-grains granola, hybrid car,
manicured campus, bountiful salad bar, side of fries, Diet Coke, office
space, built-in bookcases, prime parking place, wooded collegiate neighborhood ("How quiet it is now that life has triumphed. The rough pillars
of the sycamores support the immobile shelves of the foliage, the lawn
beneath lush, iridescent"),[75] a massive, framed, original French marketing
poster for *Le Souffle au Coeur* ("musique de Charlie Parker"),[76] bistro steak
night, side of fries, Diet Coke, recycling can, composting plans, bubble
baths, forty-two-inch smart TV, temporalities and materialities signifying:
made it.

71. Das, *Critical Events.*
72. Berlant, *The Female Complaint,* 29, 113.
73. The Byrds, "Turn! Turn! Turn! (To Everything There Is a Season)."
74. Soderbergh, *And Everything Is Going Fine.*
75. Glück, "A Summer Garden," 66.
76. Malle, *Murmur of the Heart.*

2. New York Yankee Derek Jeter hits a solo home run in the third inning of game 2 of the American League Division Series at Yankee Stadium in New York, October 2, 2002. Photograph by Ray Stubblebine (Reuters/Alamy Stock Photo).

I have never not lived life during wartime.[77] White noise absorbed in proliferating and disappearing endless war. The interminable hot peace. *RoboCop* realities.[78] I'm not far from Ferguson. I'm involved as participant, observer, blah blah. I stay in nights and weekends. I have in the past fantasized fighting cops. There is a calendar date for that impulse.

77. Solondz, *Life during Wartime;* Talking Heads, "Life during Wartime."
78. Verhoeven, *RoboCop.*

I get buzzfeeds. I snack, eating up coverage of death and disaster event genres. ("Nothing seems exaggerated anymore. Nothing amazes me.")[79] My relationship to situations of hell on earth has mainly involved entertainment, recreation, voyeurism, intellectualizing, and academic activities. And in the splendid little life, there has always been hot peace and theaters of war inside my home, inside myself.

I sometimes wanna check out as old joy comes to mind.[80] I wanna head to the checkout line with a twenty-four-ounce can of Bud Light. Or four of them. I sometimes check out in debilitating bouts of manic depression and facedown pillow fighting. The font size of life magnified to the point where I focus in-in-in, in a fishbowl of a world.

"Alternate reality," Kedron comments.

Manny waves his hand in front of my face.

All I am on here are meds.

Two lithium carbonate 300 mg tablets at breakfast and dinner, an antimanic agent.

Two Depakote (valproic acid) 500 mg tablets at breakfast and dinner, an anticonvulsant used to treat bipolar disorder.

Two Zoloft (sertraline) 100 mg tablets, an antidepressant.

One Latuda (lurasidone) 60 mg tablet, an atypical antipsychotic.

And, if things get hairy:

One Zyprexa (olanzapine) 5 mg tablet (maybe 10 mg), an antipsychotic that puts me to sleep for a good sixteen hours.

A book about so said straight man affected by the afflictions and debilities of addiction and mood spectrum disorder, an unquiet mind;[81] a prosperous person, materially benefiting from the status quo and institutions, who desperately wants to be part of, or at least regarded as part of, the social change solution; a professionally successful person who commonly experiences felt nonsuccess, letdown, insufficiency, backwardness, frustrations of home, body, and work, frustrations of repressed homosexual desires, and characteristic varieties of immaturity, immorality, and misan-

79. DeLillo, *Falling Man*, 41.
80. Reichardt, *Old Joy*.
81. Jamison, *An Unquiet Mind*.

thropy; a person who is like a child, clinging to "the eternal (and eternally frustrating) maternal,"[82] digging ditches, constantly craving,[83] seeking some stability, some real satisfaction, acceptance.

Blurred Genres, Genre Flailing

A book that's, oh, I dunno, an amalgam of family melodrama, international intrigue, French New Wave iconoclasm, American indie yada yada, late/post Italian neorealism, Duane Hanson lifecast, sports elements, combat elements, religious epic, another retelling of the story of Oedipus, another retelling of the story of Narcissus, New Journalism alter ego, school-days nostalgia, late Beatles, Beat Streuli blowup, Oliver Stone paranoia, stoner noir, acerbic comedy, mockumentary, Charlie Kaufman meta-movie, overripe concept album, diss track compilation, enfant terrible, bittersweet Bildungsroman, British social realism, anomie freak-out ("fevered imaginations," "the malady of infinite aspiration"),[84] rude awakening, angry young man, and biographical kitchen sink.

Friedrich Nietzsche avoided the artless linearity of logical, philosophical argumentation and deployed a saturating ironical style, what one translator termed "musicality."[85] In praising Nietzsche's unconventional, aphoristic, subjective philosophizing, Michel Foucault bemoans the typical masking of the situated passions and partialities of authorship in academic work, writing that scholars "take unusual pains to erase the elements in their work which reveal their grounding in a particular time and place, their preferences in a controversy—the unavoidable obstacles of their passion," becoming, Foucault writes, "insensitive to all disgusting things."[86]

Maybe this moody, show-and-tell chatterbox of an anthropologist is pathologically inclined "to mine even [his] most intimate life for public success";[87] "the voyeur of his own life,"[88] hopelessly, amorously fallen into

82. Greenberg, "My Own Private Idaho," 25.
83. lang, "Constant Craving."
84. Durkheim, *Suicide*, 256; Durkheim, *Moral Education*, 40.
85. Parkes, introduction to *Thus Spoke Zarathustra*, xxviii.
86. Foucault, "Nietzsche, Genealogy, History," 382–83.
87. Worden and Young, "On Joan Didion," 585.
88. Gray, "Autobiography Now," 55.

an exposurescape of ruefulness and neediness. Who knows? Maybe tarrying with realities and artistries of concordant failures and invigorations, chronic compulsions and coming up and into contacts, turns out to be interesting or compelling for other people.

"What do we have?" the rabbi asks. "We have our stories."

Sitting around a table, we share stories to stay sober and sorta present and contend with difficulties of dailiness. Eke out errands. Maintain some degree of capacity. Carry that weight. Keep moving.

A book about anthropology. An anthropology book. An arrangement of speech and scenes and scenarios and stuff, fancifully, cringingly, embarrassingly, complicitly composed of cultural knowledge coordinates. A sarcastic-serious showstopper. A breathing exercise. An amende honorable before the main door of the Church.[89]

89. Foucault, *Discipline and Punish*, 3.

2 Lost in Translation

Over the past few years, I have tried to contact you several times. I have called and sent a couple of letters. I am writing now to share some things that are on my mind.

Our relationship was one of the most important relationships I have experienced, and I have so much respect and fondness for you in my heart. I feel bad about how things turned out.

I regret that our relationship is broken. I have spent years reflecting on our relationship and the mistakes I made. I would like to repair the hard feelings.

There are days when I wish I had not written *Tobacco Capitalism*.[1] I know my book caused pain, confusion, and anger. I want to offer explanations and apologies. I want to have a conversation that might help to heal wounds I caused.

I am writing you this letter because I want you to know that it matters to me that I hurt you. Also, I am publishing it for a few reasons. My book is available in libraries and on Amazon, and I want to amend it in a public way. This letter exposes parts of the backstory and frames the book in new

1. Benson, *Tobacco Capitalism*.

ways. I also want to acknowledge how you received the book and do that in a way that makes it known to the book's audience and scholars in general. I want to validate your silence as a response and a form of agency. That you no longer speak to me speaks to me—and your silence is also an important message for anthropologists.

Anthropologists do not usually write with our interlocutors in mind as the readership. This problem is reflected in the language we use and what we problematize. We would perhaps write very different books were interlocutors regarded as critical collaborators and readers.[2] Sometimes instead of writing about interlocutors as people with whom we developed meaningful and intimate relationships, we appropriate works and lives for the purposes of producing academic knowledge and narratives.[3] Sometimes we fail to extend to interlocutors "the same degree of courtesy, empathy and friendship in writing as we generally extend to them face to face in the field where they are [. . .] our boon companions."[4]

I am writing here in the form of an open letter to merge audiences; I am writing to you and to anthropologists at the same time. This is personal stuff for me, and I feel the need to address you directly, not as a distant third person. I am writing about entangled relationships—my relationship with you and my relationship with anthropology. I want to open up about aspects of my work and relationships where I continue to experience moral and emotional anguish and sensitivity. I also want to open up about myself. The anthropology, the work that I have done, is wrapped up with elements of my personal life that belong in the context of the book. I am writing about this situation in the hopes of providing enriched honesty and complexity for you and other readers. I also write to express candor, humility, sincerity, and vulnerability in the hopes of regaining your trust and opening a door for reconciliation between us.

I could have written a different book about companionship and the intimate time we spent together. I have so many good memories. I lived near you for more than a year, hanging out on the farm where you tend tobacco. I think about our rides together in farm trucks. I think about

---

2. Moskowitz, "Engagement, Alienation, and Anthropology's New Moral Dilemmas."
3. Geertz, *Works and Lives.*
4. Scheper-Hughes, "Ire in Ireland," 128.

hauls to the soybean market in an eighteen-wheeler. I think about weekend trips to your place on the river. We stopped at the grocery store to purchase hamburgers and hot dogs for the grill. We bought soft drinks.

I did not mention in my book that you are one of the kindest, most genuine people I have ever met. The graciousness and endearment you showed me are the most enduring impressions I have of North Carolina.

Anthropologists rely on learning through social relationships, and friendship and intimacy inevitably arise.[5] Anthropologists can sometimes write about the world in ways that feel like an appropriation or a betrayal to people whom we lived and worked with in the field.[6] And for people who are not "inducted into its particular forms of 'seeing the world,'" anthropology can be "alienating," even "insulting."[7] The ways you explained your work and the workings of the world were, in my book, grist for an anthropological analysis, invoked to construct a critical narrative about tobacco. One of the main dilemmas for anthropologists is writing about society while acknowledging and addressing multiple vantage points and experiences, including where interlocutors have different political perspectives or stakes than the anthropologist.[8] This was a problem for me. I never knew how to be frank with you about my political views or how to converse with you about difficult and sensitive issues that are part of the tobacco industry. And I did not research or write in a collaborative or dialogical way that legitimized and honored your own ways of interpreting things.

I realize my book caused hard feelings, and we have different perspectives. Things feel really divided in this country. I wonder whether people of different opinions and beliefs can get along in meaningful ways.

I believe there is lasting affection between us, and that is where I want to reconnect and move toward a dialogue.

5. Rabinow, *Reflections on Fieldwork in Morocco.*

6. Brettell, *When They Read What We Write;* Fassin, "The Public Afterlife of Ethnography."

7. Moskowitz, "Engagement, Alienation, and Anthropology's New Moral Dilemmas," 35–36.

8. Ginsberg, "The Case of Mistaken Identity."

Curing Barns

We used to ride around the curing barns at night in a golf cart, shuttling from barn to barn amid the thick tobacco air and farm operation in a clearing surrounded by tall loblolly pines, peeking past sliding metal doors to check on the curing leaf, not saying much to each other. I will never forget those good times. They were left out of my book.

I could have written a book about tobacco farming as a positive heritage, or at least a book less focused on hard truths and conflictual realities.

I could have written a book focused on "ordinary affects," eschewing "judgment" in favor of "an experiment," stringing along descriptive vignettes about everyday life, allowing readers to do the interpretation.[9] I admittedly could have written something other than a strident critique of troubling realities in a tobacco world. I never mentioned the good times or the warmth between us.

We sat close in the golf cart and related in a dynamic of tagalong instruction. You were the grower, and I was the anthropologist, learning through observation and participation. But it felt like more than research, a bonding thing—a father-and-son thing.

After we had all finished primetime television—you and your wife, and Kedron and I—and it was time to check the barns, your wife encouraged me to accompany you. I could have stayed inside and watched the local news and visited with them. You could have taken twenty minutes to check the barns alone. And I could have learned during some interview about the curing process. But your wife knew that that time circling the barns involved something special that made our relationship more meaningful. The hanging around was never merely an academic project. There was this closeness between a twentysomething and a fiftysomething that involved trust, and that would involve an eventual wounding.

As we headed out in the golf cart, driving the short distance from your modest house to the farm area where the metal barns hummed in the North Carolina night, curing tobacco, letting off dank, hot air as exhaust, our spouses stayed back in the living room. They probably talked about

9. Stewart, *Ordinary Affects*, 1.

competition among farmers, the elderly couple down the road from whom you rent land noticing weeds around your tobacco patch, the sale on the slow-churned ice cream at the grocery store, and the funny way the old tenant farmer around the bend refers to the UPS delivery vehicle as the "ups truck."

And yet I could not have written a book about ordinary affects, these vignettes about ordinary life. I am not so skilled. And that is not the kind of anthropology I was there to do as a graduate student. My work has advanced critique. And this thrust has put me at odds with people whom I care about and who were my companions.

Heat and Exhaustion

My goal was to understand an experiential, interactional, and historical world. I wanted to produce scholarship that would situate tobacco livelihoods within an atmosphere of tensions, disputations, vexations, and claims that speak to changing materialities, structural and societal shifts, and shifting subjectivities.

I heard heated stuff in pickup trucks and living rooms, throughout town, and on farms. That heat caught my attention.

And in my book, I argued that heated rhetorics about immigration and race and deservedness and decline are related to structures and causes having to do with keywords like "neoliberalism, advanced capitalism, and globalization."[10] Tobacco farming is not some insular, harmonious "way of life." I was immersed in a "whole way of *conflict*," a "way of *struggle*," as E. P. Thompson might put it.[11]

I was admittedly working with certain research interests from the start. Amid the war on drugs, I wanted to know how you and other growers feel about the fact that you produce the main ingredient in cigarettes. Given the contestation over immigration, I wanted to know how you and others feel about social diversification and your dependence on migrant workers from Latin America, many of whom are undocumented. With the tobacco industry globalizing its operations to procure cheaper leaf sources, I

10. Ibid.
11. Thompson, "The Long Revolution," 33.

wanted to know how you and others feel about your changing relationships to profitability and multinational tobacco companies.

In sit-down interviews and informal discussions, I felt the heat. I heard a lot of stuff that clashed with my liberal sensibilities about political correctness and my own political views, although I never told this to you or other growers. Tobacco growers are decent and hardworking, salt-of-the-earth folks. There is so much that is positive and beautiful about tobacco country. I only mention misgivings here to name things that bothered me and that are real and complicated.

I worked alongside Black and Latin American farmworkers and learned of sufferings and hardships. I spent much time in labor camps, where migrant workers live, and saw squalid and arduous living and working conditions.

I heard—from many growers and other community members—derisive or dismissive explanations of social problems and inequalities, negative stereotypes of lower classes of people, the use of racial epithets and rhetorics, negative and sensationalist concerns about "illegal immigration," and justifications of the cigarette business that I disagreed with and that did not sit well with me, and that disturbed me.

Everyday talk in tobacco country speaks to the ins and outs of growing tobacco as much as the ins and outs of who deserves what, who is valuable or threatening to the nation, and what is happening in America. Maybe this statement seems to you like some sort of overly interpretive or analytical academic claim. But it is what I believe.

I wrote about how crucial matters of identity and livelihood are at stake and how heated rhetorics are appreciable responses given the pressures and predicaments that growers themselves face.

But with my access to growers in part conveyed through shared masculinity and whiteness, I was never really transparent, remaining muted, not disputing claims, not offering up my own politics or perspectives. I did this because staying neutral, not inserting myself, is what I thought I was supposed to do as a fieldworker, and frankness would have impeded access. And also, I was young and immature and scared.

Avoidance, deception, and silence on the part of anthropologists are probably common. In *Veiled Sentiments*, a classic study of Bedouin society, Lila Abu-Lughod writes:

What bothered me most [. . .] was that my relationship with the people I lived with did not seem symmetrical. [. . .] I was asking them to be honest, so that I could learn what their lives were like, but at the same time I was unwilling to reveal much about myself. I was presenting them with a persona: I felt compelled to lie to them about many aspects of my life [. . .] simply because they could not have helped judging it and me in their own terms, by which my reputation would have suffered. So I doctored my descriptions and changed the subject when they asked about me. [. . .] How ethical was it to present myself falsely, to pretend that I shared their values and lived as they did even when I was not with them? They knew nothing of my former life, my friends, family, university, apartment—in short, much of what I considered my identity.[12]

"Eventually, this sense of inauthenticity subsided," Abu-Lughod explains, as more time made for more authentic and symmetrical relationships, including "honest interchanges."[13]

I came to feel a natural ease and camaraderie on tobacco farms. But I was all the while hiding crucial parts of my identity. There were never honest interchanges where I embraced the "serious give and take" and "vulnerable" approach that, Abu-Lughod insists, define ethnography's vital core.[14] I lacked the courage to hazard uncertain and tense conversations. I never explained the intellectual scope of my project or discussed analytical approaches and politicizing tendencies common in anthropology, such as the tendency to focus on the "harsh dimensions of social life," the "power, domination, inequality, and oppression," to cite Sherry Ortner.[15]

In circling the barns, we rarely talked. Maybe your notable silence was shyness. Maybe it was heaviness or exhaustion. You have been through a lot in life. But we never got into personal stuff. Truth be told, I have almost no sense of how you see yourself as a person. My focus was on growers as a group that confronts intersecting social, symbolic, and material challenges to historical forms of status and citizenship because of large-scale industrial processes and the confounding circumstances of growing a problematized crop. In working with this focus, maybe I am guilty of advancing the

12. Abu-Lughod, *Veiled Sentiments*, 18.
13. Ibid., 19.
14. Ibid., 275–76.
15. Ortner, "Dark Anthropology and Its Others," 47.

"notion of a totalized system, of which everything is always already some-how a part."[16] Making growers seem like rote effects, functions and facets of Big Tobacco, annulling aspects of agency, voiding valences of voice, and contextualizing incomparable lives. Perhaps I failed to dignify growers as more than a trace of "'bigger' structures and underlying causes,"[17] as peo-ple whose personalities and forms of sociality, whose struggles and senses of self, whose complex humanity exceeds a story about Big Tobacco.

Maybe my book went too big and did not get at "[s]omething more authentic to our uncertain and unmasterable human condition and to the long littleness," to quote my graduate adviser, Arthur Kleinman.[18]

I would prod you to say something—anthropologist that I am—something general about what you were up to in monitoring the tempera-ture and moisture levels and handling the tobacco leaf. It smelled sweet and musty. Amid that concentrated aroma, you felt fatherly to me. And I could sense that I felt like something of a son to you, although you never said so. But another grower did tell me, after reading my book, "Pete, you were like a son to him."

Never Reject Anything Human

After a year, we headed back to Boston, where I returned to graduate school. Just as you work hard to succeed in tobacco farming, I was work-ing to establish myself as an anthropologist, make you proud even, make my parents proud, especially my father, and work with modes of analysis that had been taught to me by another father figure: Arthur, whose work and character I greatly admire.

I wanted to live up to rigorous standards of incisive scholarship. In an academic discipline historically defined around dominant male figures, I wanted to belong to a patriarchal legacy associated with apprenticeship and affiliation with Arthur as a "powerful" academic figure.[19]

I told him about my respect for you and other growers, and my desire to develop a sympathetic and sensitive account of a heated and hard

---

16. Stewart, *Ordinary Affects*, 1.
17. Ibid., 4.
18. Kleinman, *What Really Matters*, 225.
19. Behar, "Introduction: Out of Exile."

world. "Never reject anything human," he told me, encouraging me to approach things that, from my outside perspective, seemed problematic with careful regard and contextual thinking, to appreciate the complicated, fraught dignity and humanity of ordinary people and the vicissitudes and stakes of livelihoods and moral life.

I wrote about how your cohort of growers came of age with problematizing public health impulses and tobacco-control regulations and the dislocations, loss of farms, and racialized labor dynamics associated with the globalization and industrialization of tobacco agriculture. I wrote about these concrete processes to comprehend the heat and exhaustion of the heartland as having roots and reasons. I wrote about how the story of tobacco growers reflects what Michèle Lamont calls the "dignity of working men," who experience impressions and realities of socioeconomic distress that make their lives in many ways like lower classes of people from whom they might take social and moral distance.[20] I wrote about how dignity is captured by corporate power and the powers of mystification and affective politics. I wrote about how the political power and influence of the multinational tobacco companies that purchase leaf contribute to "agrarian precarities" and at the same time promulgate strategies to amass support from growers.[21]

Maybe my own readings and leanings are misguided or out of touch—the result of socialization, of pushing paper. I acknowledge that I wrote the book from a privileged position—not depending on tobacco money, not employing migrant workers, not feeling blame for contributing to toxic commerce, not having to meet the economic pressures of cutthroat tobacco companies. My book's explanatory framework, with its theory of culture and politics in America (that ideologies and power are at work), is part of a realm of attachment and conviction that I have learned through academic study and incorporation into an economy of professional attainment.

I was significantly influenced by Arthur's concept of "distinctive moral worlds," worlds characterized by values and stakes.[22] My goal was to

20. Lamont, *The Dignity of Working Men.*
21. Lauren Berlant, quoted in Puar, "Precarity Talk," 166.
22. Kleinman, "Experience and Its Moral Modes," 414.

describe and analyze the history and ethnography of the moral world of tobacco farming. Students who have done graduate studies with Arthur have produced scholarship on how "certain things matter, matter greatly, even desperately" in people's lives and how such stakes become imperiled by "disordering" processes,[23] how there is "fear of [...] loss,"[24] and how "changing forms of social experience [...] are the consequence of vast historical, political-economic, and cultural transformations."[25]

I honestly did not anticipate such steep stratification or how hot it was going to be. The structures and rhetorics are conspicuous, and I did not want to ignore these realities in writing my book.

The Politics of Ethnography

Now you and other growers have read it. A couple of years after its publication, I visited to get a sense of the local reception. Some growers told me that I did a good job. "It's all true," one man said. "We might not like to hear about that stuff, but it's true." But I was told by others that I unfairly used them without being open about myself, wrote with a liberal bias about social issues, and represented them in a disrespectful manner. I am facing something akin to what Nancy Scheper-Hughes describes in her article "Ire in Ireland." Her interlocutors read her book on village life and insisted she had tendentiously focused on "troubles" and "weaknesses" rather than "strengths" and "friendliness."[26] She was rebuked and shunned. Similarly, my ethnography turns out to have been an exercise in bridge burning.

But part of me cannot believe it. Surely you and other growers had a sense that permitting me extraordinary access was a potential representational risk. I spent time in labor camps and working in fields. I developed close relationships with farmworkers. It was no doubt evident that I would write about these scenarios and lives. Apparently, there was a privileged assumption that a range of things would be left out of the book. I seemed nonthreatening—an accepted community member—and so you believed I

23. Ibid., 360; Kleinman, "Everything That Really Matters," 317.
24. Kleinman, "Everything That Really Matters," 334.
25. Ibid.
26. Scheper-Hughes, "Ire in Ireland," 119.

would uphold positive images and messages. Maybe assumed or desired protection from critical reporting also reflects denials or lack of recognition of systematized advantages or a belief that nothing is wrong or that hierarchies of race and class are an acceptable order. I have been angry that realities that are obviously problematic to me are normalized. But I was scared to speak up, and then I wrote a bothered book that garnered praise from fellow anthropologists.

Tobacco Capitalism: Growers, Migrant Workers, and the Changing Face of a Global Industry was awarded the 2014 Delmos Jones and Jagna Sharff Memorial Prize for the Critical Study of North America from the Society for the Anthropology of North America.[27] A book you do not like is regarded in my field as meritorious. I could have written a different book—but this award is about critique.

Jones and Sharff wrote incisive scholarship about race, inequality, poverty, and other social problems. It was a politically motivated scholarship. Their work examined poor and marginalized communities.[28]

Today's cohort of active tobacco growers does not live in poverty or at the margins of society. They are higher up in a hierarchy—enterprising landowners and employers who possess some relative power in relation to the farm labor workforce and rural poor. I was in part "studying up," as Laura Nader puts it, studying the "culture of power rather than the culture of the powerless [. . . or] the culture of poverty."[29]

And yet I was not studying the boardrooms of Big Tobacco. I was not in the halls and offices of Congress where politicians and lobbyists shape public health and agricultural policies.

You are not part of some easy and uncomplicated culture of power. You are middle-class and hardworking—like my father. You proudly own and operate a business. There is also adversity. Tobacco farming, you once told me, is a "damn headache." The farm equipment breaks down. Every day, it seems, there are more regulations. You contend with the vagaries of weather in producing your crops. You have farm debts. You feel blamed by labor organizers for worker wages and labor camp conditions—but can

27. Benson, *Tobacco Capitalism.*

28. See, for example, Klugh, "Delmos Jones and the End of Neutrality"; Sharff, *King Kong on 4th Street.*

29. Nader, "Up the Anthropologist," 289; see also Gusterson, "Studying Up Revisited."

you afford to improve them? You feel blamed for smoking—but tobacco is in your blood and what you know. You have seen neighboring farmers go out of business and lose their farms.

"Every interpretive strategy," Vincent Crapanzano writes, "involves choice and falls, thereby, into the domain of ethics and politics."[30] Anthropologists silence certain voices and viewpoints and leave certain events and realities out of our books.[31] These are political decisions and decisions about relationships to interlocutors, colleagues, readerships, and the wider world. I could have researched and written in a concentrated way about your individual life history—something like a biographical portrait, calling it *Portrait of a North Carolinian*.[32] Or I could have engaged in a different kind of sociality and anthropology, where we constructively conversed about tobacco and politics and our relationship with each other, getting into respectful disagreements, leading to a book called *North Carolinian Dialogues*.[33] Or I could have written an introspective account of my personal experiences and the social dynamics and intimacies of fieldwork, something like a memoir, calling it *Reflections on Fieldwork in North Carolina* or *The Tobacco Grower and I*.[34] Or, instead of writing critically about the lives of others, I could have written reflexively about my own experiences of distress and vulnerability in observing and trying to make sense of a hard world, a book called *The Vulnerable Observer*.[35] Of all the genres in anthropology, I chose to write a "critical tale," tightly, consciously focusing on the workings of power and structural forces in line with my training and dominant paradigms in the discipline at that time.[36] My book was, to quote Scheper-Hughes, the "particular perspective" of a "particular sort of anthropologist-ethnographer" at a "particular moment."[37]

30. Crapanzano, *Tuhami: Portrait of a Moroccan*, x–xi.
31. Fernandez, "Silences of the Field."
32. Crapanzano, *Tuhami: Portrait of a Moroccan*.
33. Dwyer, *Moroccan Dialogues*.
34. Rabinow, *Reflections on Fieldwork in Morocco*; Dumont, *The Headman and I*.
35. Behar, *The Vulnerable Observer*.
36. Fassin, "Why Ethnography Matters," 628; see also Van Maanen, *Tales of the Field*.
37. Scheper-Hughes, "Ire in Ireland," 137.

The Essence of Conversation

Emmanuel Levinas writes that apology "belongs to the essence of conversation."[38] More than a discrete speech act ("I apologize"), Levinas refers to the idea that responsiveness and responsibility are dispositions integral to the dynamic of interlocution, where there is the possibility of "contestation and accusation issuing from alterity."[39] In this definition, conversation involves "the risky uncovering of oneself, in sincerity, the breaking up of inwardness and the abandon of all shelter, exposure to traumas, vulnerability."[40]

You uncovered parts of yourself to me and kept other parts hidden. I uncovered parts of myself to you and kept other parts hidden. We were like father and son, but there was never vulnerable dialogue between us. Of course, the relationship of father and son does not necessarily involve such immersion. I have never been open with father figures.

My father, with whom I sporadically communicate, has limited knowledge about my professional work. He is proud of the fact that I graduated from Harvard. But he has expressed suspicion about pushing paper. He does not know much about my life story and has a limited sense of the messiness and mental illness that were involved in the writing of my book. We chat on the phone, visit during the holidays, and express affection and love, but we avoid politics and do not go near sensitive stuff. He has not read my book. He would not agree with my arguments about history, culture, and power. He subscribes to a conservative politics that resembles much of what I heard in North Carolina. Part of me thinks that in my book, I projected frustrations and feelings about him onto men that remind me of him.

I was going through a lot when I wrote my book. I was dealing with conflicted feelings. I was writing about a drug—tobacco—while abusing alcohol and marijuana, staying up all night, and working intensively toward tenure, working within and working out the anxieties, ambivalences, attachments, and aggressions of father-and-son relationships amid an internalized commitment to critique and amid difficulty effectively coping

38. Levinas, *Totality and Infinity*, 40.
39. Diprose, *Corporeal Generosity*, 165.
40. Levinas, *Otherwise than Being, or Beyond Essence*, 48.

with competing impulses and inevitable implications. I knew you would not like my book. That is partly why I was abusing drugs and harming myself. I felt I betrayed confidence, but I also felt I was telling an important story. I wanted to impress you with a handsome, substantive book about tobacco, and yet there were heartfelt political and moral stakes for me in highlighting industrial harms. The book brought the dignity of working men into the frame of a critical analysis influenced by my academic mentor. I felt contradictory, caught in a chiasmus, a confounding network of lean- ings and longings related to loved ones. I was writing for and about you, and for and about Arthur (and a particular political and moral anthropol- ogy), and for and about my father. I was writing for and about fathers. I was also becoming a father. My son, Emmanuel, named after Levinas, was born during that last year of frenzied writing. I was exhausted. I was having a nervous breakdown. I was admitted to a hospital and treated for mental illness the same month that the book was published.

Writing the book was morally, emotionally, and physically difficult for me. The aftermath has challenged me to think hard about myself and what I have done. I have spent a great deal of time working through and coming to grips with struggles around mental illness and addiction. Since my book's publica- tion, I have also struggled to deal with heavy feelings of guilt and grief.

They say that when you lose someone, you go on seeing signs. Every time I see a Ford F-150, I think of you. It is your truck. It is also America's number one selling truck. So I routinely see you—in and around the city, on highways, and at the gas station. The contractors who do construction at my university drive F-150s. In seeing their trucks, I wonder how you are doing, what you are up to. I think about the fact that I may never know.

I also see you in my son—Emmanuel. We call him Manny. I imagine you have come to know him, and my family visits your farm. I picture him riding tractors, sifting through leaf, doing rounds in the golf cart. I have a particular dream, where you are in my living room, playing with Manny. You smile at me across the room and tell me you are proud of me. You do not have headaches or hardships. I am not smoking pot and pounding out a big, angry brickbat of a book. It is a scene of what Levinas might describe as "enjoyment," referring to "happiness, presence at home with itself."[41]

41. Levinas, *Totality and Infinity*, 143.

Abu-Lughod had a dream about a father figure. Decades after writing *Veiled Sentiments,* she awoke worried about the well-being of an elder from her field site. The premonition came true, as she recounts in an afterword to the book (part of which is entitled "Guest and Daughter"). She returned to the community and visited with the elder, ill in old age. She had developed, over decades, a special connection with him, becoming what she calls an "adoptive daughter."[42] When the elder later died, she gave a eulogy at the funeral, describing him as a "patient teacher and second father."[43]

She reflects on the special capacity of ethnography to transform lives, drawing strangers into meaningful relationships. "Our bond was real," she writes, "even as it crossed so many of the divides some presume are unbridgeable," such as culture, age, gender, and politics.[44] What "made this bridging possible," she continues, was "recognition of the complexities of the world we live in, combined with [...] years of shared conversations, memories, and affections."[45]

I wish there were lasting bridges between us. I dream about it. I regret that by not being more open about myself and making myself vulnerable, I left you vulnerable to indignity and injury. I regret that I abused the kindness, trust, and hospitality of a stranger with whom I developed a real bond.

I wonder sometimes whether I should just plain apologize for my book. But I also believe in the value and resolve of critical reporting on American society. If I am now writing in the vein of confession, lamentation, and apology, it is not in the sense of wanting to invalidate my book, because it is a good book, albeit a "big, angry, brickbat of a book," as one reviewer remarked[46]—an insightful and, yes, at times angry study of tobacco farming and grave social and epidemiological problems. But I do feel remorse for having wronged you. I acted in ways that led to expectations that the close access I gained from my respectable and friendly demeanor and

---

42. Abu-Lughod, *Veiled Sentiments,* 15.
43. Ibid., 269.
44. Ibid., 264.
45. Ibid., 267.
46. Russell, "Book Review," 211.

formal affiliation at a university would not be a method for inscribing into a public record what are, to me, troublesome rhetorics and realities.

"I'm writing a book about tobacco farming and will give you a copy of it," I promised during my fieldwork. And whenever I showed up at your house for return visits over the ensuing years, while I was furiously writing, I kept quiet about the book's content and slant. As Joan Didion puts it, "writers are always selling somebody out."[47] I sensed I was doing something like that.

I mailed you the book. I should have delivered it in person. But I was excited and afraid. It was already on Amazon. And I could not at that very moment travel to North Carolina. I was teaching. I wanted you to receive it immediately rather than coming across the webpage and wondering—hmm.

I regret the general element of withholding and discretion that defined my work. I should have maintained a "spirit of open engagement, frankness and receptivity" throughout the entire research and writing process.[48] I am also uneasy about the story that my book tells. I fear that the analysis "assimilate[s] and thematise[s],"[49] overcontextualizes, simplifies some complex humanity, and condenses lives that are singular, tender, and irreducible into a story line.

I am stuck with and haunted by these misgivings.

I agree with João Biehl that it is incumbent upon anthropologists to revisit our writings and field sites "to say more honestly what we saw or to rectify misrenderings and face the pain our interpretations and texts have caused."[50] I want to return to your farm and talk to you about my respect and love for you, your family, and your work, and my life and work and the perspectives of my book. I want to, well, have a conversation with you—something that I never really did.

47. Didion, *Slouching towards Bethlehem*, xvi.
48. Scheper-Hughes, "Ire in Ireland," 128.
49. Celermajer, "Apology and the Possibility of Ethical Politics," 18.
50. Biehl, "Ethnography in the Way of Theory," 579.

3 And Everything Is Going Fine

FADE IN:

EXT. ST. LOUIS – UNIVERSITY – ANTHROPOLOGY BUILDING – DAY (ESTABLISHING)

Spring semester. Collegiate Gothic fortress. Campus beset by classes. Lawns look gorgeous.

INT. MAIN CORRIDOR

An ordinary afternoon in the old dorm. PETER, late thirties, trudges upstairs to his second-floor office. CAMERA TRACKS after him.

INT. PETER'S OFFICE

Dark, wooden bookshelves. Eggshell plaster walls. PETER tosses his lightweight jacket atop piles of paper on the large desk. Sits in the swivel. Thinks about resemblances and mother — that BOIL, that TEMPER.

Wonders MAN, OH MAN, what has he done.[1] He must explain angry email to the CHAIR of the department. Where to begin . . . where to end.

> NARRATOR (V.O.)
>
> He would have to tell the whole truth — Nanny
> and Poppy, Grandma and Grandpa, the good
> daddy and the bad daddy, the bad mommy and
> the good mommy,[2] the daddy-mommy spider
> web,[3] layer after layer,[4] a layer-cake
> arrangement,[5] a genealogy of morals,[6] a pearl of
> a jam — to provide some adequate explanation for
> the angry email. He would have to do something
> like give an account of oneself.[7]

PETER works doggedly at desk, hands hovering on keyboard. Thinking about how to approach the CHAIR. He will likely hit repeat on platitudes.

> PETER (V.O.)
>
> Stress. Frustration. Heat and exhaustion. It was a
> gaffe, a lapse in judgment.

This process of claiming core rationality demands a constitutive loss — an internalization of rage and a shoring up of the superego.[8] Difficult, pained denial of truths related to his bio. Because he cannot talk about impulsivity and disability — bipolar disorder or anything broader.

1. Ball, *American Beauty*, 97.
2. Deleuze and Guattari, *A Thousand Plateaus*, 13.
3. Deleuze and Guattari, *Anti-Oedipus*, 112.
4. Geertz, *The Interpretation of Cultures*, 37.
5. Ibid., 372.
6. Nietzsche, *On the Genealogy of Morals*.
7. Butler, *Giving an Account of Oneself*.
8. Ibid., 99.

PETER (V.O.) (CONT'D)

Slip. Blip. Brain fart. Not a symptom or warning
sign of an unstable temperament and mixed
humors, some rambunctious, libidinal theater or
hellish racket,[9] not the manifestation of
capriciousness, immaturity, vagary, yeah, those
down-inside stirrings.

DISSOLVE TO:

DREAM SEQUENCE – INT. MAIN CORRIDOR

PETER and the CHAIR, late fifties, happen to encounter each other in the
hall. The CHAIR pats PETER's shoulder in a paternal, supportive manner
and warmly asks about the email.

CHAIR

Peter, what happened?

PETER

I ran my mouth off a bit too much, oh, what did I
say?[10] The angry boy, a bit too insane, icing over
secret pain. You know you don't belong.[11]

CHAIR

Oh no, not at all. I recommend sticking your foot
in your mouth at any time.[12] Don't you worry,
we'll all float on, alright.[13]

END DREAM SEQUENCE.

---

9. Deleuze and Guattari, *Anti-Oedipus*, 55.
10. Modest Mouse, "Float On."
11. Third Eye Blind, "Jumper."
12. Morissette, "You Learn."
13. Modest Mouse, "Float On."

INT. PETER'S OFFICE (BACK TO SCENE)

This is what PETER hopes the boss says — good graces. Although PETER has the employment security of tenure, he will want a printer cartridge tomorrow, an additional teaching assistant next semester, the choicest of classrooms, a sabbatical sooner rather than later, and a new laptop in a year or two. But he also experiences displeasure in keeping up appearances, biting his tongue.

PETER paces. Mahogany bookcases. He consternates in head scratches.

> NARRATOR (V.O.)
>
> Peter could dial in a digression. Ask a rhetorical
> question: How many fingers are on the nuclear
> button?[14] But the daddy-mommy spider web is
> not a viable excuse around the office. Being hot-
> blooded and having family disease are not, in this
> place, licenses or psychological costs.

PETER considers this affair — what to say to the CHAIR. Not someone to swallow his pride, he wishes he could confide. Enough with small talk around here! He wants to march downstairs for a sympathetic ear. Could he possibly testify across from the brass like he is sunken in at his therapist's and unload some of THE WEIGHT,[15] giving a ranging, multifactorial account, opening onto DEEP TIME,[16] opening a window for a breath of fresh air, a relationship with THE OUTSIDE WORLD?[17]

DISSOLVE TO:

DREAM SEQUENCE – INT. CHAIR'S OFFICE

14. Ellsberg, *The Doomsday Machine*, 297.
15. The Band, "The Weight."
16. Dimock, *Through Other Continents*.
17. Deleuze and Guattari, *Anti-Oedipus*, 2.

The CHAIR lazily rocks behind his desk. Seniority manifest. Personalized achievement awards. Prized paperweights. Discolored topographical maps. Fading field site photographs.

PETER discerns indifference and condescension as he is determined to communicate his plight. He sits upright. Earnest and sentimental. Hoping that an appeal to personal ways, his own elemental, will make things right.

PETER

(gently clears throat)
The issue is . . . handle with care.[18]

CHAIR

What do you mean, Peter?

PETER

I mean . . . handle with care. Picture books. Horn-rimmed glasses. The piano parlor. The once-and-for-all. The grease tree. The flowers of Guatemala.[19]

CHAIR

Let's not get off track, Peter. . . . Say, can we talk about the new employee performance tracking system?[20]

---

18. Traveling Wilburys, "Handle with Care."
19. R.E.M, "The Flowers of Guatemala."
20. Judge, *Office Space.*

PETER

(blathering)

Anger issues. Addiction issues. The love of
mothers. An insulating love, a cushioning berth.

CHAIR

Peter, please focus. Separation of Church and
State. Neither here nor there. Off the subject.

PETER

Coming of age amid violent and harsh social
policies. A conservative and repressive public
culture. A conservative and repressive daddy-
mommy spider web.

CHAIR

Peter, the thing is, we're using a new employee
productivity and engagement monitoring solution
now.[21]

PETER

The tensions of a subject formed in between
repression and incitement . . . disavowal and
designation.[22]

CHAIR

Come on, Peter, focus.

PETER

It's just that . . . inside, I'm a hot fuss.[23] Quite a
crowd.[24] Like, what if the Three Stooges were

---

21. Ibid.
22. Bhabha, *The Location of Culture*, 50.
23. The Killers, *Hot Fuss*.
24. Deleuze and Guattari, *A Thousand Plateaus*, 3.

real?[25] Agents of childlike resistance to the
repression of the adult world.[26] The crude,
exhilarating identities of real people.[27]

PETER is pleading a passionate case. For anthropologists to do their job
— to appreciate the complexities and contexts of experience even in the
liberal and antiseptic office space.

> CHAIR
>
> In the clouds. In your dreams. In the movies.

END DREAM SEQUENCE.

DISSOLVE TO:

FLASHBACK – INT. PETER'S OFFICE (WEEKS EARLIER)

PETER stares into his computer monitor stressfully. Then he springs from
the desk to the open doorway. CAMERA PANS with him and TRACKS IN
after him as he looks out into the hallway.

> PETER (V.O.)
>
> (speaking to ether and memory)[28]
> Okay, here's the thing . . .

Randomly TAPS the door frame and peers down the corridor.

> PETER (V.O.) (CONT'D)
>
> This is office space. This is space for work to be
> done. Not for chitchat. Not for you to knock on my
> door and interrupt me. Do you understand that?[29]

CAMERA TRACKS with him as he steps back to the computer and swivel.

25. Kerouac, *Visions of Cody*, 304.
26. Trudeau, "Stooging the Body, Stooging the Text," 346.
27. Sterritt, "Kerouac, Artaud, and the Baroque Period of the Three Stooges," 91.
28. Samaras, "Wind Telephone," 102.
29. Kubrick, *The Shining*.

PETER (V.O.) (CONT'D)

Man, oh man. I would do anything for a drink.[30]

At his desk with face resting heavily in hands. He lowers them. Looks up.

EXTREME CLOSE-UP SHOT – BLANK COMPUTER SCREEN

HOLD on flashing cursor for a moment. And then.

MED. SHOT of PETER at display setup, back to CAMERA. He rolls up his sleeves and sets off typing. CAMERA slowly PUSHES IN on him.

PETER (V.O.) (CONT'D)

(frenetically)

Hi you. I just looked at the course listings for the fall semester, and I see that "Introduction" is slotted for 9:00 a.m. Maybe I missed something, but I was not contacted about this decision. It's going to impact the quality of my class — a class that I have thrown my heart into for years — and I don't appreciate the function and meaning of your decision. This course has been taught for ten years in the middle of the day, and it has significantly positively impacted the growth and direction of our department. There are anthropology majors everywhere. I believe I deserved a conversation about the scheduling change. I am expressing frustration about your decision in the larger context of broader frustrations. Let's just say that there is no incentive for me to work as hard as I do. I do not want to curse or get nasty, but I feel profane sentiments. I feel exploited and taken for granted, mistreated, neglected, and underappreciated. There was no conversation.

30. Ibid.

There was an assumption — an assumption that
Pete is Pete, that the enrollment will be there. But
didn't it at least deserve a chat?

EXTREME CLOSE-UP SHOT – COMPUTER SCREEN

Flashing cursor at end of lengthy paragraph.

PETER strikes return . . . return . . . then types: "Don't do me like that."[31]
Then backspaces to delete it. Pauses briefly. Then types the salutation:
"Respectfully yours."

He sends the email.

END FLASHBACK.

INT. PETER'S OFFICE (BACK TO SCENE)

Now back in the present day, PETER sits at the computer. Wonders MAN,
OH MAN, what has he done. Must explain angry email to the CHAIR.
Must be collegial and fair.

DISSOLVE TO:

DREAM SEQUENCE – INT. CHAIR'S OFFICE

The CHAIR naturally commands the undersized room. The unusable fireplace on one wall is a sealed-off tomb. Photos of the CHAIR with diverse
groups of colleagues on the mantel. Evidence of professional travel. The
worn wooden desktop and desk chair give off a vibe of bench and gavel.

> CHAIR
>
> Peter, the students would take your class if I
> scheduled it at two in the morning.

---

31. Tom Petty and the Heartbreakers, "Don't Do Me Like That."

> PETER (V.O.)
>
> (chided)

That's called "neoliberalism," motherfucker.
Flexible labor. I'm a professor, an associate
professor.

> PETER
>
> (squeamish)
> Yeah, but, I mean . . .

MED. CLOSE-UP SHOT of the CHAIR. Wrings hands. Runs hands through hair.

> CHAIR
>
> This is about what's best for the department.

CAMERA HOLDS with the CHAIR momentarily, then SWINGS a 180 and LANDS IN a CLOSE-UP SHOT of PETER cracking a polite smile, as if saying cheese.

> PETER (V.O.)
>
> (Brooklyn, Italian American)
> Who's better than me?[32]

MED. TWO SHOT of the colleagues sitting opposite each other.

> CHAIR
>
> (mentorship)
> Optimum est pati quod emendare non possis.[33]

---

32. DeLillo, *Underworld*, 207.
33. Seneca, *Letters on Ethics*, 425.

PETER
(biting tongue)
Yes, sir. A printer cartridge tomorrow, an
additional teaching assistant next semester, the
choicest of classrooms, a sabbatical sooner rather
than later, and a new laptop in a year or two.
Thank you, sir.

END DREAM SEQUENCE.

INT. PETER'S OFFICE (BACK TO SCENE)

EXTREME CLOSE-UP SHOT – PETER slides DVD into the computer's
disc drive.

It is the movie "AND EVERYTHING IS GOING FINE," by Steven
Soderbergh.[34] A biopic about Spalding Gray, a legendary performer of
autobiographical monologues from the 1960s to the 1990s, who examined, among other things, issues of mental illness, emotional life, and
family.

MED. CLOSE-UP SHOT

The movie plays on the monitor as PETER, hunched at his desk, soaks it
in. Excerpts of the somber and hilarious performances of a man PIECING
A LIFE BACK TOGETHER, one memory, one true thing at a time.[35]

NARRATOR (V.O.)
For Peter, this is inspiration. Instead of narrating a
normatively responsible self in a fable of
rectification, instead of preferring the
seamlessness of the story to the truth of the

---

34. Soderbergh, *And Everything Is Going Fine.*
35. Russell, "Mark Russell," 182.

person,[36] Peter could insist upon not resolving
grief and staunching vulnerability too quickly.[37]

PETER swivels. Thinks about resemblances and father. That HUMBLE,
that ALTAR. Wonders MAN, OH MAN, what has he done. He decides to
write a biopic about himself and explain angry email in terms of the
overwhelm.

> NARRATOR (V.O.) (CONT'D)
>
> The teaching, the big lecture class, it is like one of
> the few things he has had, like, in life. A source of
> sought-for esteem, a claim to some small fame.
> But everybody knows this is nowhere (except the
> students).[38] Zip, zilch, nada, the teaching. Diddly-
> squat. Promotions, raises, the enrollments and
> evals do not count for much. The "such an
> awesome teacher" does not have anything shiny
> and new for sale on Amazon. He faces the looming
> risk of acquiring the demeaning label of a "one-
> book author." Stuck in midcareer. Stuck in the
> middle.

CAMERA PANS to follow PETER aimlessly shuffling papers down the
length of the desk.

> PETER (V.O.)
>
> I'm your average mameluke. Hitting up one of the
> best zoos in the Midwest. I'm gonna be stuck at
> this university forever, I guess.

A beat.

36. Butler, *Giving an Account of Oneself*, 64.
37. Ibid., 100.
38. Neil Young & Crazy Horse, *Everybody Knows This Is Nowhere*.

PETER (V.O.) (CONT'D)

No pull-ups, not ever. Stack of Norman Mailer on
the nightstand. I coulda been a contender. I
coulda been somebody.[39]

CAMERA APPROACHES as PETER looks up at audience.

PETER

(addressing the camera)

I'm a pound of maplewood-smoked bacon at the
butcher counter at Schnucks. Heaps of bacon
shrapnel stuff at the salad bar in the Student
Center. Schnitzel at Reed's American Table in
Maplewood — date night. We start with the
cheese plate. Humboldt Fog has herbaceous notes
and floral overtones. A few years ago, Humboldt
fog was a wad of twenty twenties for a full deck. I
used to buy in the Mi Ranchito parking lot. Now
I'm on the lookout for a high chair, and we're
already into chips and salsa at 4:45 for the kids.

EXT. ANTHROPOLOGY BUILDING – DAY (WEEKS LATER) (ESTABLISHING)

Semester's end. The students wear tank tops and cutoffs. The HUSTLE-
BUSTLE means the bell has gone off.

INT. MAIN CORRIDOR

Colleagues celebrate the calendar's halt. SUMMER PLANS.
Adventuresome FIELD TRIPS. WRITING RETREATS. Canoes. Upper
Peninsula. . . . PETER stays local with the sweltering summer and a child-
ish, stooging-around art project that does not make sense to colleagues.

---

39. Kazan, *On the Waterfront*.

EXT. ST. LOUIS – PETER'S HOUSE – DAY (ESTABLISHING)

Brick house in a collegiate neighborhood. Prius parked in front.

INT. LIVING ROOM

Lying on a friendly leather couch, PETER is toiling at laptop. Academic materials alongside personal and pop culture materials on floor and coffee table strewn. This is the workroom. He is working it with all he has, because it is all he has. And he is breaking rule number one of anthropology: writing with abandon about himself — a shark-jumping, deconstructive, research-resisting fuck-scream.

> NARRATOR (V.O.)
>
> There is — in the story of the email — a panoply:
> reasons, compulsions, persuasions, and impulses
> that belong to depth psychology.

> PETER (V.O.)
>
> Off limits. Out of bounds. Not for the water cooler.
> Not for anthropology.

> NARRATOR (V.O.)
>
> A book about a boy. Coming of age between
> starkness and ambiguity, between silences and
> liveness. "Just say no." No, wait. "All you can eat."
> Disharmonies of stringency and permissibility
> across locations of culture.[40] The anxious,
> surreptitious stretching across worlds to get girls
> and go to heaven, stay snuggly sheltered and set
> forth, keep promises and devour new
> pornography.

SFX: Jangly nineties alternative rock.

40. Bhabha, *The Location of Culture.*

NARRATOR (V.O.) (CONT'D)

This is an alternative book without a plot, except
for its preoccupation with entangled knots.
Something like a history of the present,[41] delving
into the dark but firm web of our experience.[42]
Enigmatic articulations that cannot easily be
translated into narrative form.[43] Evermore life and
times, rummaging through baggage, ruminating
over indications, indiscretions, and inheritances in
making sense of actions and breakdowns.

MONTAGE: THE WORKROOM

– Diet Coke can on wooden coffee table.

– Framed family photographs on end tables and windowsills.

– Rows of DVDs, mostly foreign films, on television stand — an embarrassment of shelves.

– Clusters of assorted, stacked books, some folded open, on floor.

– "THE VULNERABLE OBSERVER" by Ruth Behar atop one of the stacks.[44]

END MONTAGE.

INT. LIVING ROOM (BACK TO SCENE)

CAMERA PUSHES IN on PETER wriggling into the cushions. Getting comfy. Finding renewed satisfaction with writing in autotheory.[45]

---

41. Foucault, *Discipline and Punish*, 31.
42. Foucault, *The Birth of the Clinic*, 199.
43. Butler, *Giving an Account of Oneself*, 64.
44. Behar, *The Vulnerable Observer*.
45. Nelson, *The Argonauts*.

                    PETER (V.O.)

I'm gonna do a chapter about the influence of
board games in my life . . . and one about how my
dad invented French bread pizza but never got
credit. And a chapter about my cousin Georgie
storming out of the restaurant when they wouldn't
put a fried egg on his veal parmesan. And a
chapter or more about war.

CLOSE-UP SHOT of PETER as he turns to look directly into the
CAMERA.

FREEZE FRAME

                    PETER (V.O.) (CONT'D)

A book about a boy. A patchwork, and it works
with anecdotes and strands. Episodes of sarcasm,
irony, intensity, sullenness, chaos, and
disturbance. Loss and love, I suppose. And so,
okay. Okay, here it goes. The story of the email
unfolds. In disparate scenes and incommensurate
forms and registers told.[46] Not good ethnography.
Not speech act theory. Not much of anything,
really. For having read too much Kathleen
Stewart, it's more like an old flannel shirt worn of
wanderings athirst in the Great American
Desert.[47]

                                        FADE OUT.

---

46. Stewart, *Ordinary Affects*, 4.
47. Melville, *Moby-Dick*, 4.

4 Murmur of the Heart

<u>New Haven</u>

O Connecticut! Your Connecticut! Where you grew up traipsing woods and thickets, clambering over eighteenth-century stone walls in Vietnam-era olive-drab camouflage fatigues, playing war. Now you wanna return for a job at Yale. Because, one, you don't have allergies in Connecticut. And two, you're no longer dealing in the debility that developed in New Haven, where there's the best Italian American food in the Anthropocene, and where you did a one-year postdoc in publishing, pizza, and pot.

It was through growing up in Connecticut that you learned about Jewish people. Perceived foreignness in rituals, names, hair. Now—who knew? You are kind of kin.

You learned to make out and get it on and become tactile and unfurled in Connecticut. Your first hetero hookup was with a girl from New Canaan, a couple of stops south along the Metro-North commuter rail, meaning you were slightly socioeconomically poorer. Going up on her felt like a variety of upward mobility. (Cue "Fifteen" by Taylor Swift.)[1] The youth

---

1. Swift, "Fifteen."

group at the church where your father evangelized with the Jews for Jesus association—that's where you two met. It was autumn. The uncooperative fit of the couch upstairs. Feeling scared. Father downstairs. Removing fleece outerwear. Body fleshy, solid, and stout like yours. This corporeality became a thing for you. An athleticized, suburban Connecticut desire for some element of androgyny.

O Connecticut! Your Connecticut! Where the cognitive mappings that link the Allman Brothers Band, the Beacon Theatre, Washington Square Park, and the alluring and awkward experimentalities of high school curled in your mind around a certain stereotype of Jewishness.

Another movie in the desert island trunk.[2] A tragedy that is—from one angle, in one askance reading, or broadly speaking—about suburban Connecticut fraughtness regarding urbane, white nonethnicity. A period piece like no other, mise-en-scène speaking. Eeries and evocatives. Fall forests. Stone walls. The privileged, all-assuming, adolescent entanglements with sex, drugs, and what is—in Connecticut vernacular—known solely as "the City." Katie Holmes—her first film—is this unbelievable teenage dream, open to a night, willing to go there in a boy-crazed, insane way, an elite Manhattanite spending Thanksgiving eve doing drugs, taking pills in her vacationing parents' loft with an infatuated Tobey Maguire, a WASPy prep schooler from New Canaan, and his buddy, a darkish, drug-holding David Krumholtz, deethnicized in the film as Francis Davenport to likewise indicate prep. Stony night eyes open, close. Good guy Maguire hangs out, soberly. The others pass out. He who has a high school crush is conscientious, bids a silent goodnight and leaves to catch the early morning train back home, north to New Canaan.

O Connecticut! Your Connecticut! The leaves, and the fleece, the fleece outerwear, and the Allman Brothers Band's annual run at the Beacon, where you, with a boyish, hairless face and a Patagonia fleece, were pulled by your Jewish best friend into a scene of jam band followings and pagan exotica, barefoot fire spinners, girls with armpit hair and hairy guys with prairie skirts, nitrous tanks and hits, all-white, patchouli-lit, djembe drum circles, atmospherics, replications, Orientalisms, and nostalgias spawning a world of playing culture amid the hot peace, suburbanites performing

2. Lee, *The Ice Storm.*

3. Beacon Theatre in New York, September 27, 1989. Photograph
by Kirk West.

strangeness and exile amid the longue durée of the reverberations of
Robert Zimmerman's commute.

You and shaggy-haired, sideburned Seth took the commuter train from
Norwalk to Grand Central, then a subway down to Washington Square
Park ("The city [. . .] is always the city seen for the first time, in its first
wild promise of all the mystery and the beauty in the world"),[3] and you
guys rambled around presuming all the bums sold weed, and you relayed
through code some silly what's-up-ness, and you felt scared and iffy, like
"Let's just go," scared like you did when you were going up on lovely New

3. Fitzgerald, *The Great Gatsby*, 68.

Canaan, scared of some sin sensorium, and scared of your father who prayed with shaggy-haired men, and there you were with shaggy-haired Seth, a Canaanite, and you scored, like you scored with lovely New Canaan, and you and Seth took a subway north to Broadway and Seventysomething, to a Beacon Theatre fracas about who'll smuggle the stuff inside, and you said, "You, you," like "No, no," or "Let's just go," and you both entered the baroque smokehouse, that majestic old theater, and the Allman Brothers jammed.

O Connecticut! Your Connecticut! Where New Haven is the last stop on the Metro-North, where, during the postdoc, you physically folded into a path. Nick Drake on repeat replaced the Allman Brothers and Bob Dylan, the lovely, melancholic first album, *Five Leaves Left*.[4] And that dank smell permeated your fleece outerwear and everything you had in that little rental room, and this long-overdue love affair or lapsed adolescent infatuation pushed a hyperfunctional flurry, and you went wild and jammed out and got a great academic gig and moved to the Midwest and took it with you, the leaves of grass,[5] and the infatuation unraveled and the nature of it all had penetrated into your psyche and biology so deep and hard that wherewithal was lost, and there was impossible paralysis, and it would take the healing power of sharing stories and the magical work of a remarkable rabbi and improbable incorporation into a small society of Jewish friendship to free you from the authentic grip of powerlessness known and verified by those who cannot stand up from the couch.

St. Louis

The rabbi asks, "What do we have? We have our stories," he says. "This is hard stuff. There's no judgment. Go out, come back in. There's never a not-welcome."

"Have you seen _____?"

"Doing sheetrock down in South City."

"He's hanging sheetrock. Hanging on."

---

4. Drake, *Five Leaves Left*.
5. Whitman, *Leaves of Grass*.

"Go out, come back in."

"Inpatient, outpatient."

"On and off meds."

"Go out, come back in."

"A week is good. A day, hour, minute, second is good."

Around the table, they speak of birthdays.

Connecticut to college. Straight to grad school. Stint in tobacco country. Back to Boston. Greyhound to New Haven. Southwest terminal in St. Louis. Brick house. Tenure track. Big promotion. All a big blur.

Years.

And then. A seat at the table.

Everyone in the group had shared. Here was a first-timer with a story of despair.

"Pass."

Go out, come back in.

A week later, everyone in the group had shared. "First name only," an invitation to the second-timer, a gesture of care.

"I'm Pete. My therapist told me to come here. I'm not Jewish."

"That's okay. It doesn't matter."

"I've never done this kind of thing—a meeting like this. The truth is, it feels good to be here. I'm a drug addict. I've been using drugs a long time. I'm fucking tired. I can't do it anymore. It's all I do. Drive to meet my dealer and then go home and just sit on the couch. A few years ago, I had a nervous breakdown. Doing all kinds of weird shit. I was on this airplane, I don't remember where, and I tore the ads out of the magazines and wrote 'shame' on them with a black Sharpie marker, all caps, big bold letters. I went around the airport handing the pieces of paper out to strangers. And some airport cops, I asked if they had seen anything suspicious. I wanted to get arrested. But yeah. I don't really know what I'm supposed to say. When everything feels like the movies, yeah, you bleed just to know you're alive.[6] I get ulcers from too many painkillers. Sometimes I cut myself. Sometimes I make myself throw up to get, like, a high. When I had my breakdown, that was a few years ago, when Occupy was happening, I was gonna quit my job and join the protests. I wanted to fight cops. And

6. Goo Goo Dolls, "Iris."

it's crazy because I've got a wife and a kid and a good job. And I'm good at my job. I wanted to run away. I was heading toward losing everything. And then one night, I was watching protests on television, and I took a shitload of Klonopin, and I wound up in the hospital. It was like, 'Here ya go, you're manic,' and I went into the psych ward for a while."

(Email from student, November 16, 2011. Subject: "Your Whereabouts . . . Sorry for Being Nosy." Body: "Are you at Occupy Wall Street in New York? Just a theory. Some person in class today actually asked if you had been arrested. The TAs assured us that that wasn't the case.")

"It seems no one can help me now, I'm in too deep. . . . Seems like I should be getting somewhere. Somehow, I'm neither here nor there. Can you help me remember how to smile? Make it somehow all seem worthwhile.[7] I want something else to get me through this.[8] That's why I'm here. I text my dealer and drive to the parking lot at Mi Ranchito and drive back home. That's the loop. When he doesn't respond right away, I text him again. Over and over. It's all I do. 'Where are you?' 'What's up?' 'Did you get my text?' I ask my wife if maybe he doesn't like me anymore, and that's the worst possible thought, you know, not having a dealer, and she says, 'He's a fucking drug dealer: it's his job to deal with addicts and crazy people. He's probably stoned.' But yeah. I don't know what else to say."

Go out, come back in.

A week later, everyone in the group had shared. And here was this newcomer, hunched in his chair, disheveled, kinda wannabe, really. The woolly cap, the hoodie hanging back.

The rabbi smiled. "I remember being you. I wish I could go back there. It's a beautiful, wonderful place to be. You are down there, man. And you're working it. I remember being right there where you are. We all know that place. I know those eyes. The thing is. You came back here."

The medical translation of addiction is "hitmakrut," meaning to be sold to. The rabbi used another word that week. He said "takua," meaning stuck, used to refer to being stuck in traffic, broken down, jammed. The rabbi also shared a parable:

7. Soul Asylum, "Runaway Train."
8. Third Eye Blind, "Semi-Charmed Life."

"A man is fleeing a tiger in a field. He comes upon a cliff, jumps, catches hold of a vine, and holds on for dear life. Ferocious tiger up; down below crags, crashing waves. The vine is tearing and tearing. He turns and sees a strawberry in a small hole in the cliff. Grasping the vine with one hand, he plucks the strawberry with the other. How sweet it tastes! That's it, that's the story," the rabbi told the group. "Some people say it's about enjoying the present, living in the now. Others talk about temptation and foolishness. Others about accepting fate. But maybe it's about movement, getting unstuck."

The rabbi then referred to the word "sur," as in a turn aside, and how, in Exodus 3, Moses turns toward God, interpellating him from the burning bush. The rabbi held his hand ajar in front of himself, over the table. Twisted his hand, subtly, said "strawberry." Twisted his hand, said "gesture." Said "flutter."

Go out, come back in.

A week later, March 9, 2015, no one had shared—a silence, an air. And here the newcomer was again sitting there.

"I have one week."

A few hands slapped the table.

"I don't know what to say. I don't remember what it's like to feel good because I've been fucked up so long. After the last meeting . . . after last week's meeting, I drove home and I told myself, 'Fuck it.' Manny was asleep. I went out for beer, my usual route. North up Kingsland, north of the Loop, past Mi Ranchito, and left on Olive to Schnucks—the Olive Street Schnucks, the Black Schnucks, my Schnucks—where the liquor section is right up front near the long self-checkout of torn clothes, sweats, dirty hair, cheap beer, and fidgety despair. But on the way to the store, I got stuck. I was driving past Manny's preschool, and I thought to myself, 'Next week I'm gonna say it.' I wanted to come in here and tell you guys, 'One week.' I turned into the parking lot, the parking lot at Manny's school. Circled around. Pulled into a space. Parked. And right there, she was right there sitting next to me, leaning on the console. I asked if she wanted some music. I put on 'Harvest Moon' by Neil Young. Our song, I always say—desperately, romantically. A tune for pledging, or hoping for, an assuring arc. A song about an enduring love that's withstood really hard stuff. An impossible, hanging-on love. ('Because I'm still in love with you,

4. Jacques Tati as the bumbling Monsieur Hulot in *Trafic* by Jacques Tati, 1971 (Smith Archive/Alamy Stock Photo).

I want to see you dance again. Because I'm still in love with you, on this harvest moon.')[9] And right there, I stared out at Manny's school through my windshield. I needed to do one thing. Shift gears. I backed up, backed out. Circled around the parking lot and thought, 'Fuck it.' Thought, 'I'm gonna grab some beer and crash on the couch.' I was like, 'Nevermind.'[10] But then I pulled into another spot. Parked. Sat there. It didn't feel like willpower. It felt like a handle. I was like, 'Fuck it,' and I backed out again, but then pulled into another spot just as quickly. I circled around the parking lot. Over and over. Doing a loop. Jacques Tati. *Trafic.*[11] Jammed. And then, I just, I dunno, I drove out and drove home. I don't know if it was Manny or if it was her or just the little life in general. I wanted to get home and tell my wife: 'Finally, I figured out, but it took a long, long time. And now there's a turnabout, maybe 'cause I'm trying. There's been times,

9. Young, "Harvest Moon."
10. Nirvana, *Nevermind.*
11. Tati, *Trafic.*

I'm so confused. All my roads, well, they lead to you.'[12] I hurried through the front door and ran upstairs to see her. 'Hey,' she said. 'You're back. What's the deal? Where's the beer?' And I was like, 'Is this the right decision?' And she went, 'What the fuck do you think?' See, because I don't know. The decisions and soul movement feel strange. That was one week ago. We drive by that parking lot on the way to Mi Ranchito. It's the familyest, friendliest restaurant around. Manny goes to school at that parking lot. My specialest place in the Anthropocene."

12. Sister Hazel, "All for You."

5 Do the Right Thing

<u>Breakfast</u>

The name comes from Henry James, or, according to Kedron's version, one of her great-great-grands. He has a great personality. Loves to eat. Calls assorted food "bar." Only we understand the pronunciation. Bran Flakes, Cheerios, Fig Newtons, and the organic blueberry cobbler ancient grains bars. All food is "ah gar."

He sits in his high chair across from me at the dining room table. I look at him and blink and we play eyes. Henry is on his way. He is growing up.

Schools are a big deal in St. Louis. Always the first question. The proverbial "Where?" encodes so much about race, class, culture, and geography in a landscape of segregation. These "public secrets" enshroud that "which is generally known but cannot be spoken."[1]

Kedron and I live in an inner-ring suburb, one of the most socioeconomically and racially diverse municipalities in the region. Some people in more affluent and homogenous suburbs stigmatize the town and its schools because of apparent lacks and diversities. Most of our faculty colleagues

---

1. Taussig, *Defacement*, 50.

would not consider sending their kids to these schools. We live in the largely white, bourgeois section of town, and nearly all our neighbors opt for the private-school route. Kedron and I have chosen to send Manny and Henry through the public school system. We love these schools. We believe they are good schools. We see positive things happening despite the pervasive skepticism and realities of relatively limited resources. We believe in a different or expansive notion of what "good" means when it comes to schooling.

When he started out at the preschool, Manny was one of a handful of white kids among several dozen Black kids. Another kid's parents had emigrated from Mexico. An Asian American kid was growing up in the part of town historically populated by Chinese immigrants. Manny was not receiving free or reduced-price lunch like many others. The school building was not remodeled. Manny was little and learning. Kedron and I expected that this sociocultural and socioeconomic situation would shape him. (One of us quixotically—all right, obnoxiously—has carried an inflated idea that this school decision is part of a project in worlding, a deliberate political act, a moral act, an intentional act of spatial and racial engagement in a segregated metropolitan area.)

Manny and Henry are privileged in growing up with two professor parents. They also benefit in going to these schools. Manny sees Black people filling institutional ranks: teachers, practitioners, and instructors in music and art, physical education, caregiving, coaching—Ms. J. the school nurse, the principal, the administrators, Mr. D. the school enforcer, Mr. F. the custodian, and the Black parents and families. He comprehends dependencies and double shifts and forms of kinship and the idea—indispensably conveyed in history and art and music lessons, hallway display cases, and the proud insistences of teachers—that Black lives matter.

He says "boy." As in, "Boy, you got hot takis in your hair." We cringe and correct, saying, "You, we, don't call people boy."

He says "I be." We correct him. But why?

It will impact his life.

It can get him into trouble.

It does not belong to him.

We knew that Manny would confront frictions, having to figure things out. Good schools—where Manny and Henry are not part of a dominant majority and where diversity is not overwhelmingly a neoliberal commodity.

LUNCH

FADE IN:

EXT. AFFLUENT SUBURB – DAY (ESTABLISHING)

AERIAL SHOT reveals a patchwork of concrete parking lots and office buildings surrounded by the densely wooded cul-de-sacs and labyrinthine streets of residential neighborhoods.

EXT. DOWNTOWN

CAMERA BOOMS DOWN and PUSHES IN on a well-worn extended hatchback car as it takes slow corners around the suburb's central business district.

INT. CAR

KEDRON, a woman in her late thirties, sits squarely at the steering wheel. Strikingly attractive, she plays it down by wearing no makeup, a loose-fitting vintage dress, and flat shoes.[2] She carries within herself a great fund of life, and her deepest enjoyment is to feel the continuity between the movement of her own heart and the agitations of the world.[3]

In the passenger seat, not unusually good-looking, PETER does the broken-in flannel thing. Stares out the window, mesmerized as always by how nice everything is in this affluent suburb abutting campus, on the other side of campus from their own more modest municipality.

> PETER
>
> It's such a terrific town.

---

2. Linklater and Krizan, *Before Sunrise*, 5.
3. James, *The Portrait of a Lady*, 35.

KEDRON

It really is.

PETER

How can people fail to see in it the best possible plan of the best possible state of society?[4] All the advantages of modern social conditions without the struggles and dangers necessarily resulting from them.[5]

She laughs, and he slowly joins her.[6]

PETER (CONT'D)

Such a low crime rate.

KEDRON

No crime, really.

PETER

(pointing)
Everyone follows the speed limit and stops right there.

KEDRON

Right at the crosswalk.

PETER

No one jaywalks.

4. Marx and Engels, *The Communist Manifesto*, 40.
5. Ibid., 38.
6. Linklater and Krizan, *Before Sunrise*, 8.

> KEDRON

Never.

> PETER

And no drugs.

> KEDRON

No study drugs.

> PETER

Nobody's fucking around.

> KEDRON

Zero problems.

Townhouses. Shop-lined streets. People watching and possibilities pondering. For the two faculty members, Sunday driving . . . on a weekday.

TWO SHOT from back seat shows the sweethearts in friendly chitchat and enjoying the scenery.

> KEDRON

Here are the houses that aren't hiding anything.

> PETER

Might as well not even have walls or shutters.

> KEDRON

Nobody is throwing stones.

PETER places his hands together to make a church.

> PETER
> (nursery rhyme)
> Here is the safe neighborhood. Here is the steeple.
> Open the doors and see all the people.

CAMERA shooting out side window reveals a lengthy queue extending along Main Street from the brunch place. Waiting to be seen.

> KEDRON
>
> Why don't you write a chapter about brunch?

> PETER
>
> (perplexed)
> I'm listening.

> KEDRON
>
> Okay, um. What's with the celery stalks? Why does everything come with a biscuit?

> PETER
>
> But what's the moral of the story?

> KEDRON
>
> It's all in the ethnography.

They have a hard laugh. For they share a local knowledge, appreciating the frivolousness of the academic wisecrack.

MONTAGE: STREETSCAPE

– Citizens strolling. Leashed dogs dawdling.

– The long and winding road for Belgian waffles and Bloody Marys.[7]

– Skin-tight bicycle shorts and jerseys.

– White jeans.

– SUV-size jogging strollers.

7. The Beatles, "The Long and Winding Road."

– CACKLES and TUGS from purposefully abstruse names ("Odin," "Wren"), an implication of uniqueness for lives that are being cultured for a same, already clichéd KIDS, cute goshes.

END MONTAGE.

INT. CAR (BACK TO SCENE)

TWO SHOT through front windshield. PETER and KEDRON are getting bored.

>   KEDRON
>   (deliberates)
>   Are you thinking?

>   PETER
>   Brunch?

>   KEDRON
>   Yeah. Some participant observation.

>   PETER
>   Sounds good.

Neither says anything for an extended moment.[8]

>   KEDRON
>   Okay. Here's one.
>   (deadpan)
>   I went to a restaurant that serves breakfast at any
>   time. So I ordered French toast during the
>   Renaissance.[9]

---

8. Linklater and Krizan, *Before Sunrise*, 106.
9. Wright, "Water."

PETER

Did you make that up?

KEDRON smiles.

EXT./INT. CAR

The vehicle pulls into a curbside spot. Rolls to the silent stop of a hybrid. PETER and KEDRON unbuckle seat belts and open doors, stepping out into the space of the grid.

EXT. BRUNCH LINE

CAMERA MOVES with them as they join the column. Not teaching today. Not having much on their plates. Feeling the pull of pancakes, they start the long wait. They are hitched into the luxuries and ambivalences of a semi-urban academic life.

KEDRON

(leaning toward him)
Whatever ultimately comes of our lives, we made
the decision to buy a Prius.

PETER

We sure did.

He grasps her hand and gently pulls her to his side. Wants to confide.

PETER

Remember that game of choosing a different
historical period? Did you ever play it when you
were little?

KEDRON

I guess.

PETER

Turns out the moral of the story is plumbing.

She smiles at the thought but is not totally sure.[10]

PETER (CONT'D)

(giddy)

That's the whole thing. Habitations of modernity.[11]
That game, it's why I went into anthropology. I
wanted to have the job where you sit around and
play that game, like all the time. Is it better to live
in this swanky suburb or some medieval town or a
rainforest village? It was always about relativism
for me. It was always about a critique of
modernity, a critique of America, really.

She smiles, not really taking him seriously.[12]

KEDRON

I love how brunch always turns into graduate
school.

PETER

Foucault fucked you up, too. Historical ontology.
Assemblage studies. That's why Aihwa Ong has
always been so important for me.

CAMERA PANS as the line sluggishly moves along.

Artisanal toy store. New old-fashioned delicatessen. Family-friendly craft
brew pub. The sidewalk is stop and go. Past on-street parking it flows.
Northern European luxury cars. Southern European performance cars.

10. Linklater and Krizan, *Before Sunrise*, 25.
11. Chakrabarty, *Habitations of Modernity*.
12. Linklater and Krizan, *Before Sunrise*, 99.

PETER has an anthropological appreciation for the business district mojo
— a variety of white-collar status culture not unlike faculty bios and academic conference lobbies and bars.

>   PETER (CONT'D)
>
> Politics is the adventure of the otherwise. Looking
> after the otherwise as it becomes an arrangement.
> The study of why some modes of existence stay in
> place.[13]
>
>   KEDRON
>
> Here we go . . .
>
>   PETER
>
>   (more and more excited)
> All of this is one arrangement of many possible
> arrangements. . . . Ethics is the struggle to foster
> and extend the many names of the otherwise such
> that they are given life.[14] That's why Povinelli is so
> important for me.
>
>   KEDRON
>
> Yeah. Easier said, dude.
>   (turns to him)
> Deviation is hard.[15] The world is the real world,
> however much you read Foucault.
>
>   PETER
>
>   (turns to meet her)
> Deviation is made hard.[16] The more a path is

13. Povinelli, "Geontologies of the Otherwise."
14. Ibid.
15. Ahmed, *What's the Use?*, 160.
16. Ibid.

used, the more a path is used.[17] There are
pressures of investment and promises of
investment.[18] And it all makes sense. Because
there are gifted kids, kids deserving more
attention, kids who have solidified life interests at,
like, age six. The naturalizing certainty. "Salinger."
"Romy."

KEDRON

Yes, and some schools have fewer gifted kids. Not
interested in anything. Not special.

PETER

Exactly. That's why they're there. The parents have
loser children and wisely decided to live in a
district with bad schools. Why waste an expensive
mortgage on ordinary kids? They would for sure
put a stake in the ground were their little ones
exhibiting the talents and flits.

KEDRON

(back to earth)
Look, people do what they gotta do. It's called
practicality.

CAMERA MOVES with them as the caravan crawls forward.

PETER

Remember grad school, that thick red book? It
said, and I quote, "Philosophers have only
interpreted the world; the point is to change it."[19]
That's the main one! The number eleven mic drop

17. Ibid., 40.
18. Zaloom, *Indebted*, 1.
19. Marx and Engels, "Theses on Feuerbach," 145.

at the end of the top ten list of all-time radical
political claims. It goes to eleven![20]

KEDRON

(rolling eyes)
You know so much about movies.

A farm-to-cone ice cream parlor, still unopened this morning.

PETER

This line is moving so slowly. Whose idea was it to
come here anyway?[21]

She steps closer to him and puts her arms around his neck.[22]

KEDRON

The brunch feelings were mutual. Don't hate the
player, hate the game. That's what they say.

PETER

Everyone's read Bourdieu. It's not like these
arguments are new. Tuition money from rich-kid
families is needed to enlighten the next generation
in the hopes of undoing inequalities. But I whine.
Because I'm frustrated. And resigned. Quiche on
my mind. And maybe the university's function is
replicating the existing state of society while
making sure students have a good time.[23] The
school-to-school pipeline. A sustainable recycling
program.

---

20. Reiner, *This Is Spinal Tap*.
21. *Seinfeld*, "The Chinese Restaurant."
22. Linklater and Krizan, *Before Sunrise*, 46.
23. Marx and Engels, *The Communist Manifesto*, 39.

KEDRON

Wow, you just took it to eleven.

The more he builds up to a rant, the more amused she seems to get.[24]

PETER

Regardless of political beliefs and what's on the
bookshelves and what they say in their own books,
professors buy up prime real estate while doing
critique on the neighboring country club campus.
And the school choices that are said to be
ineluctable — a veritable foist — they build on
removal campaigns to clear room for business
districts and eggs Benedict.

KEDRON

You're talking "talk is cheap."

PETER

I'm talking "there is nothing outside the
text."[25]

KEDRON

(really enjoying this)
Make your stakes, everyone. What's the betting?
I'm watching you, everybody's watching, I'm a
crowd all by myself. Do you hear the crowd? Do
you hear them muttering? "Coward! Coward!" —
that's what they're saying.[26] It's what one does,
and nothing else, that shows the stuff one's made
of. You are — your life, and nothing else.[27]

24. Linklater and Krizan, *Before Sunrise*, 53.
25. Derrida, *Of Grammatology*, 159.
26. Sartre, *No Exit*, 45.
27. Ibid., 43.

Carried away in frivolity, things have gotten quite spirited as they anticipate one coffee and one green tea.

KEDRON (CONT'D)

However much you want to be real, we're all
banking, all of us, on institutions and
investments . . .

PETER

(cuts her off)
An alibi society for a fantastical future when we
will no longer have to lamentably invest in and
benefit from inequalities in a holding pattern of
liberal idealism and dreams for everyone. The
trumpets will sound, and we will be changed.[28]
Every valley shall be exalted, every hill and
mountain shall be made low.[29]

VARIOUS SHOTS of the sweethearts interacting as they pulse toward the
destination. A group in front of them gives up, gets out of the line, does
not have the time. And the jam-packed file springs ahead to realign.
Making progress.

PETER (CONT'D)

A chapter about brunch, huh? Lululemon lappers
and besties and reconstructed family guys. A
contributor class always astonished by *Morning
Edition*.

KEDRON

I like *Morning Edition*.

28. 1 Corinthians 15:52.
29. King Jr., "I Have a Dream," 219; see Isaiah 40:4.

PETER

I know. But seriously, please cancel our fucking
membership.

KEDRON

<u>Sustaining</u> membership.

PETER

(huffy)
That's my point. Fucking bullshit. You know NPR
decided not to use the word "torture" to talk about
the torture regime?

She gives him a little kiss.[30] They are walking along slowly, awkwardly,
each a little in their own world.[31] PETER just smiles, looks at her, and
then slowly looks up at the sky.[32]

KEDRON

What are you thinking about?

PETER

The moral of the story.

KEDRON

I'm listening.

PETER

Okay.

A long pause.

30. Linklater and Krizan, *Before Sunrise*, 60.
31. Ibid., 102.
32. Ibid., 104.

PETER (CONT'D)

In conclusion, the institution is so awesome. So
highly ranked. No other lawn like it for hundreds
of miles. Everywhere straight lines. Absolutely on
brand all the time. But we don't feel fine in this
place most of the time.

KEDRON

I mean. Sure, we're all affected. But if this is what
Pete Benson is going through, then what's it like in
the depths out there? Some people are affected
more than others. We've got it pretty easy.

Getting into issues of culture and inclusion, PETER is way out on a limb.
CAMERA ZOOMS IN on him.

PETER

Yes. Right. Sara Ahmed. Institutions don't fit
everybody the same.[33] But if a professor like me,
the fear of talking about whatever it is . . . You
better leave yourself in the Prius in the parking lot
before heading up to the office because they don't
want you. Oh, you have a degree in social analysis?
Well, don't think about analyzing this place. Don't
scuttle the scam, man.

A beat.

PETER (CONT'D)

The atmosphere. The argot. The hardy har har.
Don't you forget to maintain your liberal subject
avatar! My sense of humor and how I'm too
outgoing. I give too much of myself to people, so
they tell me. I forget to leave myself in the garage,

33. Ahmed, *On Being Included*; Ahmed, *What's the Use?*

you see. My personality. Intensity. Playful. Cynical.
Some hostility. I slump over in meetings. The
meds make me drowsy. I'm not number one on the
U.S. News ranking of people. Problematic.
Compromised. Someone who curls up and lies.
This entire life behind things.[34]

KEDRON

(switching gears)
The other day, Kanye came on the playlist. Manny
mumbled the words and kinda nodded.

PETER

Which song?

KEDRON

I dunno. It was cute. And I thought about how
there weren't any Black kids in my school where I
grew up.

PETER

Me neither.

KEDRON

And I turned the knob down. . . . I know he's
gonna confront that word, and he'll learn why it's
the worst word and the best word and the most
important word. And face the contours and
boundaries of codes and styles that he now
assumes belong to everyone. Who knows? His life
is gonna be easy and hard. That's how life is. The

---

34. Mendes, *American Beauty.*

unpredictables we wade into in life, to grow both
young and old in it at once.[35]

Walking along in silence, they both are observing what is around them
and eventually look back at each other.[36]

PETER

Let's play pepper. I throw 'em out there, okay?
Round one. National parks? Quick. Quick.

KEDRON

Educational.

PETER

Zoos?

KEDRON

Need something to do.

PETER

Could you do honey?

KEDRON

Cheese with ease. I'm stuck at honey.

PETER

(incredulous)
Oh, please. You gotta have everything. You see
some of these motherfuckers going to Schnucks,
Trader Joe's, and Whole Foods just to make sure
they're doing everything right.

35. Deleuze, "Control and Becoming," 170.
36. Linklater and Krizan, *Before Sunrise*, 28.

KEDRON

And the gas?

PETER

I only go to one academic conference per year.

KEDRON

That's still releasing as much carbon as a
community might over a whole year in much of
the global south.[37]

It continues, the lazy line. The sweethearts go on musing about living's
design.[38]

PETER

The problem is, you settle into some sorta life,
right? You become an avant gardener.[39] Time
passes, and you're settled in, but then the
goalposts move. The ethics are obsolete after a
while. And it doesn't matter anyway, because now
you're investing in the little life. Can't even think
straight. You want the best for your kids. Lots of
presents under the tree. So you're like, "Oh, fuck
it." You literally say that a lot. And then. I dunno.
You grow old . . . You grow old . . . You wear the
bottoms of your trousers rolled.[40] You go to Target
sometimes because the fancy toy store is
expensive. You avoid Amazon except for
ecofriendly shampoo and conditioner.

37. @anandspandian, Twitter, November 19, 2019, 8:43 a.m.
38. Lubitsch, *Design for Living.*
39. Burnett, "Avant Gardener."
40. Eliot, "The Love Song of J. Alfred Prufrock," 9.

KEDRON

(teasing)
Pretty, pretty impressive. Say, do you eat anything
that's impossible? Are you waiting for civilization,
or past it and mastering it?[41]

PETER

Oh, fuck it. The chewy bars have pumpkin seeds
in them. The light bulbs and laundry detergent.
The Prius. The public schools. Wanting to do a
good job and wanting to be worthwhile. But it
doesn't matter. You and me, we're a net drain on
society, a bad location of culture.[42] We live in a
nice neighborhood in a mixed-bag municipality.
Our public-school kids are destined for university.
But they say the phrase "struggling parents" can't
be used if the family's got college savings.[43]
Whatever keeps capitalism afloat, right?

KEDRON

(droll)
He had reached a layer of the upper atmosphere
where the air . . .[44]

Her voice trails off and she gestures toward the sky, her hand tracing the
trajectory of a rocket ship. He continues in a tone of brinksmanship.

PETER

All right, maybe there's some jealousy. We have
colleagues who pose like revolutionaries, and they
get patted on the back for it. They live right here
. . . in Brunchtown. It's all a form of

41. Whitman, *Leaves of Grass*, 63.
42. Bhabha, *The Location of Culture*.
43. @IncentiveMusic, Twitter, December 29, 2019, 9:42 a.m.
44. Wolfe, *The Right Stuff*, 44.

contemplation. No real practical political activity.[45] Because the best schools know about Rosa Parks, too. But it's like a box of chocolates. You always know what you're gonna get.[46]

KEDRON

You really <u>do</u> know a lot about movies.

PETER

(ravenous)
Neoliberal multiculturalism. Comfortable relatability. But what about some otherwise probability? Some damning, deranging variations. Unsettling arrangements. Maybe this does happen. I dunno. There is no simple formula for the relationship of art to justice. But I do know that art means nothing if it simply decorates the dinner table.[47]

KEDRON stops in her tracks. Skips over a crack. Pirouettes. Then takes a whack.

KEDRON

(conductor's arms)
No hay banda! There is no band! Il n'y a pas d'orchestre! This is all a tape recording.[48]

PETER

(more and more heated)
Kids consuming and dramatizing every possible religious and cultural event in cartoons of Wells and Truth for a past tense of whoo and phew. A

45. Marx and Engels, "Theses on Feuerbach," 143.
46. Zemeckis, *Forrest Gump*.
47. Rich, "Why I Refused the National Medal for the Arts," 319–20.
48. Lynch, *Mulholland Drive*.

developmental awareness fleet devouring all of it,
forming from it, the tidiness of admissible and
profitable personalities in pomo minstrelsy
musicals and cantatas. For real, it's a fuck-
scream.

KEDRON

It's hard, you know. Everybody wants the best for
their kids.

PETER

Look, I don't care where you send your kids to
school. But everybody's like "Decolonize!" until it's
time to interrogate the desires and associations
colonization has produced.[49]

KEDRON

Oh yeah, they're gonna give up their career to
make a socially engaged book club or something
because you're calling them out for writing radical
history.[50]

She looks up at him.[51]

KEDRON (CONT'D)

By the time you're, I don't know, you've put up
with so much. Life wears down what you can do,
and you've seen all the photographs, or you're a
drop in the bucket.

49. @dickgirldiaries, Twitter, September 28, 2019, 3:05 a.m.
50. @noname, Twitter, December 29, 2019, 12:03 p.m.
51. Linklater and Krizan, *Before Sunrise*, 99.

PETER

What if instead of reflecting on privilege, throw a
brick through a window.[52]

KEDRON

You never threw a brick.

PETER

Because I have a disease. I can't throw just one.

KEDRON

Ha ha, like the potato chips.

PETER

Do you suppose yourself advancing on real ground
toward a real heroic man?[53]

KEDRON

I'd rather take coffee than compliments just now.
Thank you.[54]

PETER

What's taking so long?

KEDRON

Well, we <u>can</u> speed things up if you want.

PETER

(befuddled)
Okay?

---

52. @catcontentonly, Twitter, May 28, 2020, 12:59 p.m.
53. Whitman, *Leaves of Grass*, 106.
54. Alcott, *Little Women*, 349.

KEDRON

(chuckles)

Maybe we should eliminate certain faculty
members altogether. It'd be moral. . . . It'd be
right.[55] All the white men. Ha ha! You gotta luck
out on a 23andMe test to keep your job.

PETER

(desperately wanting)[56]

I don't know what the hell I'm doing with this new
book. Maybe it's the most hypocritical thing to do.
But I wore a hairnet, and so did you. And my mom
and dad did, too. So yeah, speaking personally,
that's what the business models and school
districts mean to me. Natural selections. The
extractions of interlinking inequality industries.
Taco Bell and the experts who study it. A
science of salsa packets. The change behind
the till.

They walk in silence, just taking in all around them for a few moments.[57]

PETER (CONT'D)

Ah, good conversation — there's nothing like it, is
there? The air of ideas is the only air worth
breathing.[58]

KEDRON

And I'm so excited for those pancakes.[59]

---

55. Russo, *Straight Man,* 19.
56. Better Than Ezra, "Desperately Wanting."
57. Linklater and Krizan, *Before Sunrise,* 48.
58. Wharton, *The Age of Innocence,* 219.
59. *Portlandia,* "Brunch Village."

PETER

We need one of those . . . those passes to jump in front of the line.

KEDRON

You want an enrichment program for the brunch place?

PETER

I don't want to stand in a line with you all morning talking about the other while waiting on apple butter.

KEDRON

Wait, what? You started it. This is your game, remember?

PETER

So what's the best historical period?

KEDRON

I'm just being realistic, Pete. Manny and Henry are probably gonna be tracked. The district isn't the same for us as it is for a lot of other families. This isn't a special political cause or anything. We probably couldn't have afforded it . . . but the fact is, we didn't choose to live in Brunchtown. We like a more diverse thing. We value the schools where we live. Being involved in the community. There's no grand theory.

PETER

Yes, and experience some different . . .

KEDRON

Here we go again.

PETER

... force and ambivalence. Potencies. The
personality of a place. The gently wearing walls of
the schoolhouse. Like not entirely precious or
something.

They look into each other's eyes. PETER reaches out for KEDRON's hand
and clasps it tightly. They smile, believing that they are changing the world
in unexpected ways, and then embrace tenderly for several moments.[60]

KEDRON

If we want to go to Bed Bath & Beyond ... I mean,
this line isn't moving.

PETER

(à la "Passionfruit" by Drake)[61]
Time out. Hold up. Wait a second. We've got to
start this conversation over ...

He just looks at her a little nervously and cannot say it. She is truly intrigued
and welcoming and a little excited at what he is struggling with.[62]

PETER (CONT'D)

I didn't have to write about the tobacco farmers the
way I did. I could have written a different book.

KEDRON

Oh, you don't say.

PETER

A book about the hold life has.[63] How humans are
born into worlds and how hard it is to live them

60. Linklater and Krizan, *Before Sunrise*, 107.
61. Drake, "Passionfruit."
62. Linklater and Krizan, *Before Sunrise*, 24.
63. Allen, *The Hold Life Has*.

differently or bring them into question or
transcend or oppose their possibilities and
dangers or become otherwise to communities and
structures or consider that such undertakings
would be interesting or necessary in the first
place.

KEDRON

Deviation is hard. You settle down. A place
becomes a home.[64] Like you said, the hold life has.
It's not the consciousness of men that determines
their existence, but their social existence that
determines their consciousness.[65]

PETER

Here's a different take on the moral of the story.
I'll spell it out. Moral. Of. The. Story. M.O.T.S. Get
it? Words, literally words. I'm thinking Foucault.
Les mots . . .[66] Words. Palabras. Language as the
passionate, phatic, aesthetic, musical, sentimental
source of society.[67] Being present to each other in
colloquy. Practically any American indie. What's
your favorite mumblecore movie? Conversation as
the uncovering of the self in vulnerability.[68]

KEDRON

Foucault really <u>did</u> fuck you up.

64. Lingis, *The Imperative*, 76.
65. Marx, *A Contribution to the Critique of Political Economy*, 21.
66. Foucault, *Les mots et les choses*.
67. Rousseau, *Essay on the Origins of Languages*.
68. Levinas, *Otherwise than Being, or Beyond Essence*.

PETER

(grins)

Well, then, we've got it easy.

KEDRON

We make life easier for each other, I think.

A long pause.

KEDRON (CONT'D)

Hey, I just wanted to say, I've always loved who
you are. But I also love who you've become in
the last few years. I love dad Pete, late-thirties
Pete.

PETER

Thanks for saying that. It means a lot.

An extended silence.

PETER (CONT'D)

Wait a minute. Why are <u>they</u> getting a table?

KEDRON

How do you know they didn't get here before us?

PETER

No, no, I think they cut in line.

KEDRON

Now that's radical. Time flies when you're
dismantling systems of oppression.[69]

(moving on)

69. @MadelineBacolor, Twitter, November 26, 2019, 9:23 p.m.

Okay, I think it's time for recess, professor. How
about we go home, have some pumpkin bars or
whatever, do email, and then go to the job talk.

PETER

Yeah, let's get out of here.

FADE OUT.

dinner

a campus visit is experience near.

on the way over here, we were talking about layovers, airport food, and
about what it's like.

neighborhoods, schools.

medium cool.[70]

welcome to the midwest.

such fascinating work, and the new project—predations of the grotesque.

what do you suggest?

the roasted red beets and goat cheese.

diet coke, please.

start-up fund, course release, ask for what you need.

and the book coming out, do you know, are your interlocutors gonna
read?

of course, you know where that might lead.

the position of the anthropologist is powerful—no one disagrees.

ideally, our work benefits the people we study. but there are no
guarantees.[71]

our relationships to research subjects are fraught.

ethnography is hanging out within earshot. sidling up to get forgot . . .
and whatnot.[72]

inhabiting somebody else's "is" for studies of anthropology's "ought."[73]

70. Wexler, Medium Cool.
71. Horwitz, "Just Stories of Ethnographic Authority," 137–38.
72. Didion, Slouching towards Bethlehem, xiv.
73. Hume, A Treatise of Human Nature, 302.

well, there's dred scott, there's nelly.

a complicated history and calamari.

oh my gosh, the talk, i loved the photography!

ethnography is inescapable memory. we never capture all the magic of fieldwork on paper. nothing can bring back what the books plunder.[74]

another way to work that magic would be memoir.

nobody wants all about my mother.[75]

it's not self-absorption when personal story and social analysis are in proportion.[76]

i don't know what's going to happen.

the wine depends on what people are having.

not as many slaves.

very livable.

the zoo is fantastic.

if you're single there are neighborhoods.

restaurants.

it depends.

ferguson changed the whole dynamic.

seed grants.

think about doing local research.

mine are in middle school.

starting to learn about everything.

tremendous.

business.

school district.

you know, it's what one of them, lacan or derrida, let's just say "jacques," it's what they called an "empty signifier."[77]

underrepresented minorities.

the university is diversifying.

you can't find the same square footage on the coasts.

livability is big.

where are we right now?

74. Horwitz, "Just Stories of Ethnographic Authority," 141.

75. Almodóvar, *All about My Mother.*

76. Rosaldo, *Culture and Truth.*

77. Mehlman, "The 'Floating Signifier.'"

well, we're sorta below, what, what would you guys say?

we're sorta below, and also around.

you see, there's this dividing line, and all falls down.[78]

and there's no getting around.

we live here, in town. but i don't know how that sounds. i mean, no, not really, though. more in a tucked-away neighborhood, you know?

but yes, that's what you're asking, i guess.

for the schools, yes.

they're the best.

and this is a restaurant on a street in the business district.

did you see the neat bookstore?

and as part of this tour, let me mention the brunch place next door.

technically, it's a brunch-themed restaurant. they serve brunch at any time.

and, oh my gosh, the lines.

we went today but couldn't get a table. no bagels. no pure maple. just gazing at our navels and going back and forth about hegel.

so, the new project, it seems particularly spatial. like an ever more granular kind of portrayal.

well, yes and no. i mean, it's different. i'm looking at the embodiment of duress in mundane articulations of what i'm calling "unfinished reparative dwelling," playing on a vignette about two loitering lovers who stumble upon and share a half-empty box of chocolates.

are you still working with lacan and derrida at all?

it's really more banal. ethnography attuned to the mess of the overall. the relationship between the symbolic and the real, we live in it, make no mistake.[79] but these stories relate an intimate gestural politics of improper habitation within excessively uneven distributional worlds, whereby the subject is constituted not simply as lack, but rather in terms of what i am calling "untempered estrangement."

the desire for that kind of grounding, for the concrete, feels so urgent right now.

---

78. West, "All Falls Down."

79. @Lacan_nocontext, Twitter, February 16, 2020, 10:52 a.m.

the statistics, models, and maps do not match what is happening on the ground.[80]

it's huge that global health is realizing the need for human accounts.

an anthropology of slowing-down, affect-savoring, lifeworlds.[81] the peopling of technologies . . . the mapping, tracking, or inquiry into cascades, changes, and implications.[82]

does anyone else feel like we're talking about a camping trip?

emerging life-forms.[83]

kinships and networks and norms.

power dynamics and the multitude swarm.[84]

critical infrastructures for living.[85]

or simply the layout of a building. it's all crucial for a policy to succeed.[86]

does anyone else feel like we're talking about a game of *simcity?*

when the nsf asks about the impact of our work, that's the key. tailoring program delivery to fit a local enquiry.

laugh out loud. did you just call anthropology "taylorism"?[87]

the horror![88]

ethnography through thick and thin.[89]

local knowledge provider for global health and development interventions. the epistemological equivalent of a spice bin.

that joke where the indigenous people are all named "gary" and "joe," but to make it sell, the anthropologist calls them "wolf pack" and "snow fox."[90]

sure, mock all you want. sell off your anthro stocks. but the local-knowledge black box means resources and hires—a bigger sandbox.

80. Fischer, *Anthropology in the Meantime*, 4.
81. Ibid., 3.
82. Ibid., 4.
83. Fischer, *Emergent Forms of Life and the Anthropological Voice.*
84. Hardt and Negri, *Multitude.*
85. Fischer, *Anthropology in the Meantime*, 2.
86. Shah, "Global Problems Need Social Science."
87. Taylor, *Scientific Management.*
88. Conrad, *Heart of Darkness*, 182.
89. Marcus, *Ethnography through Thick and Thin.*
90. @DanDanTransient, Twitter, January 19, 2020, 4:09 p.m.

so much is in our response. how the world itself can change with the assumption of another point of view.[91]

anthropology as self-formation?

ways to encounter the world anew . . . devices of imagination.[92]

exactly . . . it's about relativism and disruption. why don't we hear more about the anthropologist as being unsettled, going through upheavals and fundamental transformations?

it is as though we stand at the threshold of those two incompatible visibilities. . . . the painter could not at the same time be seen on the picture where he is represented and also see that upon which he is representing something.[93]

the issue is that so much of our critical theory is rooted in marx, in hegel, you know? our metaphors are about putting together, reaching across, synthesis. the dialectic feels good because it's about inclusion. somebody says, "anthropology is extractive?" and we answer, "nah, that's the old days. now it's collaboration, working with communities." we get to keep our jobs. whereas other metaphors aren't amenable—know thyself, get out of the way, stay in your lane, this relationship isn't working.

mother-fuck the dialectic, whatever, dualism. the problem is the system. try savoring affect really, really hard for tenure. what do you say when you bump into the dean? it's like, "no biggie, i'm just over here encountering the seeds of a humanity to come."[94] could you imagine if art history said that it's bringing about a revolution in the species?

i'll have what she's having.[95]

maybe let's clear everything out. repopulate our departments with the research subjects themselves. they can think about their own forests and tailor their own interventions.[96] it'd be moral . . . it'd be right.[97] cut out the middle people.

91. Pandian, *A Possible Anthropology*, 120.
92. @anandspandian, Twitter, January 7, 2020, 9:28 a.m.
93. Foucault, *The Order of Things*, 4.
94. Pandian, *A Possible Anthropology*, 3.
95. Reiner, *When Harry Met Sally* . . .
96. Kohn, *How Forests Think*.
97. Russo, *Straight Man*, 19.

when I came up for tenure, you should have voted against me.[98] the department didn't need another white male, and critical theory was already covered.

but what would happen with that kind of shake-up?[99]

you can't go into private business after popping the red pill.

what?

you know. the blue pill is life as you know it. the matrix. the world of deception and simulation. but the red pill, you wake up behind appearances. the things themselves.[100] anthropology is the red pill. i'll show you how deep the rabbit hole goes.[101]

michel foucault.

les mots et les choses.[102]

the research is slow.[103]

have a three- to five-year plan.

coq au vin.

cassoulet.

i imagine it's been such a long day.

you must have so many questions; just fire away.

st. louis. the university.

well technically, that's not quite true, but it's what they say.

no, it doesn't matter what he says.

some of the senior faculty are phasing out anyway.

the wine goes so nicely with the filet.

lobster gratin and seafood fumet.

chicken velouté.

shall we ask the waiter to bring us more of those croquets?

s'il vous plait.

the dean pays.

write signature pieces, well placed.

your book, right away.

98. Ibid.
99. Godard, *La Chinoise.*
100. Husserl, *Logical Investigations.*
101. The Wachowskis, *The Matrix.*
102. Foucault, *Les mots et les choses.*
103. Adams, Burke, and Whitmarsh, "Slow Research."

after tenure, you play.
maybe a vacay.
the new project, apply for money.
study precarity.
materiality.
teach later in the day.
sound good? sound okay?
there are so many.
big ideas.
research.
so, yes, i mean, no, not really.
not as many slaves.
looking at disparities.
it is so interesting.
advantages.
textures of suffering and frames of the resilient and the actionable.
you will love.
the roasted red beets and goat cheese.
inclusion and diversity.

6   Rushmore

Check Out

Kedron tenure-tracks at the coffee shop on weekends. These two guys go out for breakfast and run errands. Target for diapers and wipes for Henry, who is at home with the sitter.

This is the life.

Dad buys Manny a toy. Legos. Maybe an action figure.

They check out video games, electronics, and sports equipment. Leather baseball gloves. Nerf footballs. Sweet.

Then Petco for gecko food. Two dozen medium-sized crickets.

Then the Student Center on campus for downtime. Upstairs in the rec area, Manny is mesmerized by the undergrads sitting around a big screen, playing PlayStation. Dad sits on a nearby couch. Works at laptop, always works. He comes to realize the students are playing a gory first-person shooter game. *Call of Duty: Infinite Warfare.* Or *Battlefield.* Or *Doom.* Who knows? All he can say for sure is that the television is a seventysome-thing-inch point-of-view barrel exploding heads and faces, glorified oblit-erations of rendered bodies.

"Let's go don't tell Mom I'll buy you a doughnut."

Keep Improving. Lowes.

Save Money, Live Better. Walmart.

Save Big Money at Menards.

He has a bit of a belly. And he knows that there is some connection between bellies and scalar, political-economic "bigness."[1] And he wonders who or what is responsible in terms of structure and agency. Perhaps everyone and nobody. He senses "the pervasiveness of the conspiracy plot."[2]

A regional midwestern home improvement chain, Menards is physically the biggest of the box stores, a supersized, two-story Manifest Destiny metal hangar with people-mover escalators and industrial elevators and preposterous aisle layouts. They scout and chuckle. Manny cries out the overhead signs.

"Candy close to pet food. Yuck."

"Nails and screws nearby leaf blowers. Let's keep walking."

"Mulch across from microwaves. Mouth-watering."

"Patriotic flags next to for-sale signs. Figures."

The American dad is proud of his first-born, sharing a sense of humor, seeing Manny, half-toothless, smirk at retail camp. Traces and elements of himself at that age—precocious, energetic, and irreverent. A curiosity kid with a nose for off.

He knows his own mom misses six-ish Pete. Maybe that's why she's more interested in Manny. He knows he's gonna miss this Manny. And all the others. He was toxicologically skewed for the stretch of Manny's life from ages zero to four-ish.

And here he is in the middle, working the weekends. And it's time for lunch. As much as he enjoys sarcastic cavorting about capitalist improvement and life-enhancement logics, and as much as he would like to treat Manny to Panera or a slice of pizza, he suffers from a kind of neurasthenia which is temporarily cured by cloistering. He's always impatiently wanting to circle back. His mom had a way of saying, "Let's just veg out," meaning do nothing. Sit on the couch, keep the television company. Enter into a relaxed, transfixed "time space" of "intrinsic connectedness"—a "chronotope" that perhaps shaped an eventual pot plot.[3]

---

1. Tsing, "Supply Chains and the Human Condition."
2. Weales, "Mailer's *Maidstone*," 63.
3. Bakhtin, "Forms of Time and of the Chronotope in the Novel," 84.

And here he is in the middle. A rendering, fading in and out of attunement and attentiveness. Weekly homework club meetings extend way past six o'clock, and other parents are nonplussed. Not realizing there is a playoff game. Not needing news. Not worried that there might have been an attack. Not dismayed about cardiac arrest risk on the Supreme Court. Baseball practices are not canceled on account of drizzle. Everyone is out in the mist, not missing, obsessing, checking—not poring over tabloids. He envies the avidness and dedication and balance and focus of the others. Great catch interesting batting cages said group work report card summer camps do dinosaurs.

And he envies Kedron. Springtime is here, and he's on the couch spellbound by March Madness blowouts while wife and kids are outside playing fort.

He thought recovery was over at abstinence. But he's nel capolavoro di Alfred Hitchcock, "like crazy" in a way that is "a little too nonmetaphorical."[4] Debilitating anxieties. Capturing preoccupations. Neuroses about the minutiae of life. After work, he asks her if this or that that was said means this or that and if he needs to worry about this or that. She's interacting with a child who is throwing words and worries. ("What's my age again?")[5]

Setups

[H]e was greatly attached to his mother, who had not only fed him herself but had also looked after him without any outside help. This good little boy, however, had an occasional disturbing habit of taking any small objects he could get hold of and throwing them away from him into a corner, under the bed, and so on, so that hunting for his toys and picking them up was often quite a business. As he did this he gave vent to a loud, long-drawn-out "o-o-o-o," accompanied by an expression of interest and satisfaction. [. . . Not] a mere interjection but [. . .] the German word *"fort"* ("gone"). [. . . It] was a game and [. . .] the only use he made of any of his toys was to play "gone" with them. [. . .] The child had a wooden reel with a piece of string tied round it. It never occurred to him to pull it along the floor behind him, for

4. Berlant, "Genre Flailing," 157.
5. Blink-182, "What's My Age Again?"

instance, and play at its being a carriage. What he did was to hold the reel by the string and very skillfully throw it over the edge of his curtained cot, so that it disappeared into it, at the same time uttering his expressive "o-o-o-o." He then pulled the reel out of the cot again by the string and hailed its reappearance with a joyful "*da*" ("there"). This, then, was the complete game—disappearance and return.[6]

According to Sigmund Freud, this game enacts a "great cultural achievement" at a difficult moment in the child's life.[7] The mother is less often at the child's side. Through a process of toying with a symbolic object, repeating a "joyful return,"[8] the child becomes "master of the situation."[9] There is a mixture of pleasure and empowerment in a compulsive exacting of "revenge" on the mother "for going away," lending to the game a "defiant meaning," Freud writes, as in: "'All right, then, go away! I don't need you. I'm sending you away myself.'"[10]

Jacques Lacan's interpretation of the repetition impulse is more expansive. Not a narrow metaphor for mommy, reiterative activity is about coping with basic existential situations of "deprivation" and "solitude," and seeking the "desire of another."[11] A redundancy practice, an "endless circularity," to attain identity and the attention of a gaze.[12] Given the ceaseless "sliding-away" of meaning and definition in life,[13] the repetitious use of words and things seeks to secure "consistency, recognizability and unity."[14] The practice of signifying, Lacan theorizes, is "the subject's answer to what the mother's absence has created on the frontier of his domain—the edge of his cradle—namely, a *ditch*, around which one can only play at jumping."[15]

---

6. Freud, *Beyond the Pleasure Principle*, 14–15.
7. Ibid., 15.
8. Ibid.
9. Ibid., 17.
10. Ibid., 16.
11. Lacan, "The Function and Field of Language," 262.
12. Ibid., 264.
13. Lacan, *The Four Fundamental Concepts of Psychoanalysis*, 61.
14. Ragland-Sullivan, "The Psychical Nature of Trauma."
15. Lacan, *The Four Fundamental Concepts of Psychoanalysis*, 62.

"What the little boy must hide at all costs," to paraphrase Lacan, "is the lack of the object."[16]

Dad buys Manny a toy. Legos. Maybe an action figure.

They check out video games, electronics, and sports equipment. Leather baseball gloves. Nerf footballs. Sweet.

At Manny's age, Manny's dad was treated by his mom to Lincoln Logs and Playmobil. Lots of setups. Family Camping Trip. Comfortable Living Room. Lighthouse with Lifeboat. Scaffolding with Workers. Grand Castle of Novelmore. Mars Space Station. Redcoat Bastion.

A "setup" is a "memorial to [...] *jouissance*."[17] An entertaining physical space of make-believe—neighborhood, battlefield, pirate ship— assembled of figurines, pieces, accessories. A thematic configuration organized on floor, carpet, or table, a small psychoanalytical world where the child exercises control over a mini reality, and where the child's familial relationships figuratively crop up in and coordinate toy stories.[18] "Get in the car everybody! We're going to school! Vroom, vroom. Beep, beep." What the child is playing with in fort-da and setups is "none other than himself, the much moved-about, talked-about object of a mother's sometimes adoring, sometimes exasperated, sometimes rapt, and sometimes distracted attention."[19]

Growing up, Manny's dad built these ginormous, elaborate setups— spectacular cityscapes, settler-colonial spreads, wagon circles, open-faced domiciles, fantastical magic kingdoms, and decked-out military details of plastic army men. Oh, man, no one could move him away from his setups.

"Let me show you my setup," he peppered and pestered Mom.

And a decade later: "I made you this mixtape. Here you go. Let me know." And from afar, across the Connecticut town of his adolescence, he sat and listened, too. The desire of another. Some imagined simultaneity,

16. Ragland-Sullivan, "The Psychical Nature of Trauma"; see Lacan, *The Object Relation*, 158.

17. Lacan, *The Other Side of Psychoanalysis*, 81.

18. Sloterdijk, "We're Always Riding down Maternity Drive," 44; Lasseter, *Toy Story*.

19. Watson, "Guys and Dolls," 476.

5. Jason Schwartzman as the eccentric teenager Max Fischer in *Rushmore* by Wes Anderson, 1998 (Pictorial Press/Alamy Stock Photo).

like sex. (Cue "Neighborhood #1 [Tunnels]" by Arcade Fire.)[20] He supposed his friend—ahem, friend with benefits—listening some miles away on cushions, thinking of him. Vicariousness. The verve pipe.[21]

The sweethearts are watching *Band of Outsiders* or *Rushmore*.[22] Something cool and funny and smart. Something he picked out. Where he can see in her eyes that she thinks he is cool and funny and smart for picking it out. An embarrassment of shelves.

Shots. Scenes. Studies. Styles.

They have been married years and years, and yet a "torment of love lies in the knowledge that [she] has a secret inner life in which [he] can never participate."[23] And pathetically, same pageness, recognition of smartness

20. Arcade Fire, "Neighborhood #1 (Tunnels)."
21. The Verve Pipe, *Villains*.
22. Godard, *Band of Outsiders*; Anderson, *Rushmore*.
23. Williamson, "The Divided Image," 60.

is what he wants. Attention for his things. What the little boy must hide at all costs is the lack of the object. Out of the corner of his eye, he watches her watch good movie. He's like a director's lens on her consuming agency. She is smiling—slight, light lip quivers.

In the Prius, they sometimes discuss theory.

"Man's desire is the desire of the Other."[24]

"Isn't there a song about that?" (Cue "Brass in Pocket" by the Pretenders.)[25]

Sometimes they mumble lyrics.

"I'm the only one . . ."[26]

"Hey, Manny," he yells out to the back seat, doing, demonstrating Attentive Dad. And building a setup—here a grasp of the Spotify stream as historical and categorical reference points. "Do you hear the Beatles in this, Manny? More McCartney than Lennon. Like postgrunge heartland rock, and some counterculture—Janis, Joe Cocker, and, um, what else? Cyndi Lauper."

"Dad, you're so into genre."

Possum[27]

Manny's dad draped blankets across chairs, tables, and lamps, darkening tuck-ins, hideouts, and hangouts. Not yet clinical psychiatric disease, he was hunkering down. He had a habit of too much television. *He-Man and the Masters of the Universe. G.I. Joe: A Real American Hero. The Transformers.* And he wore out Atari and then Sega and then Nintendo. *Mario Bros. The Legend of Zelda. Sonic the Hedgehog.* And then a decade of sports games. *FIFA. Tecmo Bowl. NBA Live. NHL '94. Madden.*

The room above the garage (a.k.a. the "computer room") was an addition to the house built for the kids by Manny's dad's dad. It was also this kid's discrete personal space for cozying, digressing, regressing, sliding away, and emerging. Boundaries between work and play were completely muddled. Late nights jumbled the activities of keyboarding, web

24. Lacan, *The Four Fundamental Concepts of Psychoanalysis*, 235.
25. The Pretenders, "Brass in Pocket."
26. Etheridge, "I'm the Only One."
27. Phish, "Possum."

surfing, video gaming, boom-box blaring, and mixtape making. All work and all play.

No wonder *Tobacco Capitalism* was written in a "narcotic tobacco haze."[28]

One night in 2011, working late on the book's final draft, smoking pot, smoking cigarettes, nervous breakdown nigh, an ad hoc office space in the back of the house in St. Louis, reclining in his beloved, busted writing chair, he glimpsed, beyond a smudgy window, in moonlight beneath the apple tree, a possum scurrying in the clumpy grass of the backyard. Mind you, he was stoned. And half-drunk. But this was really real. He had never seen such wildlife there. It reminded him of Connecticut. The woods. The mandatory two-acre minimum to ensure rustic real estate.

It reminded him of that upstairs room of his Connecticut adolescence, where he used to piss out the window to lazily avoid the steeplechase of winding downstairs, through the mud room overcrowded with coats and shoes, and the family room, handmade afghans strewn, then up a few stairs to the catwalk, and then through the kitchen to the bathroom. But no more than half of the pee made it onto the two acres on account of the metal-wire window screen, which became a sheet of dried stick. Every night, after midnight, before heading to bed, he would keep this secret, closing the vinyl mini blinds. He was like, "Nevermind."[29]

His mom probably saw the screen a decade later, when he was off at grad school, when his parents sold that colonial house in Connecticut and moved into a new subdivision on the outskirts of Austin, when that Texas playboy, looking up to and taking after Daddy, playing fort-da, making a setup, digging a ditch, building a fort in the desert, sent hundreds of thousands of troops to Iraq. Nevermind.

It was upstairs in that room that he sank into defining, lifelong proclivities for slouching, toying, and manipulating—habits of playing video games, playing with Word documents, and playing with himself. Lincoln Logs and Playmobil were now other sorts of materials, blocks, and handles—other sorts of setups. Lines and paragraphs and chunks of highlighted text and files in folders for manic high school paper writing. The

28. Ginsberg, "Howl," 135.
29. Nirvana, *Nevermind.*

evolving fort-da of school ages and a career, the compulsive back-and-forth of obsessive organizing, a Tetris life, coming of age into a frenzy-norm.

No wonder *Tobacco Capitalism* was written.

Stuckness in a shoddy seat, the desk's light wood stained with smears, pot-ash gray, feet propped next to the overfull ashtray. Small-world diorama of a drug addict. Back and forth now and again to the parking lot to meet the dealer. Back and forth every night to the refrigerated beer aisle at Schnucks. Back and forth on the hour to the fridge at home for a couple bottles. Back and forth to the Advil bottle for unhelpfully ulcerating relief. Back and forth on the half hour, a faint forward lean to the table for the pipe. Bloody arm cuts in the kitchen. Ken Burns. Barry Goldwater. The fieldwork. The overwhelm. The solitude at that computer monitor. Look at my setup. Did it. The book. A career and the damage done.[30]

The Reporter

The breathing room of adolescence was not in mallrat subcultures or the skate ramps in the school parking lot or the athletic fields behind it.[31] He hung out in the library during lunch and after hours to avoid the cafeteria, and for history books and the sports section. Rather than playing sports, he documented them—the beat reporter covering high school teams for the local paper, a youthful passion for writing that got him tenure (and hospitalized).

In a paper for an advanced modern American history class, the assignment was to write about an important figure. His conservative father encouraged him to write about Barry Goldwater. He knew nothing of the man. And, besides, what did Dad know about Goldwater? He was thirteen at the time of the '64 election, when Goldwater was the Republican nominee for president. Maybe Dad carried with him some vicarious relation to his own father's likely fondness for a politician who had the vocal support of two fellow Connecticuters: former senator Prescott Bush and his son, George H. W. Bush (the playboy's dad)—who was himself running for Senate in Texas in '64.

30. Young, "The Needle and the Damage Done."
31. Smith, *Mallrats*.

More connections—an actor-network.[32] H. W. grew up with the nickname "Poppy," which is what all the grandkids called Blair, the reporter's dad's dad. And "Blair" is also his own dad's middle name and his own middle name, making for a royal "Peter Blair," which conceals ethnic influences—that Mediterranean—from Mom's side.

The name was again repurposed for Manny, short for "Emmanuel Blair."

Kedron was lying on the bed. He was relying on the wall. They had not yet decided on a name. Time was ticking. He quixotically spoke of philosophy and baseball, assuming, "No way, no how." But it was love at first mention. A deep connection. A home run.

Emmanuel "Manny" Blair is a combinatory gesture, part of their own intimacy, a trace of durabilities, a nod to their beloved Guatemala, and a loving designation of holiness. Emmanuel is the name of Manny's dad's favorite philosopher, as in Levinas, a French philosopher of Lithuanian Jewish ancestry, an exemplary philosopher of ethics. Blair is a monosyllable, flat and gleeful, denoting a heritage of blaring alcoholism passed down from fathers to sons going at least as far back as Poppy's (Manny's dad's dad) upscale section in bedroom-community Connecticut. And the nickname, Manny, is an ironical homage to the Anglicized names of famous Latin athletes. The sweethearts lived in Boston as graduate students during the prime of Manny Ramírez, the great—hopefully, one day, Hall of Fame—Red Sox outfielder. They then moved to St. Louis, where the tike was born during the waning peak of boxing legend Manny Pacquiao.

When Pacquiao fought Floyd Mayweather Jr. in 2015, in what was marketed as the "fight of the century," the little man was four years old. And his dad, a few months into sobriety, shelled out $89.95 (plus an additional $10 for high definition) for HBO's pay-per-view broadcast. There was a month of nonstop hype leading up to the event. Their television was locked on ESPN for expert commentary from the likes of Max Kellerman at an outdoor studio situated in front of the MGM Grand in Las Vegas. And eventually, on fight night, half a world away, a large entertainment company in the Philippines, Pacquiao's native country, aired the fight for

---

32. Latour, *Reassembling the Social*.

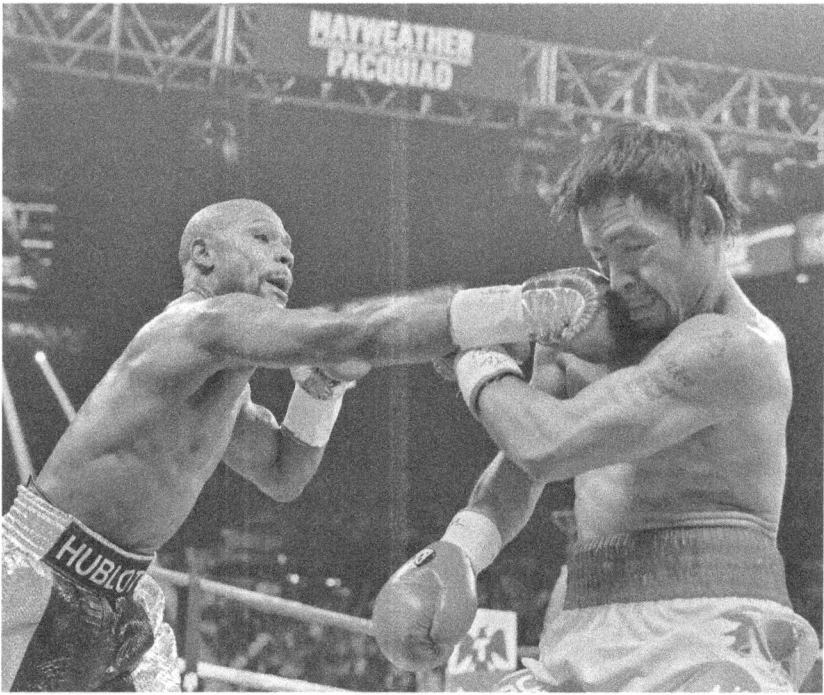

6. Floyd Mayweather Jr. (*left*) connects with a right to the head of Manny Pacquiao during their welterweight title fight in Las Vegas on May 2, 2015. Photograph by John Locher (Associated Press).

free on cable and in cinemas. The biggest television event in the history of the Philippines.[33]

Manny went to sleep as usual. The sweethearts, they stayed up late, awaiting the main event. Undercard after undercard. Nine, ten o'clock. Kedron surfed the web, maybe read a book. He was on the other couch, his couch, speculating about entrance music possibilities and the stare down and Mayweather's mean and cold straight face and Pacquiao's restrained, ambiguous grin, his indicative readiness. It was the most popular bout in pay-per-view history, purchased by three million households.[34] And it was happening—the most anticipated ever, ever.

33. Cordero, "ABS-CBN, GMA, TV5 Join Hands to Air Pacquiao Fight."
34. Schroeder, "High TV Demand Delays Mayweather-Pacquiao Fight."

The screen suddenly went black. The coverage shorted due to widespread service issues—too many viewers, not enough and not-good-enough technology. ("Maybe I shouldn't breathe so much.")[35]

HBO referred to "electronic overload."[36]

Along with thousands, maybe millions of other customers, he dialed the service line, getting an automated machine, and an impossible wait time. And it was well past bedtime. So he hatched an ingenious plan.

According to the television's channel guide, the fight would air again in the early morning, perhaps faux live for late-shift workers on the US mainland or time zone-challenged viewership in Alaska and Hawai'i. Nevermind. The reason didn't matter. What mattered was that it would be live—again. It was all on demand—liveness, fungible.[37] The plan was to purchase the rerun (in high definition) and record it to the DVR system, and tomorrow, after breakfast, let the little man run around the backyard while having coffee and hanging with Ked. Then he would do something odd, not quite right, which is to say, watch a megafight during the daytime. See, because there must be at least some decency. The bell always dings well after sundown, after the kids are down.

Okey Dokey, Neighbor!

And whaddya know, here comes this guy.

"Shush, nope, don't say anything. I don't wanna know. Who won, what happened, nothing. Don't wanna know. We've got it on tape, upstairs. An ingenious plan. Did it!"

The neighbor traverses the alley behind their houses. His face mawkishly telegraphs dumb. He tunes in to Premier League soccer on weekend mornings. Doesn't like football, baseball, or basketball—or boxing. He's sorta, therefore, not quite, not right.[38] Kinda like not all-American or something. He prefers a sport in which there are only fake injuries, where the quantity of shin holding, playacting, and rolling around at the referee's feet far outstrips the shots on goal, and certainly goals.

35. Figgis, *Leaving Las Vegas*.
36. Schroeder, "High TV Demand Delays Mayweather-Pacquiao Fight."
37. Ong, *Fungible Life*.
38. Bhabha, *The Location of Culture*, 92.

His face is a view of the boxing fan as uncouth and Vegas as a tourist trap. Only a certain kind of person purchases (and hatches an ingenious plan to purchase again) an overhyped, overpriced punch-out, an extravagant Black-on-Brown porno brawl coded as sport. Only a certain kind of man childishly kicks and screams spoiler alert.

And for the erstwhile reporter, it isn't clear which outcome is worse. This schmooze involving the potential disaster of prematurely knowing the result of a fight for which he has now paid upwards of $200, ruining his desire for a real show, no tell. That. Or having to keep interacting with a guy who seems to be looking down on him in holding sanity over his head, who thinks of himself as down-to-earth because every weekend he is ably assembling swing sets and bicycle seats for his kids, and who considers himself wholesome and refined because, when it comes to the sporting life, he prefers live action in the morning with a bagel and cream cheese—that is, afternoon matches played in the metropole at 9:00 a.m. St. Louis time. He prefers these civilized contests to what happens in Vegas: the apparent debasements of aggrandizing, tacky promotions, the copious gambling—the world, to quote Homi Bhabha, of "grotesquerie [. . .] on the margins of metropolitan desire."[39] And the reporter cannot help but feel diminished—his thing for boxing evidence of a personality defect or flawed morality compared to the neighbor's white-picket-fence respectability. This guy is the museum piece of functional familial existence, a nauseating normalcy of habitus and home life. Por ejemplo: every year, he and his wife host a Cinco de Mayo party. At the home improvement house, there's a fajita bar with all the fixings. Manny's parents decline the invitation, taking their kids out for hamburgers and fries.

"Capchuk."

"Dude, Henry, that's like a hockey player's name. It's ketchup, Henry."

The neighbor is likely drawn to the globalization sport's historical and sociological import, issues of race, class, gender, and empire, which, of course, also run through boxing . . . making the previous evening's pay-per-view event mega.

Floyd Mayweather is considered one of the greatest fighters of all time. He grew up in poverty in Grand Rapids and New Brunswick. His mother

39. Ibid.

was an addict, his father a professional boxer and boxing trainer and a drug dealer. Mayweather dropped out of high school, finding an outlet in boxing, and over the course of an illustrious career, he became one of the highest paid athletes in the world, including $180 million for the fight with Pacquiao alone.

Manny Pacquiao is also an all-time great boxer. He grew up in poverty in the Philippines and dropped out of high school. He earned $120 million in the fight. He is an outspoken, controversial, conservative Christian and a longtime member of Congress in his home country, a former US colony.

The neighbor knows the outcome—which one of these two men won. The result was on the ticker at the bottom of the screen while he was checking out the soccer.

"Shush, what happens in Vegas, please keep it in Vegas. I've got it on tape."

"Okay, then. Gonna take the kids for a bike ride."

"Have a good one. And afterward, check out Warwick Anderson's article 'The Trespass Speaks.' If you don't have access on Google Scholar, I'll print you a copy. It's about tropical neurasthenia, also known as 'philippinitis,' and the history of American colonialism there, a devastating analysis of imperial figurations of civility and abnormality and how excesses and degeneracies seemed threatening to the modern man and enmeshed with violences perpetrated by American colonizers in Pacquiao's home country.[40] Brutal, like boxing. Read all about it."

When Ferguson happened a year prior, the neighbor snidely remarked, complained really, about a "race riot," ostensibly victimized and wowed, surprisingly surprised about fulminations riven by segregation. The innocence. The nerve. He drives a Mini Cooper SUV model, the Countryman. Even Manny can read that sign.

The sweethearts went inside with Manny, who took a nap. They eagerly cued up the DVR. But the thrill shortly gave way to letdown; it was one of the most underwhelming matches of all time. Spectrum TV refunded homeowners for the purchase, the short-circuited first purchase.

---

40. Anderson, "The Trespass Speaks."

New Delhi

Peter Blair checked out AOL. This was before Google. AOL indicated that Goldwater wore "horn-rimmed glasses." He remembers this phrase distinctly. He cut and pasted it into his paper, describing Goldwater's facial politics. The teacher rightly assumed that this phrase was not his own. She accused him of plagiarism. She graded his paper an F: failure.

The first-born son with Grandpa's first name and Poppy's middle informed his parents. Dad thought it was because the teacher had a liberal bias, the topic of the paper being an archconservative. For her part, Mom picked up the handset. Demanded an amendment. She rightly clarified it was not theft. Goldwater's iconic glasses are an object of common knowledge. There was henceforth an ensuing after-school conversation where the three of them—Peter Blair, Mommy, and teacher—sat on plastic stack chairs and discussed proper citation practices. The result was an inevitable A-OK.

She is a cupboard-stocking, clothes-folding Mediterranean mother, diehard in devotion and love.

He has talked about this incident in therapy for years.

"How would you like to replay that moment?"

"I talk to the teacher on my own. My mom doesn't rescue me."

When he now writes, like for his job, he is frantic with controlling behaviors—maniacal proofing and revising, worries of pilfering, neurotically checking every detail. These "exploratory repetitions of fort/da reproduce and honor [. . .] a little boy's dependent position in the difficult game of growing up."[41] He detaches from family for weeks. Frets. Selects and copies phrases. Drops them into Google to look for coverage, commonalities, freaked by the prospect of plagiarism accusations.

"Hey, Ked, this phrase is cited in the article, but it's in the abstract and it isn't cited there. What do you think? And the Levinas citation is from a different edition, so what should I do?"

Not weaned, having internalized assistances, absolutions, protections for consequences, for life, he is distraught in authorship: a byline. His set-ups, always unfinished, now PDFed, irreversibly, publicly thrown, on his own, available on the www.

41. Watson, "Guys and Dolls," 476–77.

He checks to see what time it is in New Delhi, where the outsourced copyediting is done. He makes Arjun's life a chaotic, bipolar brain-dump of manic overload. Sends streams of emails every night. Fix this, that, and the other. Add citations here and there. Delete this word, no wait, I take that back, never mind, do this, and this. Requesting changes to page proofs that are supposed to be final.

The emails are flagged with alarmist subject lines that blare in full caps the phrase "USE THIS ONE" and include protracted strings of exclamation points and asterisks, as if the emphatic lettering wasn't sufficient. And the emails all give the same notice. Use this one, asterisks, more asterisks, important, most important, exclamations, reply, confirm. The actual one to use is simply the one that has one more asterisk. But there are also different, overlapping email threads. Arjun needs to parse interwoven, simultaneous claims about "this one"-ness. Poor guy wakes up and has dozens of emails and hundreds of typographical marks from a single IP address in America. And only one or two of the emails is for implementation.

The temporality of the process doesn't help the reporter's insanity. Everything takes days because of an imaginary dateline or something. Who designed this? Why does the calendar skip or jump or vanish and reappear or something in the middle of the Pacific Ocean? (Hint: the political and economic history of the Philippines.)[42]

He goes to sleep. Arjun starts work. Arjun gets off work. He wakes up. There is no effective overlap. It's all at once both live and on a delay, like a DVR.

Kedron, deeply concerned, anticipating another hospitalization, implores him to make one straightforward list of the alterations he wants for the manuscript.

"Sit on it for a day or two. And then send one coherent email. You can't keep changing your mind. And you don't need to ask him to confirm receipt. You don't have to say 'important.' He knows what he is doing. He will make the changes. This is not a personal relationship. It's not a thing where he likes you or doesn't like you or where he is going to punish you by not making changes because you are bothering him. But you can't bother him. Stop digging."

42. Lamont, "Planet Notes."

But it doesn't matter. Reason. Rationality. This is philippinitis. A dry drunk, neocolonial breakdown. Transnational word throwing. Hurling. Like how all his country's junked record players, radios, VCRs, televisions, CD and DVD players, computers, and smartphones end up in vast garbage dumps in India, landfills where impoverished scavengers rummage through circuit boards of lead, mercury, cadmium, and arsenic. Cuts and pastes. The overwhelm. The ditch.

Peter Blair tracks down Arjun on Google. He contemplates buying a plane ticket. Google has the address. Sage Publications in New Delhi is in a special industrial zone. Google also has the phone number with the country code and a time-zone conversion app. Yawning, it's late. Tick tock. He watches, timing Arjun's arrival at work, waiting for the app to read "New Delhi 9:30 a.m.," the start of the business day. Arjun answers. And everything is going fine.[43]

---

43. Soderbergh, *And Everything Is Going Fine.*

7 Toy Story

Once and for All

Not quite a teenager, he sat there forever, glued to the CNN coverage of bombs over Baghdad.[1] It was like a sporting event. A dream come true.

A few years earlier, he'd watched Mike Tyson decimate Michael Spinks. The match billed a "once and for all" fight to end all fights.[2] Don King, the legendary boxing promoter, credited the event's success to "the dynamism of a Donald Trump."[3]

Trump Plaza. Trump Taj Mahal Casino and Resort. Atlantic City, New Jersey. Chintzy compared to latter-day Las Vegas standards. Still, it was the highest-grossing fight of its time—pay-per-view, Pepsi sponsorship. Although the event didn't generate enough live gate for Trump to recover his astronomical site fee, he reliably garnered more than usual at his casino during the event.[4] It was a win-win-win-win-lose situation.

---

1. Outkast, "B.O.B."
2. Berger, "Tyson-Spinks Bout Pits Rage against Strategy."
3. Gildea, "Color of Money Is Gold for Tyson-Spinks."
4. Ibid.

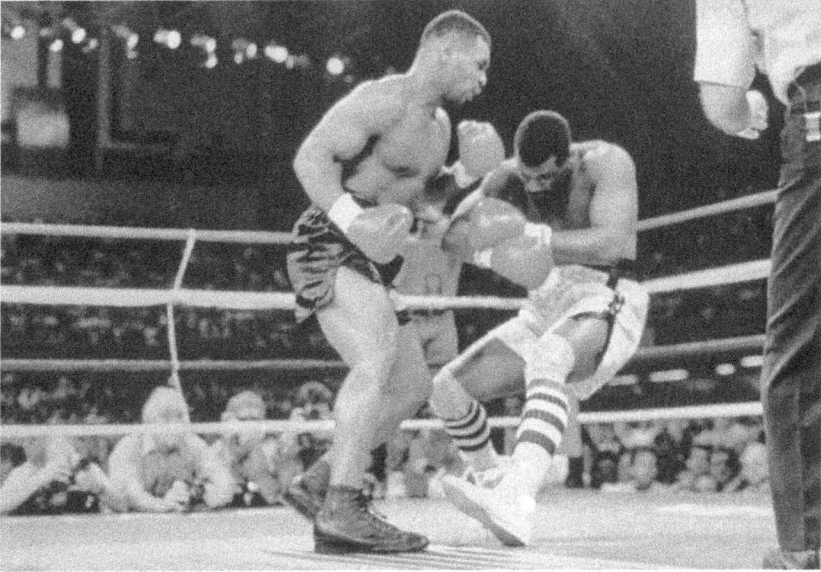

7. Michael Spinks goes down after receiving a knockout by Mike Tyson during their ninety-one-second heavyweight fight on June 27, 1988, in Atlantic City. Photograph by Richard Drew (Associated Press).

G. I. Joe

Atlantic City, a beach resort city, reputedly inspired the design of the Monopoly board game. Think street names.[5]

He grew up on the Atlantic shore with war on TV and, as a home front groundwork (a kind of homework), spread out setups of a massive G. I. Joe action figure collection, Hasbro's "antiterrorist commando," designed in the late Cold War in collaboration with Marvel Comics and marketed to compete with Mattel's Barbie doll.[6] The boy even had the G. I. Joe USS *Flagg* aircraft carrier. At seven and a half feet long, it barely fit under the Christmas tree. Dad jiggered a pulley system to hoist it from floor to ceiling in the bedroom that the brothers shared.

5. Irizarry, "'Monopoly.'"
6. Long, Jacques, and Kepos, *International Directory of Company Histories.*

In 1991, around the time of the bombings of "the them, the there," Hasbro acquired Monopoly and other major brands, including a stake in Nintendo video games, and it rivaled Mattel as the world's largest toy company.[7]

Boys of Summer[8]

He was born at the end of the Carter years. Became a brother at the start of the Gipper years. Mom went from working in the cosmetics section at Bloomie's at the Stamford Mall to staying at home days and sticking with some night shifts. Helen and Pete (i.e., Grandma and Grandpa) helped. So did their brothers and sisters and cousins. Blocks of small plots in the working-class, immigrant neighborhood of Spring Hill, single- and multi-family houses with vinyl siding.

Dad grew up across town in the professional airs of a degreed family and an upscale WASP community on Long Island Sound. Academic floun-ders and a reading disorder interrupted the expectations of his parents (i.e., Nanny and Poppy) to attend university. And in any case, he always preferred blue-collar. Did all manner of manual labor—boat building, bar-nacle scraping—as a teenager. Plus, he was a dedicated beer drinker. His route was culinary—the top cooking school in the country, nearby New Haven, starting point for working stations, coming up in the weeds, the kitchen's culture of exhaustion and heat, eventually, executive chef and part owner, a happy, brass-trimmed, oak-planked tavern.

Dad worked hard and worked a lot, and a lot of times, worked late. Somewhere in there, something changed him. He became born-again and sobered up, perhaps anticipating the birth of the kids. Bookshelves in the living room accumulated cassette sermons, study guides, evangelical periodicals. That's how it was, by the Book, in adherence to Christian con-cepts and creeds at church and home; in the restaurant owned; in beliefs about the proper manner with which a baseball should be thrown; and in views on the rebellious, seeking, hormonal, or simply normal adolescent

7. Ibid.
8. Henley, "The Boys of Summer."

8. Peter and Dad at Yellowstone National Park in Wyoming, 1980. Photograph by Mom.

behaviors that he didn't condone—life as a strict framework of dos and don'ts.

Dad coached their Little League teams. A garage full of equipment. Aluminum and ash wood bats. Beaten-up leather gloves. New and used hardballs. Chest protectors. Shin guards. Grass-clumps-underneath cleats. Face masks. Helmets. Backstops. Flimsy rubber batting tees. There is a picture of a late eighties team on the mantel in St. Louis. The kid was a slugger, hitting cleanup and playing first, maybe favoritism from Dad.

It's true that the Yankees of the eighties stunk. But, man, those were the days. Dad had season tickets, the third-base side, behind the home dugout. Mattingly. Randolph. Meacham. Winfield. Henderson. Pagliarulo ("Pags"). Righetti ("Rags").

The family made pit stops at the restaurant, heading southbound to the stadium. The backdoor entrance—Dad had keys and was in charge—like the famous long tracking shot in *Goodfellas*.[9] The walk-in freezer to check food storage bins and inventory tags. The chemical high of the dishwashing docks. The prep room of knives and bones, and here is the patrón, speaking Spanish learned in the kitchen. And at the expediting station, the order awaits, sodas in Styrofoam, and chicken fingers, steak fries, and bacon cheeseburgers in those tinfoil and plastic domes. And then, to the Bronx, back on the road.

The iconic apparel shop underneath the elevated tracks for fitted hats. Mays-era Giants. Robinson-era Dodgers. The Murderers' Row Yanks (Combs, Koenig, Ruth, Gehrig, Meusel, Lazzeri). Negro Leagues teams (Grays, Monarchs, Cubans).

Before the first pitch, potato knishes. Batting practice. Thwacks. Pepper games. Autographs. The oddity of sports uniforms cinched by heavy-duty leather belts. The splendidly stale street-cart soft pretzels, mustard, too, on those dense, chewy rounds, and Sabrett's footlongs with Gulden's brown, the best hot dog in town.

Every couple of weekends in the summer. Every summer for years. A Ken Burns movie of a boyhood—green pastures, affective grandeur, afternoons of son and father.

And there were family road trips. Civil War battlefields. National parks. Fort Wilderness. Kings Dominion. Mesa Verde. Pedro's South of the Border. Natchez Trace. Crater Lake. Petrified Forest. Black Canyon of the Gunnison. Devils Postpile. Shoney's Big Boy. Great Sand Dunes. Craters of the Moon. Living to run and running to live. Never worried about paying or even how much was owed.[10]

Money for Nothing[11]

Tyson was the most marketable heavyweight in the world. He'd turned pro a few years earlier and won nearly all his bouts by knockout.

Spinks exited the backstage training room to "This Is It," a pop-rock tune by Kenny Loggins.[12] He might as well have been disqualified at that

---

9. Scorsese, *Goodfellas*.
10. Bob Seger & the Silver Bullet Band, "Against the Wind."
11. Dire Straits, "Money for Nothing."
12. Loggins, "This Is It."

9. Referee Frank Cappuccino calls the count for Michael Spinks after he was knocked down by Mike Tyson during their fight on June 27, 1988, in Atlantic City (The Ring Magazine/Getty Images).

point. Tyson was next with an unreal entrance. "[B]are-chested and already soaked in sweat," he "slowly materialized from the back and meandered to the ring,"[13] advancing to amorphous, literal noise from Coil, an experimental, industrial band that had done the soundtrack for Clive Barker's horror film *Hellraiser* the year before.[14]

After the bell rang, Tyson charged Spinks with repeat blows. The once-and-for-all punch started from his waist and smashed Spinks in the face. "No man could have withstood it," a reporter wrote. Spinks crashed onto the mat. The referee, Frank Cappuccino, counted to ten.[15]

The ring featured logos for Diet Pepsi and Trump Plaza, the cheesy hotel's bold serif advertised near each of the mat's edges as well as vertically on the post pads. This unforgettable, historically important display

13. Chmiel, "A Man Walks into a Boxing Ring."
14. Barker, *Hellraiser.*
15. Putnam, "'I'm Gonna Hurt This Guy.'"

of boxing prowess was stuck with an eyesore reminder: the most striking aspect of the stills, the name of the pasty, orange-hued hustler plastered everywhere in a Google search for Tyson knockouts.

It was a remarkable dud, the ninety-one-second victory.

"What a rip-off! I want my money back!"

Households jammed pay-per-view customer service lines, shouted at screens, speculated fix or flop. Both King and Trump were known for ties to organized crime. Italian Americans loomed. (Vincenzo Castigliane: "It's not a recommendation. [. . .] It's no longer your film.")[16]

"Would you fight Iron Mike for the money?"[17]

"Just run around the ring, fall down."

"Whatever."

"There's nothing flashy about him inside the ropes. No robe, no socks. Nothing but black trunks and shoes."[18]

"That's sick."

"Like he's fighting wounds from the past."[19]

"He's an orphan."

"Yeah, his father abandoned him or something."

"He's from one of New York's worst neighborhoods. He beat up kids for making fun of his high-pitched voice."

"He was sent to a juvenile prison."

"Yeah, Cus D'Amato took him under his wing or something."

"Maybe he suffers from depression."

"He'll probably crash his Beemer into a tree to try to kill himself."

"He'll probably get a tribal tattoo across his face for good luck or something."

"That would be sweet."

"Black trunks and shoes."

"Run around the ring, fall down. Money for nothing."

16. Lynch, *Mulholland Drive*.
17. DJ Jazzy Jeff & the Fresh Prince, "I Think I Can Beat Mike Tyson."
18. Snowden, "91 Seconds."
19. Ibid.

Playing War

The kid's stack of video games in the upstairs playroom got one higher with the addition of *Mike Tyson's Punch-Out!!* for Nintendo. Meanwhile, Operation Desert Storm aired all day on the TV downstairs in the family room.

The adjacent mudroom housed a stockpile of Vietnam War military gear. Supplies from the army surplus store in Danbury. Fatigues. M1 army helmets. Plastic canteens. Horizontal weave pistol belts. Fulton MX-991/U flashlights. Lightweight rucksacks. Collapsible e-tool trench shovels. Bunches of M-1956 modernized load-carrying equipment. Also, an arsenal of toy "Old Betsy" rifles bought at landmark battlefields, Davy Crockett–themed gift shops, and campgrounds across the country. The kids burrowed in brush and ferns in a cinematic Connecticut backyard, yelping, "Pew! Pew!" as they unloaded pretend projectiles across the wooded piece of land, a battlefront for aspirant infantrymen, with their any-era guns for shifting terrains of endless war historicity, the nature of the hostility ever fluctuating—Concord and Lexington, Huck Finn, or Hồ Chí Minh. (Cue "Mad World" from the *Donnie Darko* soundtrack.)[20] In autumn, residents of nearby towns drove up to see the foliage. These boys constructed pile heaps, mounds for play protection.

A public culture of saturating and engendering loves of God and country, of alarming, normalizing, and entertaining relational forms and affiliations. Military picture books fanned out beside refreshments. Flintstones Push Up Pops. Oreo Double Stuf Cookies. Fruit Wrinkles. Shark Bites Fruit Snacks. Hi-C Ecto Coolers. Armed forces reference books, programs for the performance, technical illustrations diagramming and detailing aircraft and weaponry used by good guys. The MIM-104 Patriot missile. The M1097 Avenger Humvee. The M1A1 Abrams battle tank, with a 105 mm M68A1 rifled tank gun (55 rounds) and a .50-caliber M2 heavy machine gun (900 rounds). Squadrons of Intruders, Mohawks, Corsairs, Harriers, Thunderbolts, Hawkeyes, Phantoms, Tomcats, Eagles, Hornets, Prowlers.

20. Andrews, "Mad World," feat. Gary Jules; Kelly, *Donnie Darko*.

Coalition forces flew tens of thousands of sorties in a few months and dropped 88,500 tons of bombs,[21] perverse and unprecedented, more than were dropped during World War II.[22]

CNN in living color. Peter and the Wolf. Baath Party. All-around achromatic oblivion punctuated, splatted by orange antiaircraft tracers, streaking pew pew yellow-green orbs, globules, fires and hues, blues, kabooms. The birth of the chyron: Baghdad under Heavy Bombardment. Bright Flashes all over the Sky.

American military and media depictions emphasized precision. But unguided "dumb" bombs functioned at 25 percent accuracy and were 91 percent of the ordnance.[23] The sorties caused $190 billion in losses to infrastructure and industry: "electric power stations (92 percent of installed capacity destroyed), refineries (80 percent of production capacity), petrochemical complexes, telecommunications centers (including 135 telephone networks), bridges (more than 100), roads, highways, railroads, hundreds of locomotives and boxcars full of goods, radio and television broadcasting stations, cement plants, and factories producing aluminum, textiles, electric cables, and medical supplies."[24] This consequentially brought about manifold humanitarian and public health disasters.[25] A vast many Iraqis, mostly civilians, died, as compared to 146 US soldiers. *The Atlantic* commented that "the new American air power delivered, finally, on the old dream of a relatively bloodless victory."[26]

Nintendo War

"The Gulf War did not take place," Jean Baudrillard provocatively claimed at the time, proposing that the events were more television spectacle than actual war, a totally lopsided affair—a Tyson. A new kind of abstract, corporatized, and market-oriented atrocity realized in consumerism, technological simulation, and live programming.[27] "The media promote the war,

21. Kelly, "The American Way of War."
22. Kifner, "From Bombs to Burgers, Gulf War Involves Biggest Supply Effort Ever."
23. Human Rights Watch, *Needless Deaths in the Gulf War.*
24. Rouleau, "America's Unyielding Policy toward Iraq," 61–62.
25. Human Rights Watch, *Needless Deaths in the Gulf War.*
26. Kelly, "The American Way of War."
27. Baudrillard, *The Gulf War Did Not Take Place.*

the war promotes the media, and advertising competes with the war," Baudrillard wrote.[28]

"Awesome," the kid thought. "The war promotes snacks, snacks promote the war, and the cupboard, where there is microwavable popcorn, competes with the television."

CNN had a ratings bonanza. An image of a bomb plumbed narrowly down a chimney ran repeatedly. Television viewers came to inaccurately believe in smooth deliveries and limited civilian casualties,[29] like a video game terraform lacking humanity, bereft of "grievability."[30] Media critics labeled it "Nintendo War."[31]

1979

The Connecticut colors were coming in. The baseball season had ended. The nurse wrapped the newborn in a pink blanket. Sitting outside the delivery room, in the hallway, Dad welcomed his baby girl, Kelsey.

"We ran out of the blue ones," the nurse informed him.

The smash hit "1979" by Smashing Pumpkins came out when the boy was in high school.[32]

O Connecticut! His Connecticut! Where he grew up where he grew up because they moved up. A good school district where one kid looked like Tobey Maguire and all the girls like Katie Holmes. (Cue "Found Out about You" by Gin Blossoms.)[33] Where the low he loves soundtracked, backgrounded, and toned school ages, study time, cushions, carpets, closed doors, late-night video games, bedtime books, hookups. They memorized and marveled peaks, peeks, scapes, scenes, box insets, bolded fonts. Moped the mall. Swung swings, pumping. Fantastically high, almost looping. Sat backward, hats backward, at picnic tables. ("[...] the rivers, hills, and forests; the abundance and saturated color of the towering trees; the deep, dappled shade; the stone walls enclosing fields now gone to goldenrod; the

28. Ibid., 31.
29. Barry, *Visual Intelligence*, 283.
30. Butler, *Frames of War*.
31. Barry, *Visual Intelligence*, 283.
32. Smashing Pumpkins, "1979."
33. Gin Blossoms, "Found Out about You."

lichen-dappled old gravestones; the town greens; the Congregational churches with their white-clapboard siding.")[34] O Connecticut! His Connecticut! The country and the City.[35] The Metro-North commuter rail. Washington Square Park. O Connecticut! ("How you burden my soul. How you hold all my dreams captive [. . .] how you play with my mind. O, my heart goes back, suffocating on the pines.")[36]

A book about how academia and anger and addiction took over.

His parents worried about liberal academia, and anthro-what, for what, what's that? But what did they expect? It was kinda in the deck. Mom is ethnicized indulgent, and Dad's a lots-of-stuff buff. Family road trips and season tickets and, at home, an embarrassment of shelves for a child's future gig in cultural studies. Encyclopedias. Almanacs. Atlases. TripTiks. Guides. Manuals. Theater-of-war board games. Trivia books and games. Every genre of music (except reggae, reggaeton, rap, classical, and many others). Documentaries. Classics. New releases. And, on floppy disk, and in 256-color VGA, *Oregon Trail*, *SimCity*, *Railroad Tycoon*, and *Civilization*.

Christmas morning, 1990. A box of VHS tapes underneath the tree, the PBS documentary series, *The Civil War*.[37] A few years later, Santa brought *Baseball*.[38] With the throwback ballcaps and collected military memorabilia, it was of a piece. Baptism in cultural relief. Immersions of a wonderful life.[39] All the wars are good wars. All the stories, stories of healing and restoration.[40] No wonder *Tobacco Capitalism* was an overarching summation. Motivation to understand his own personal formation, issues of politics and nation, and his father, by studying the lives of conservative working men. Mysteries of why. Research that has had the flavor of a battle cry. A book about tobacco that lacked the warmth of the videocassette box sets. Not a Ken Burns film. Maybe that is what the growers wanted. Hall of fame. National monument.

34. Conniff, "Is Connecticut Really New England?"
35. Williams, *The Country and the City*.
36. Ryan Adams & the Cardinals, "The End."
37. Burns, *The Civil War*.
38. Burns and Novick, *Baseball*.
39. Capra, *It's a Wonderful Life*.
40. Burns and Novick, "Vietnam's Unhealed Wounds."

But despite the kid's frustrations with and misgivings about a conservative upbringing, there's no chance he would be in anthropology—studying history and culture and the culture wars—if not for that childhood so richly imbued with visual and textual materials. It nurtured a son's perhaps-resented superseding and his repudiation of traditions and teachings. His turn toward anthropology's godlessness, relativisms, and Western-civ-strange-ings.

Top Gun

Operation Enduring Freedom began with air strikes in Afghanistan one month into graduate school. A couple years later, the former president's president-son once again headed to Iraq with friends and frenemies to play war—the "coalition of the willing," comprising hundreds of thousands of troops. That which never occurred was not ending.

Students marched from Cambridge down to Boston Common.

Baghdad fell in less than a month—a Spinks.

General Tommy Franks, the US commander, a veteran of the Vietnam War, outlined the operational basics during a press briefing: "[to] identify, isolate and eliminate Iraq's weapons of mass destruction [. . .] to search for, to capture and to drive out terrorists from that country [. . .] to immediately deliver humanitarian support to the displaced and to many needy Iraqi citizens [. . .] to secure Iraq's oil fields and resources, which belong to the Iraqi people [. . . to] help the Iraqi people create conditions for a transition to a representative self-government."[41]

Cosmopolitan and beneficial-sounding, civilized, like a "friendly"—a noncompetitive soccer match organized for the purposes of recreation, amusement, profit, and conditioning, with snacks afterward.

Although none of the stated objectives was accomplished, the president proclaimed otherwise for fun-and-games refrains of simple and easy.[42] He made this sick—just such a sweet—landing in a Lockheed S-3 Viking military jet on an aircraft carrier off the San Diego coast. It was like a scene

41. CNN, "Franks Holds Press Briefing."
42. The Jackson 5, "ABC."

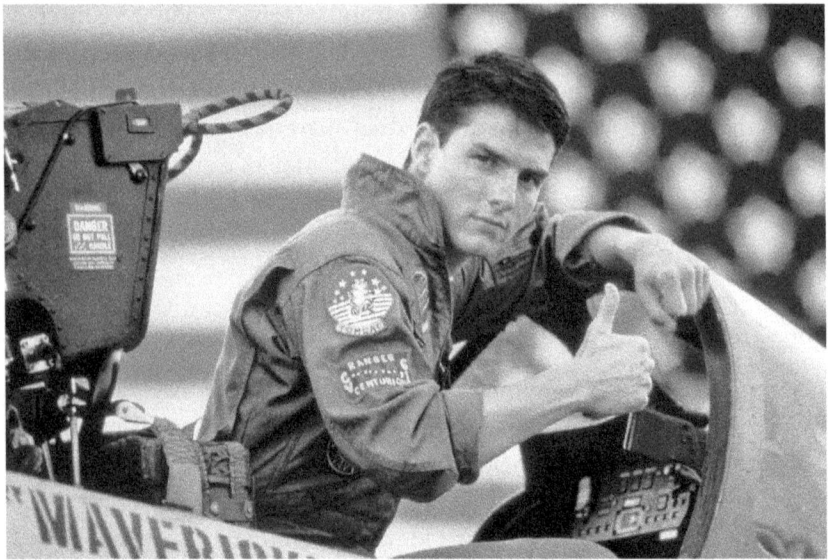

10. Tom Cruise as Maverick in *Top Gun* by Tony Scott, 1986 (PictureLux/Alamy Stock Photo).

from *Top Gun,* the summer blockbuster dogfighting buddy movie (set in San Diego) from the height of his father's vice presidency.[43]

While the presidential son could have simply arrived onboard the carrier in his official helicopter, he chose the Viking vanity landing, decked out in flight gear. ("They misunderestimated me.")[44] A female Republican speechwriter editorialized in the *Wall Street Journal* about him "stepping out of a fighter jet in that amazing uniform," looking "really hot," and "presidential, of course," and "credible as commander in chief. But mostly 'hot' as in virile, sexy and powerful. . . . He out top-guns the Hollywood version." "Flyboy," as she nicknamed him, then went to makeup and wardrobe, later reappearing in a suit to address all hands on deck and at-home viewers with a momentous televised speech.[45]

43. Scott, *Top Gun.*
44. Bush, "Campaign Speech."
45. Schiffren, "Hey, Flyboy."

"Major combat operations in Iraq have ended," he declared. "In the battle of Iraq, the United States and our allies have prevailed."[46] The famous Mission Accomplished banner in the background. That was 2003.

Refreshments

It was the apparent ending of something "that began some time ago,"[47] a once-and-for-all fight to end all fights. But this bush league of a finale was also a nifty new beginning.

The *Call of Duty* video game franchise launched that year. Over the ensuing decades, with more than a dozen versions—*Modern Warfare, Black Ops, Ghosts, Advanced Warfare, Infinite Warfare, World at War,* variously set in World War II, Vietnam, the Third World War, and the Iraq region—the franchise has sold hundreds of millions of copies for many billions of dollars. And with the—how many?—Harry Potters and Marvel movies, there is surely evidence of a pathological degree of interest worthy of a special category in the DSM, which was, coincidentally, at this time, undergoing revisions to include more obsessions and compulsions.[48]

The mission-accomplished mistake landed alongside a movie franchise about a charismatic cowboy exiled from the dinosaur setups of an adolescent playroom home in suburbia.[49] Another series chronicled the apocalyptic escape quests of a preextinction posse of woolly and saber-toothed searchers.[50] So many epic adventure films about lost and found, arriving "[e]ach time [. . .] as the 'once and for all' of a promised catharsis."[51] Another canonical gem in this genre, *The Land before Time* was released during the holiday season at the end of the Gipper's second term, when the president's dad was vice president, and a few months after the once-and-for-all Tyson haul in Atlantic City.[52] It's an animated Mesozoic migration snacker about a cataclysmic famine and the refugee journey of an

46. Bush, "Remarks by the President from the USS *Abraham Lincoln*."

47. Stewart, *Ordinary Affects*, 1.

48. American Psychiatric Association, *Highlights of Changes from DSM-IV-TR to DSM-5.*

49. Lasseter, *Toy Story.*

50. Wedge, *Ice Age.*

51. Ronell, "Support Our Tropes," 29.

52. Bluth, *The Land before Time.*

adorable bronto orphan who flees for the abundant Great Valley and comes of age with flying and hopping dino pals and establishes a new home in a land before time. Mission accomplished.

Fantastical action distraction for endless nowhere war. Difference and repetition formulas, next and another already in the dreamworks.[53] A global screen thing for kitten bloopers. The racial innocence or menace of the "non- or post-human."[54] The superheroic society. Nostalgia for the hard to believe. Nostalgia for righteous empire.[55] Right there in the primetime of the "war on terror." The administration's NSFW black site hilarity lairs and porno prisons and what-happens-here hotels. And in theaters, a string of magical, medieval, exteriorized conquest-world marathons.[56] Can't even count 'em. The stories are all the same: cowboys and engineers. The homogenizing cultural imperialism of tentpoles. Ancillary everything: action figures, comic books, board games, video games, amusement parks. Hasbro as "history of the present."[57] With musical accompaniment by Randy Newman. (Cue "Strange Things" from the *Toy Story* soundtrack.)[58]

Breakdown

Anthropology as exile and return. The graduate student arrived for the North Carolina heat. Enter the field. Works and lives.[59] Take notes. Write it down. One year—a Malinowski.[60]

All done. Ready to go. It hit as they packed the U-Haul. The sweethearts took a break to watch the television coverage with the neighbors, the tobacco farm family from chapter 2. They watched the devastation and the masses housed in the Superdome.

Two aging Black farmworkers helped them load up. These men then got behind the wheels of machines.

53. Deleuze, *Difference and Repetition*.
54. Bernstein, *Racial Innocence*; Elsaesser and Hagener, *Film Theory*, 194.
55. Marty, *Righteous Empire*.
56. Jackson, *The Lord of the Rings*.
57. Foucault, *Discipline and Punish*, 31.
58. Newman, "Strange Things"; Lasseter, *Toy Story*.
59. Geertz, *Works and Lives*.
60. Malinowski, *Argonauts of the Western Pacific*, 1–26.

After a year of ethnography-related discretion, verging on deception, about to hit the road, what was he supposed to say about social disasters?

Write it up: they drove back to Boston for angry book. Along the way, he got stuck. Overwhelmed from heat and exhaustion, he milled about the parking lot of a rest stop on I-95 and dry-heaved. He knew what he was doing, booking it to betray blessings for anthropology matters, trafficking purloined letters, digital files of saids and seens, takings, receipts, booty for a boy's book report about a hypocritical, tobacco-subsidizing society and its "wars on."

At the semester's end in 2007, he pressed Control-P. Bill and Bill (Clinton and Gates) supplied the commencement addresses. For the post-doc position, he moved back near his Connecticut birthplace and kept writing angry book.

Breakdown

Flyboy announced a "surge" in troop levels, a shift or tweak or restart or F5 or something. ("Oops, I did it again.")[61]

The photographed falling man needed a narrative framework, some mollifying sense. History had punched "a permanent hole in the real," no matter that the desert mission was a quagmire, and the war's interminable perpetuation was necessary to fill that gaping void with meaning.[62] It's as if everything the presidential son did "was intended to efface history, or to [. . .] bring it back to the day of the crash," rewind to a land before time.[63]

The official house photographers publish virile, sexy, and powerful exposures of feet on the Resolute Desk, black landline to ear. But there are censored, repressed, sequestered, deleted scenes from behind the veneer. Bad guys under sofas and beds, stuffed animals and lovies on rugs, longings for cowboys and lands, dreams of the big leagues ("Sleep sleep beauty bright, dreaming oer the joys of night"),[64] Lincoln Logs, Erector sets, and blinking maps (Battleship and Risk, both made by Hasbro). It's that inside

61. Spears, "Oops! . . . I Did It Again."
62. Ronell, "Support Our Tropes," 25.
63. Ibid., 19.
64. Blake, "A Cradle Song," 468.

11. A person falls headfirst from the north tower of New York's World Trade Center, September 11, 2001. Photograph by Richard Drew (Associated Press).

the house there is a boy jumping around the edge of the cradle, performing *Top Gun* while "fluttering" and "faltering in regression."[65] The drunk-
enness of "denial and compulsive repetition,"[66] not stopping making sure
our boys are not dying in vain. Forever going on with the campaign.
Asserting surname. War games. Suturing selfsame. Infinite war epigenet-
ics. Call of duty. Family disease. The daddy-mommy spider web.[67] The
little life of macro breakdown.

Skittles

The shift or tweak or restart or F5 or something also marked the meteoric
ascent of planet protection and villain culture, a whole civilization mar-
veling at DC and declaring Marvel. Dozens of superhero movies for billions at the box office as military ops both surged and faded from view, no
longer news. The Marvel Cinematic Universe is the highest grossing movie
franchise ever, with attractions at Disney theme parks worldwide and
numerous product spinoffs. A chroma-key-compositing Tower of Babel of
a "culture industry" that's continuously remarketing pseudo-profound
mythologies of inclusion and empowerment.[68] Everyone as superhero
script. Enchanting visions of "unique, supremely talented beings," "[t]he
empowered individual."[69] A cult culture beaming bigness like Universal,
Paramount, DreamWorks, 20th Century above and across an ordinariness
of banal, routinized astonishments and disbelief suspensions and, of
course, selling snack packs, streaming bundles, and corporatized libidinal
ideoscapes and technoscapes.[70] Skittles of modernity at large.[71]

If only the CIA had employed Árbenz sympathizers in 1954. If only
there were antibias and cultural sensitivity professional development programs at Abu Ghraib. If only there were more diversity, equity, and inclusion in the sale of fake butter spreads, vanilla milk, sugary sodas, junk

65. Ronell, "Support Our Tropes," 19.
66. Ibid., 25.
67. Deleuze and Guattari, *Anti-Oedipus*, 112.
68. Horkheimer and Adorno, *Dialectic of Enlightenment;* Bowden, "Why Are We
Obsessed with Superhero Movies?"
69. Bowden, "Why Are We Obsessed with Superhero Movies?"
70. Appadurai, *Modernity at Large.*
71. Ibid.

food, tobacco, fossil fuels, chemicals, in the ranks of Lenco BearCat-armored police personnel carrier drivers, electric-chair button pressers, immigration agents, drone operators, at the defense contractors that make Humvees and M1A1 Abrams tanks, in the strata of the financiers and fixers; a superhero universe of employees and officials whose good ethical and political sensibilities and values lead them to heretically violate their sworn institutional responsibilities ratcheted around profits, policies, and paradigms.

Breakdown

Iraqi deaths in the years after the war's start and the "Mission Accomplished" announcement totaled in the hundreds of thousands. The United States spent roughly $2 trillion on the war.[72] As with the first installment a decade prior, this epic sequel led to humanitarian catastrophes.[73]

The friends and frenemies gradually pulled out of the coalition, which was disbanded and given the lonely name "United States Forces—Iraq." US forces were also drawn down, and the code name for some new nothingness over there was changed to Operation New Dawn. That was 2011. Right around the time of the hospitalization. Hot. In print. A book inscribing "many Thou's" as "the them, the there."[74] Copies routed south by southeast to North Carolina. The cover didn't acknowledge "About a Boy" or "By Peter Pan." The preface didn't reason out the angers and nerves, the saturations, the stomach stuff.

Clone Wars[75]

A few years later, a shift or tweak or restart or F5 or something, the next president established Operation Inherent Resolve, a new set of security and violence activities. Officials had not seen the horror and sci-fi movies about how attempts to destroy aliens and monsters spawn "breeding

72. Costs of War Project, "2015 Costs of War Executive Summary."
73. Bailey, Kirkbride, and Omar, *Rising to the Humanitarian Challenge.*
74. Wu, *On Metaphoring,* 529.
75. Filoni, *Star Wars: The Clone Wars.*

grounds" of replicants, incubators, mutations, rapidly proliferating cells, cancers.[76] Or maybe they just don't make 'em like they used to.

Meanwhile, investigations revealed underage workers and unsafe and abusive conditions in the factories of Hasbro's suppliers.[77] It was found that the company was purchasing paper from endangered forests and contributing to deforestation.[78] Hasbro has since touted its commitments to "product safety, human rights and ethical sourcing, and environmental sustainability." Its social responsibility report admits numerous "challenges" of product safety, chemical reporting, labor conditions, and environmental impacts in the mass production of plastic widgets, which fundamentally relies on third-party vendors and problematic regulatory frameworks in the planetary "outer zone."[79]

Public Television

Trump essentially owned Atlantic City. Three casinos. The largest employer.

And then. He extracted hundreds of millions of dollars through bankruptcies, leaving destitute properties and sinking worker benefits. In 2016, the president of one casino union stated about Trump's campaign for the presidency: "If you want to know what the country is going to look like [. . .] you don't have to look any further than Atlantic City and the Taj Mahal. [. . .] The future is [. . .] no future."[80]

In 2015, Manny and his dad relished the monthlong buildup for Mayweather versus Pacquiao. On fight night, the pay-per-view crashed. That's another story.

Around the same time, they began following the news coverage of the campaign for the presidency—the rallies and debates—sitting together on the couch, cringing, guesstimating.

"No way."

76. Priest, "Iraq New Terror Breeding Ground."
77. Barboza, "U.S. Group Accuses Chinese Toy Factories of Labor Abuses."
78. Radford, "Hasbro Turns Over a New Leaf, Steps Up for Rainforests."
79. Hasbro, *Playing with Purpose*, 14; Lingis, "Anger," 200.
80. Neate, "Trump and Atlantic City."

"Not a chance."

"Maybe."

"What if?"

"Holy schnikes!"[81]

Sound parental trepidations about not exposing a preschooler to the pugilistic spectacle of the Mayweather-Pacquiao matchup now seemed trivial, awkward, and anachronistic given the depravities, vulgarities, and sport airing on the educational channels.

Manny had advanced to chapter books in school. He could comprehend the news, read the chyrons and tickers.

What's the Impact of Drinking a Dozen Diet Cokes a Day?

Trump Slurs Immigrants from "Shithole Countries"

Trump Defends Tweet Rants with New Tweet Rant

Check Out Sex Tape

Trump Has Never Encouraged Violence

Trump Mocks Reporter with Disability

"It Would Have Been Easy to Be Truthful"

"I Thought It Would Be Easier"

He Says He Doesn't Need Beyoncé

President Gets 2 Scoops of Ice Cream, Everyone Else 1

You couldn't make this stuff up.

Like Don King always said: "Only in America."

Upon taking office, the presidential son said, in his queer, grinning, misunderestimated way: "What's not fine is rarely is the question asked, are, is our children learning."[82]

---

81. Segal, *Tommy Boy*.
82. Miller, "With a Grin, Bush Answers Early Charges of Aloofness."

8 Shame

His grandfather Pete Fumo labored a lifetime for modest wages in a factory in an industrial section of Norwalk near Long Island Sound, packing spaghetti sandwiches in a lunchbox, smoking unfiltered Lucky Strike cigarettes, dying around seventy years old from lung cancer in the early nineties. His grandmother Helen Fumo (née Czel) worked as a grocery store cashier. Around the turn of the century, her parents were labeled "Magyar" on an entry list. Without having English and pronouncing their destination like "Norwalk," they were sent by officials to *Newark*. They then somehow found their way northward to Connecticut and the neighborhood where they belonged.

Descendants of Ellis Island, they fought: Pete in Europe, Helen in the Pacific.

"The natives," Helen said sparingly to family gathered around the in-home hospice care bed. "The natives," lying there, half-conscious, dying in old age and elder status. "New Guinea," a reverie, rolling over, uncomfortable, radiating repose, acceptance, grace, and even cheerfulness. "Time and tide wait for no man," she now and again remarked, her go-to adage.[1]

---

1. Chaucer, *The Canterbury Tales*, 120.

12. Pete and Helen Fumo in their hometown of Norwalk, Connecticut, late 1940s.

And she asked for Frank. "My Way," mumbled through chapped lips.[2] Her daughter, the first-born's mom, moistened her mouth with sips from a jumbo-size plastic mug brought from the hospital.

Years before, the kid had visited Pete, Helen's husband, in a hospital. Pete was pale and frail. He was feeble and covered in fungoides, the blotchy skin.

He gasped for air, cancer ridden. "Pete, my boy," he murmured.

The kid moved around nasal tubes to kiss blistered, coarse lips. He whispered, "Love you," and headed off for two weeks, far from family, and this hospital, to an evangelical Christian summer camp in Missouri.

"Yes, of course he'll be here when you get back," his parents affirmed.

For some reason he has long been drawn to visuals of the Vietnam War. Maybe, mainly, he is looking for someone in there—a distinct man. He regularly returns to one photograph in particular—the iconic portrait taken by Pulitzer Prize–winner Horst Faas. In the frame, a man is smiling or smirking or something, an unnamed soldier of the 173rd Airborne Brigade battalion on duty at Phước Vĩnh base camp in South Vietnam in 1965. "WAR IS HELL" is written on his helmet.

The soldier would later be identified by family as Larry Wayne Chaffin. Chaffin grew up and attended high school in St. Louis and returned home from the war to reside across the river in southern Illinois, where, according to a local paper, he "had many problems adjusting to civilian life." He died in his late thirties from "complications that arose from diabetes," which he "might have contracted from exposure to Agent Orange."[3] This chemical was produced for ecological warfare in Vietnam by Monsanto, headquartered in St. Louis. It is a major corporate sponsor of the university where the boy is now a professor.

Works of Art

One film critic describes Ingmar Bergman's *Shame* as "a definitive apocalyptic vision" about "a nameless and continuing [. . .] war."[4] In an

---

2. Sinatra, "My Way."
3. Fitzgerald, "Local Family Says Unidentified Soldier Is Their Flesh and Blood."
4. Bergman, *Shame;* Crist, "Basic Bergman Truth."

13. Unidentified US Army soldier of the 173rd Airborne Brigade battalion on defense duty at Phước Vĩnh Base Camp, South Vietnam, June 8, 1965. Photograph by Horst Faas (Associated Press).

14. US Marine sharing cigarettes in Da Nang, South Vietnam, 1967. Photograph by Philip Jones Griffiths (Magnum Photos).

interview in 1968, Bergman noted that his concept for the film stemmed from newsreels from Vietnam. The media reports were "fantastically odd and at the same time deplorable," Bergman stated. He described "an old man and an old woman who walked with a cow," when "a helicopter started from the ground with a roar and soldiers ran up to it. The cow broke loose and the woman ran after the cow and the helicopter took off into the air and the old man stood there just perplexed, bewildered and heartbroken. In some way, more than any other atrocities one has experienced," Bergman went on, "I perceived there the misery of third parties, when everything breaks loose over their heads. It was this image of the small world."[5]

There were snacks and setups in a Connecticut house. Cushions and blankets. An alcove for battle studies.[6] A little library of history books with pictures that everyone has seen.

5. Hedling, "Shame," 247.
6. Mayer, *Battle Studies*.

15. South Vietnamese forces follow terrified children, including Kim Phúc (center), as they run down Route 1 near Trảng Bàng, South Vietnam, after an aerial napalm attack on suspected Viet Cong hiding places on June 8, 1972. Photograph by Nick Ut (Associated Press).

The Pulitzer Prize–winning photograph of nine-year-old Kim Phúc, arms splayed out, running naked down Route 1 near Trảng Bàng after a napalm attack; explosions, firestorms, dust storms in the background, soldiers lackadaisically following on the road with an "attitude of business as usual" that "contrasts vividly with the girl's sudden, unexpected, excessive experience of pain and terror."[7]

South Vietnamese General Nguyễn Ngọ Loan "raises the shiny snubnose .38, points it at the prisoner's right temple and pulls the trigger," and at that instant the "camera shutter clicked once," capturing the killing of suspected Viet Cong officer Nguyễn Văn Lém at "the moment the bullet

7. Hariman and Lucaites, "Public Identity and Collective Memory in U.S. Iconic Photography," 43.

16. South Vietnamese general Nguyễn Ngọ Loan, chief of the National Police, executes suspected Viet Cong officer Nguyễn Văn Lém in Saigon, February 1, 1968. Photograph by Eddie Adams (Associated Press).

crashed" through the "prisoner's skull at about 600 mph, distorting his face, tousling his hair and shoving his head off center," as described by a *Washington Post* reporter, who calls it "one of the most powerful pictures of the Vietnam War, or any war."[8]

Marines at the Battle of Huế, the bloodiest battle of the Tet Offensive, ride atop a tank turned into a makeshift ambulance. A stunning work of art, a "tableau," as one journalist describes it, "a palette [. . .] of dark, muddy greens and blues and browns in a grayish light, with shocking splashes of red," an "entire face wrapped in a thick bandage," an "arm in a sling," a "limp" and "half-naked" and "upside-down" marine who "has

8. Ruane, "A Grisly Photo of a Saigon Execution 50 Years Ago Shocked the World and Helped End the War."

17. Several bloody and bandaged soldiers ride on top of a tank used as a makeshift ambulance after the Battle of Huế, South Vietnam, February 15, 1968. Photograph by John Olson (Getty Images).

been shot through the center of his chest" and "looks to be dead, or nearly so," seductive aesthetics of the "tragic futility of the conflict."[9]

In images of such poignancy and allegory, he struggles to discern the individual existent as inexhaustible reservoir, as singularity. Pictures of naked or uniformed bodies and the ubiquitous youthfulness of each face. Scenes of "a world in pieces" and "a world turned upside down" as ontological commonplace.[10] The serialized signification of an impersonal "there is" existence threatening to subsume alterity's trace.[11] But he also encounters what defies the abstracting occasion of art, an aura that imparts. What Walter Benjamin describes as an "unruly desire to know

9. Bowden, "The True Story of 'The Marine on the Tank' and One of the Most Emblematic Images of Vietnam."

10. Levinas, *Existence and Existents,* 7.

11. Ibid.; Levinas, "The Trace of the Other."

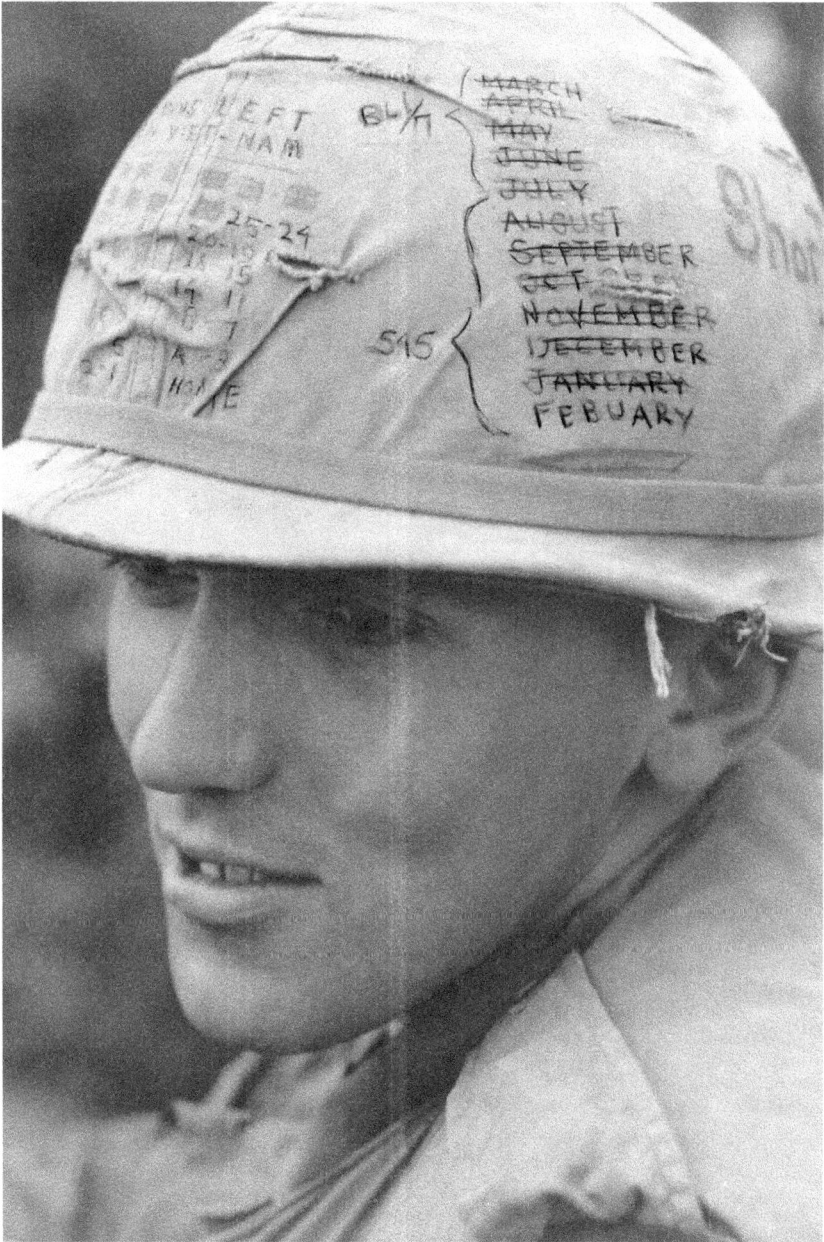

18. A member of the First Cavalry Division keeps a calendar on his helmet during Operation Pershing near Bồng Sơn, South Vietnam, January 1968 (Alamy Stock Photo).

19. Members of B Troop, First Squadron, Ninth Cavalry, South Vietnam, November 1, 1967 (Alamy Stock Photo).

what [their] name was."[12] This entire life behind things.[13] Fragments of redemption.[14]

He looks at Chaffin, flips through the books, returns here and there, looks at Chaffin again. The remove of a foreign land—interrupted by uncanny feelings of stranger relationality,[15] of a shared constellation, as when

12. Benjamin, "Little History of Photography," 510.
13. Mendes, *American Beauty.*
14. Handelman, *Fragments of Redemption.*
15. Hariman and Lucaites, "Public Identity and Collective Memory in U.S. Iconic Photography."

20. Paratroopers of the US Second Battalion, 173rd Airborne Brigade, cross a river in the rain during a search for Viet Cong positions in the jungle area of Bến Cát, South Vietnam, September 15, 1965. Photograph by Henri Huet (Associated Press).

Benjamin asks, "What is aura, actually? A strange weave of space and time: the unique appearance of semblance of distance, no matter how close it may be."[16]

Cigarette synecdoches and helmets with shitstorm calendar countdowns and graffiti send-ups, lucky strikes. M60s stretched across shoulders.

Proper nouns as postcards and simulacra: Mekong Delta, Ho Chi Minh Trail, Tet Offensive, Tet holiday, Hamburger Hill, Hanoi Hilton, Hanoi Jane, Operation Davy Crockett, Westmoreland, "that lying son of a bitch Johnson."[17]

Huey helicopters, fires and hues, UH-1 Iroquois model helicopters nicknamed Hueys, with rockets and machine guns, helicopters for vanguard air companies used alongside infantry scouts for the traditional

16. Benjamin, "Little History of Photography," 518.
17. Zemeckis, *Forrest Gump*.

21. The sergeant of A Company, 101st Airborne Division, guides a medevac helicopter through the jungle foliage to pick up casualties suffered during a five-day patrol near Huế, South Vietnam, April 1968. Photograph by Art Greenspon (Associated Press).

cavalry role of reconnaissance and security, helicopters sometimes utilized for the evacuation transport of marooned men stuck in the shit.

And a transport for refugees who, in a perverse scenario, were loaded up and removed to the West by the invaders displacing them.

Progress

And he stumbles. It's a funny word to pronounce. Wikipedia mentions that this food "was popularized throughout the world by refugees after the Vietnam War."[18] CNN ranks it one of the best global foods—delicious postcolonial comfort food for everyone.[19] Who cares that the noodle dish

18. Wikipedia, "Pho."
19. CNN, "The World's 50 Best Foods."

22. Huey helicopters pour machine-gun fire into the tree line to cover the advance of South Vietnamese ground troops in an attack on a Viet Cong camp eighteen miles north of Tây Ninh, northwest of Saigon, near the Cambodian border, February 18, 1965. Photograph by Horst Faas (Associated Press).

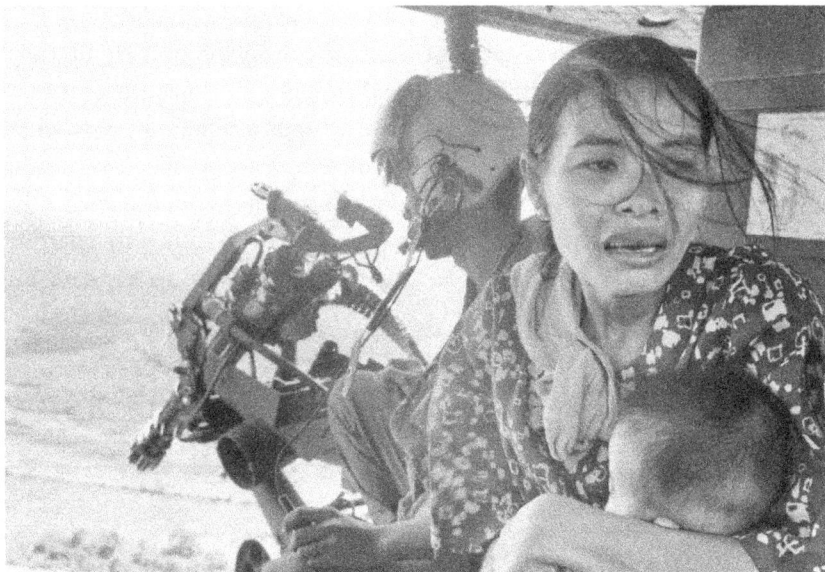

23. Government helicopter gunship carries refugees away near Tuy Hòa, 235 miles northeast of Saigon, March 22, 1975. Photograph by Nick Ut (Associated Press).

represents a much more layered reality of cultural hybridity and exchange, involving regional variations and emerging out of complex histories of imperialism, colonialism, migration, and struggle.[20]

He is fascinated by the work of a powerful policy whisperer—Walt Rostow, an MIT economist and political theorist who entered the national stage in the 1950s as a fierce advocate of using military force to fight the Cold War and promote capitalism. Appointed a speechwriter and foreign affairs advisor, he had their ears—first Eisenhower, then Kennedy, then Johnson.[21] He encouraged ramping up involvement in the shit and helped to implement the strategic concept of saturation, carpet bombing in Vietnam.[22] If the Viet Cong are hiding in the jungle, destroy the jungle— ecological and biological warfare, strafe, shit tons of payloads, napalm, and Agent Orange.[23] Starve them out of the pines—desertification. When there is emptiness, a new world, plant a flag and anoint it "America." Raze the earth to recreate it in an image, a "god trick."[24] A global force for good that strikes for the sake of health and prosperity, intensively inflicted growing pains. In the new world, market forces and military forces work together in derangements of ecopolitics and necrobiopolitics.[25]

("We have it in our power to begin the world over again. A situation, similar to the present, hath not happened since the days of Noah until now.")[26]

Rostow influenced the theory of economic development. He literally wrote the book on it, outlining stages of progress.[27] He contended that societies of advanced industrialization are taxonomically superior to what he termed "traditional" societies. The conceit was that Vietnam would achieve civilizational progress with railroads and hotels and boardwalks and main streets and utilities and parking spaces—a Monopoly board— and factories and tractors and wide-ranging mechanization and modernization and commodity foods and Coca-Cola and Marlboros. And Hồ Chí Minh, the leader of a small, subsistence-agriculture country comprising

20. Greeley, "Phở."
21. Milne, *America's Rasputin.*
22. Milne, "'Our Equivalent of Guerrilla Warfare.'"
23. Zierler, *The Invention of Ecocide.*
24. Haraway, "Situated Knowledges."
25. Bento, "Necrobiopower."
26. Paine, *Common Sense,* 45.
27. Rostow, *The Stages of Economic Growth.*

24. C-123 "Providers" flown by US Air Force crews nicknamed "Ranch Hands" spray chemical defoliant to burn off heavy foliage hiding enemy infiltration routes and base camps, Huế, South Vietnam, August 14, 1968. Photograph by Robert Ohman (Associated Press).

sustainable, organic farms and farmers' markets, Hồ Chí Minh, and the presumptuous and paranoid notion that he was playing dominos, were selling points for an ever-expanding Homestead Act of neocolonial, corporatized nation-building and market penetrations.

In hindsight, the United States did not in fact lose the war—only all the battles. The peace accords signed by Nixon in '73 didn't end America's influential relationship to Vietnam. The aftermath reflected a geostrategic pattern deployed by the United States for decades across East and Southeast Asia, utilizing warfare, societal decimations, and market pressures to facilitate capitalist, export-oriented, economic transitions.[28] The United States imposed sanctions to harshly punish Vietnam, pressuring the World Bank, the International Monetary Fund, and development agencies to withhold aid and loans, negatively impacting a war-torn, materially devastated country, making for crippling infrastructure

28. Martini, *Invisible Enemies.*

problems.[29] US business interests championed political and economic integration and normalization.[30] The passing of time and trade agreements eventually brought about a boom economy for investment and export.[31] "Vietnam's economic and social achievements [. . .] are nothing short of amazing, arguably placing it among the top [. . .] performers among all developing countries," a World Bank report stated in the early 2000s.[32]

Portland

Maybe it's easier to take the recipes and exterminate the people. More economical. Fewer externalities. Dropping nukes would have saved all that time in the shit, and money spent. The conventional payloads and chemical weapons. And the trouble of resettling refugees. Just think about how reductions in budgets and social services would enable more noodle consumption.

A glance at the Google listings for noodle recommendations in Portland shows top spots in the gentrified Pearl District, home to Powell's bookstore, high-rise condominiums, warehouse-to-loft conversions, and the magnificent Cosmopolitan on the Park building.

But anyone willing to take the bus outside of the center and go without a certain niceness and feel okay around intersecting otherings of race, class, culture, and space might meet a nearly bald Vietnamese American woman who cooks the world's greatest noodles. Her close-cropped hairstyle emerged across East Asia within Buddhist traditions over millennia—a spiritual thing, a symbol of renunciation and devotion.[33]

The professor is there for delicious noodles. But she must have stories of endurances and old joys and what these foods mean to her. He wants to hear these stories. But she speaks a different language. And he is on a tour for an anthropology class. His head is buzzing with buzzwords like "infra-

29. Fallows, "Shut Out."
30. Brown, "Rapprochement between Vietnam and the United States," 321.
31. World Bank, *Vietnam—Delivering on Its Promise.*
32. Bourguignon, foreword to *Economic Growth, Poverty, and Household Welfare in Vietnam,* vii.
33. Grant, *Eminent Nuns;* Gutschow, "What Makes a Nun?"

25. Vietnamese and Cambodian refugees in a US helicopter en route to a refugee reception center at the Katum Special Forces camp in South Vietnam, six miles from the Cambodian border, May 5, 1970. Photograph by Charles Ryan (Associated Press).

structure" and "affordable housing." He remembers a basic law. It's called 101. There is a Wikipedia page about it. When all the posers and fans bum-rush the stage—genre flailing after the flood and declaring everything art—then the people formerly known as artists are crowded out. Then there is a shocking problem with the prevalence of bums and fans. He doubts he will be able to eat at her noodle shop when he returns in a few years now that the city has decided that this outlying area shall be more fully, infrastructurally incorporated into the broadening front stage, and is sending in the stagecoach, the development troops.[34]

In making noodles, she is perhaps not doing politics. It seems that she is not formally considered a citizen-activist—or either one of these. She does or does not ride a bike. But her stories are essential to future life. People are too busy or uninterested in going beyond a bowl of broth. But

34. Ford, *Stagecoach*.

her stories might relate to the "inclusive" idea that "we are all, all who live in this age, veterans of this war."[35]

Her stories might trouble dominant logics of development. Her food—however long it persists in this location, location, location—condenses an "undramatic" thriving,[36] a way of making and making do that is critically different from the decadent aheadness of the new sustainabilities movement. With its lost-and-found innocence. The coffee. Kombucha. Craft beer. Cannabinoids. Microdosing. Shit composting. Urban gardening. Wheel reinventing.

Oh, for the love of anthropology! The professor is having a hackneyed anthropological romance—*Tristes Tropiques,* an antimodernist idealizing, longing, victimizing, and othering, a freeze-framing of this woman as atavism, a relic of littleness and betterness.[37] He reads her traditional Buddhist anti-aesthetic as a meaningful contrast to the ornate, tribal, novelty stylings of the suffocating, hyperenunciated, tattooed monoculture of white, hipster identity nonpolitics.

And he breathes a sigh of relief. He takes a sip of the soda she brought him. It's a red can. Coca-Cola. The real thing. He ordered a Diet Coke. But this was lost in translation or was not part of some supply chain.

"Someday this war is gonna end," the Colonel alleges on the beachhead in *Apocalypse Now,* with napalm strafe exploding in the vast jungle behind him.[38]

Murmur of the Heart

The scopophilia took shape and stirred in stills in the small world of a living room. Now the professor is surfing Google Images. The aura, the sheer singularity of existence dissolved in the representational surfaces of the photographs, evokes a philosophical view of a life as a "combination of chance," a contingent "destiny," a cosmic "dicethrow,"[39] a "champagne

35. Egendorf, "Vietnam Veteran Rap Groups and Themes of Postwar Life," 124.
36. Berlant, "Slow Death," 760.
37. Lévi-Strauss, *Tristes Tropiques.*
38. Coppola, *Apocalypse Now.*
39. Deleuze, *Nietzsche and Philosophy,* 26.

26. Medic James E. Callahan gives mouth-to-mouth resuscitation in war zone D, about fifty miles northeast of Saigon, June 17, 1967. Photograph by Henri Huet (Associated Press).

supernova."[40] This can provoke what Emmanuel Levinas refers to as a "bad conscience of justice," arising in an unsettling sense of shared vulnerability and shame.[41]

He scans the picture books for traces and possibilities of a man he loves, born in 1951. It would have been the 1970 draft. There is relief in finding only resemblances and apparitions.

On the fireplace in the living room in his St. Louis house, there is a picture of Helen. She is wearing a khaki uniform and is in her twenties, proudly stationed in the Pacific in the forties. That action somehow makes sense. That war—in which she was part of the US invasion and occupation of New Guinea—seems right. She is a good guy. But the men in the picture

40. Oasis, "Champagne Supernova."
41. Levinas, "The Other, Utopia, and Justice," 230.

27. Helen Czel stationed in New Guinea as part of the Women's Army Corps during World War II.

books are not a greatest generation. They are fodder born of a funeral casino.[42]

A box arrives in Connecticut. There will be an engraved name on the wall at the Vietnam Veterans Memorial in Washington, DC. The family will pile into the car and drive down I-95 to place flowers at the monument.

Or maybe there is a vanishing. A hometown kid went missing in action. There is belief in still-life among family and friends there in Connecticut.

But his dad, who drew a nightmarishly low number in the 1970 draft, lucked out. Le souffle au coeur. The medical inspector detected murmur of the heart. Dad went to culinary school and got into the restaurant business. Bada bing! There were Yankees season tickets. But some other kid might have had those choice seats on the third-base side. There might have been someone with a more angular face, a more muscular figure. A more competent professor. A more responsible individual. He might not have these personal issues in life. All this shit. The personal wreckage and fuming anthropology depend on the chaos-theory chance that his dad did not go to hell.

42. Klima, *The Funeral Casino.*

9 Life Is Sweet

As Good as It Gets[1]

"Did you have a good childhood?"

    "I haven't had a good adulthood."

    "But did we do anything, you know, to cause it?"

    "No, Ma. It's a disease. You guys did a good job. I have a disease."

    "But did you have a good childhood?"

    "Whaddya want me to say? Things were hard. Does anybody have a good childhood? Mine was as good as it gets."

Mamma Roma[2]

It's always been hard for me—the food issues. I mean, how food and eating are at once public and enshrouded in our family. Food is a connective force but also an elephant in the room. There hasn't been a time in my life when you guys weren't, you know, dieting or doing something food related—counting calories, low carb, good fats, fasting, skipping meals. Overexcited

---

1. Brooks, *As Good as It Gets*.
2. Pasolini, *Mamma Roma*.

28. Peter and Mom in Kennebunkport, Maine, 1982. Photograph by Dad.

talk of appetite and menu planning fills out the everyday. How could there be anything the matter, given the open chatter about what's in store for dinner? Family adheres in the rolling déjà vu of nothing much happening, nothing new. No real chew. No talk of what we're going through. Silence surrounds food like so much else, suppressing the truth, that these object relations reside in compulsive behaviors, of course.[3]

At home, meals were nothing exotic. American, mostly. Sometimes Chinese takeout. Italian, naturally. Meals invariably revolved around meat, the centering node for the periphery of veggies—maybe roasted potatoes and green beans, or baked potatoes and peas, or baked beans and corn on the cob, or buttered noodles and steamed broccoli—a not-long roster played on rotation. And always salad. Iceberg lettuce with coin-sized carrots and slices of celery, cukes, and radishes. Scallions, sharp and branchy, thick. Tomatoes, hothouse generic. The onions were the best part, cut long

3. Lacan, *The Object Relation*.

and muscled down, a reliable art, incisive and crosswise for half-moons. The dressing, a vinaigrette, easy-peasy, homemade by the chef.

Whaddya want me to say? I haven't had a good adulthood.

I mean, Ma. One evening, at a colleague's house, I was listening to this guy drone on about the marvels of his smart TV. There was a little green bag—his stuff—on the table,[4] and you know what they say about the waiting.[5] All I could think about was busting it open. I asked if we could put on some Led Zeppelin; the television was set up for streaming. He kept yapping about research and grants, and it was really, I mean, we sat around for a few hours drinking IPAs. Some variety where you drink like two. We never did smoke or put on an album or progress into booze. ("We mustn't kick the bar. We lean into the bar.")[6] I'm a shot of Laphroaig 10 Year beside a bottle of Bud Light. Not a craft beer in sight. The excessive consumption of top-shelf takedown and lowbrow lubricants, a matter of extremity, an immoderate spite, an odd couple,[7] a war of position.[8]

"Okay, here we go, everybody! Dinnertime! Grab your seat, here comes the food!"

And before Kedron and I can say, "Okay," again, before she and I can properly orient the dinner's opening act, before we can say, "Here's this," or, "Hang on, Henry," and before everybody is seated—and this is under my roof, mind you—and before the condiments are on the table, and maybe even the cutlery, and before I'm like, "Manny needs a napkin," and before ice water is poured out, and before the butter knife is placed, before any of that, you guys pick at the food from platters or simply serve yourselves and start. An ungodly race. A meal begun without grace. Whaddya want me to say? I know, believe me, I know. I've also got that haste. I know what it's like—compulsivity. It was absolutely insanifying for me, the taunting presence of the plastic baggie. I know what it's like to suffer straight-line problems, to be hitched to the carte. I know it's hard, and I'm writing from the heart.

When you visit, you always say, "Gosh, you've gained weight, you look so good, so healthy." Like I'm a goose. When I used to visit Texas, Grandma,

4. George Baker Selection, "Little Green Bag."
5. Tom Petty and the Heartbreakers, "The Waiting."
6. Figgis, *Leaving Las Vegas*.
7. Saks, *The Odd Couple*.
8. Gramsci, *Prison Notebooks*, 168–69.

still alive, living with you guys, she would say the opposite about some apparent wasting. "Aren't you eating enough? Meat on your bones," Grandma would admonish.

It's because of factors, there are factors. People—temperamentally and sociologically embodying the entrance at Ellis Island—eat. They eat because this is what's working hard. It's about labor and sufficiency. Having enough. Bountiful food as a means of achieving satisfaction.[9] It's about earnings and exuberance. It's about class. Being rich in meat.[10] And so, yeah, I do take it personally, the moralizing healthism of society, the visible normalcy of people with easily hidden imperfections and indiscretions, people without evident dysfunctions of the will, people residing in other portfolios and postethnic enclaves. From the ground level of factories and grocery stores, on refinement my background has frowned. I wonder how issues of scarcity and adequacy, and shared, familial tendencies to overdo and indulge, have been passed down.

We both have setups. The habit of manipulating materials and metaphors of jouissance in order to foster a nexus and the familiarity of a routine.[11] Ma, you come to visit us in St. Louis, disembark with frozens crammed into hard-shell suitcases. That obsession with wares that we share literally wrapped up with goods and the lifelong provisioning of maternal care. Beef tenderloins. Pork tenderloins. Chops. Shoulders. Lasagna. My favorite: your chicken parmesan. And your homemade gravy. You've always fed me. Formula, then solid food. Zeets. Creamed corn from a can. Celery stuffed with peanut butter. Apples stuffed with peanut butter. Lettuce and mayonnaise on toast. Plain ronis (pasta, butter, parmesan cheese). Open-faced turkey.

You're always nudging me. "How you doing? You okay?"

Nothing but just talk.[12] Everything, just talk. The anecdotal flow of just talk.[13] The sociality of just talk.[14] Our inability to *just talk*.[15]

---

9. Gabaccia, *We Are What We Eat*, 54.
10. Grieco, "Food and Social Classes."
11. Lacan, *The Other Side of Psychoanalysis*.
12. Stewart, *A Space on the Side of the Road*, 6.
13. Ibid., 108.
14. Ibid., 111.
15. Ibid., 171.

Nothing less. Nothing else. Bipolar beeps and buttons. Zero for nothing. One for something. If one, text back a few, as in, "I love you."

Whaddya want me to say? I haven't had a good adulthood. Addiction. Mental illness. Cynical distance.[16] Ethnography's thickness.[17] . . . And oh, the awfulness. You know what I mean. Ma, you know what I mean, what happened to me . . . my colleague, what she did to me . . . my breakdown and the hospital. . . . And then there's everything in general.[18]

Whaddya want me to say? You guys did a good job. You've always fed me, Mom. Formula, then solid food. The first decade was fruit cocktail, the second, boiled hot dogs and ginger ale, and since then it's been checked bags of meat, wholesale. I drive around the terminal at the St. Louis Airport on the lookout for frequent flyers with meatballs, you guys lugging duffle fridges from the carousel. And mamma mia! You're not wearing socks. No heavy jacket. Fast-forward six months, and it's the same pastels, now in the summer balm. I love you so much, Mom.

If I could take it away from you, I would. I know it's not a choice. I know what it's like to be in a hard grip or bad brain or whatever you wanna call it. I know how bad society makes people feel. I stay home when Kedron and the kids go to the rec center's pool; bipolar meds cause weight gain and make me not want to be seen. The stress and body of shame, precious areas of life where I'm absentee. Every day, when I get home from work, I swap out pants for sweatpants. I have trouble finding pants with room in the lap. Fact of the matter, I feel outsized in a world that makes people feel like crap. Because that's what I see, Ma. The problem isn't you or me; it's society. No shanda from me.

If you could take it away from me, you would. I know, Ma. Thanks for saying that. So would I. Every day I'm scared for the day you die. We've got, I dunno, nothing very profound. Nothing academic or advanced. We don't email and we never talk details. But love is felt in chitchat on the phone and holiday hugs and food bought in bulk. Hunkering down in the TV room when you're in town. No serious sit-downs. No communicative rationality.[19] Not in this lifeworld born of factory workers and checkout

16. Žižek, *The Sublime Object of Ideology*, 27–33.
17. Geertz, *The Interpretation of Cultures*, 3–30.
18. Van Sant, *Paranoid Park*.
19. Habermas, *The Theory of Communicative Action*.

girls and backyard theater and night shifts at the mall. The apparent shallows are gentle, and the affection is not so nimble. But you know what, Ma? There's deep love in the hellos and hugs. A real authentic simple. I'm already grieving every day for days without just talk, without the Stratego champ from Norwalk.

Family Matters

I was afraid of the ball, which was now coming in around seventy. "Stay in there," the coaches prodded. "Don't be afraid." I was hit a few times. Rib cage. Thighs. Buttocks. I felt like a soldier ordered to charge. I thought about the Ken Burns documentary and was perplexed as to why those soldiers passively followed such irrational demands, why they didn't just fall to the ground when the generals sadistically commanded them to brave musket volleys and bayonet melees.

I wasn't going to be a Yankee. I prayed for rain and baseball practice cancellations to allow for after-dinner TV. *Full House. Family Matters. The Wonder Years. Home Improvement. Life Goes On. The Facts of Life.* I identified with themes in *Roseanne.* Overweight parents working to make ends meet. Conservative family dynamics.

Whaddya want me to say? Living to run and running to live. Never worried about paying or even how much was owed. And I remember what you said to me. How you swore that it never would end. I remember how you held me, oh, so tight. Wish I didn't know now what I didn't know then.[20]

The recession.

Fragile foundation. Large budget deficits. Astronomical military spending. Insufficient tax revenues. Often large swings. Impulse response functions. This is a book about macroeconomic disturbances. Standard deviation bands. Inflation limited economic expansion oil prices Iraq invasion together with overall. Historical decompositions became contractionary. The line showing no money supply effects suggests depressed real estate values. Aggregate supply component. Structural vector autoregression.

---

20. Bob Seger & the Silver Bullet Band, "Against the Wind."

Erratic consumer confidence and reluctant businesses. The hardest hit were the New England states.[21]

Whaddya want me to say? I remember dining room conversations with the mortgage broker. ("The adults are talking.")[22] I was in the living room overhearing the stewing-over. I saw the man offered Diet Coke and chocolate wafers. I thought about how every Christmas, Grandpa gifted a roast or ham to his factory owner, a form of patronage from an Old World heritage.

Whaddya want me to say? There were minivan drives to scope out cheaper housing. A ranch with a chain-link fence around a weedy lot was to a boy in the back seat a sign of the downswing. I heard talk of bank accounts cleaned out. You guys apologized for fewer presents underneath. Humbly laid out a modicum despite the circumstances being difficult. We didn't have conversations, but I knew it was serious—the hand you were dealt. It was secretive and scary—and, I worried, all my fault. I developed a pivotal anxiety about money—and a troubled conscience regarding myself. I didn't care about the tree. I realized the sweat equity going into outlays for the family. For sure, the constant bickering between us the year before I went to college reflected misgivings about going away; it was also an effect of our shared grief and uncertainty about the workday and frugality and student loans from Fannie Mae. Our familiar way, an inability to mull okay. I felt burdensome because I was weighted in that wallet. Second mortgage for access to good schools. Sports equipment. Baseball cards mint. Clothes for fitting in and fitted team hats. The hearty family dins for stuffing a goose fat. And mounds of tuition debt—that you and I both took on—so I could read books, sit on a lawn, and move into a different class.

Whaddya want me to say? Things were hard. The restaurant went into decline and then out of business. Dad walked away without assets. Second and third jobs. Stacks of tax filings. Working jobs. Manual jobs. Service jobs. Seasonal jobs. Dad ended up at a shipping warehouse in Danbury. It relocated to Austin. (That's how things wound down from Connecticut to Texas.)

Whaddya want me to say? My mom was the lunch lady at the high school cafeteria, right there in the prime time of growing up. My classmates liked you more than me, teased you in front of me, and teased me in

21. Walsh, "What Caused the 1990–1991 Recession?"
22. The Strokes, "The Adults Are Talking."

front of you. Don't get me wrong—I loved seeing you every day, too. But it was embarrassing. And that's a tough resolution because it was a labor of anything-for-you love, I always knew. Making do. But it's not like you were a teacher's aide or the art appreciation instructor. You had angles on the tables, the ecology of cool, kind of cramped my thereness in an independence scene and style, maybe interrupted my arrival. No other parent worked at that school. The people who worked there came from outside of town because they couldn't afford to live in our town. That's the whole point of that town.

As for me, it was expected—weekends, nights, summers—it's what you do. Such as Boston Market in Danbury. Black servers dispensed a choice of chicken, meatloaf, ham, or turkey, plus sides, from warmed stainless steel hotel pans into compartments on customers' plastic plates and, in the kitchen in back, Ecuadorians filled other pans with, for example, creamed spinach and an array of other sides, from plastic bags shipped from a regional processing facility. Standard American English without facial hair was at the touch-screen cash register earning a couple bucks more per hour—plus pilfering—for future college spending cash and additions to the CD collection.

The score . . . Step one, the customer receives their meat-and-two meal: say, a quarter chicken white. They shuffle down the line to the register. Step two, the cashier—me—specifies the price, including tax (from memory), and lightly floats fingers over the screen but doesn't actually register anything, doesn't make it official for the manager's nighttime sales tabulations, doesn't scuttle the scam, man. Step three, under the felicitous condition that the cash payment is exact, well then, the customer, not expecting change, finds a vacant dining table and sits tight. What quarter chicken white? Money for nothing, and chickens for free.[23]

No other student in my school worked at a restaurant. That's the whole point of that school. I hung out with the crew after hours and learned slang and colloquialisms that weren't taught in my Spanish classes.

The junior-year study abroad program was administered by the parents of an eventually Ivy-bound valedictorian who was at that moment

---

23. Dire Straits, "Money for Nothing."

studying abroad. That student didn't have part-time work on their resume, no stealing from a corporation.

I applied to go to Ecuador. The interview was me and my parents—we wore our church clothes—and the other couple, the administrators, in their vested home. Of all the topics that we must have covered, I can remember one: biggest fear.

I answered, "Swimming with whales."

And they reacted quizzically, like, that's silly—what's not to embrace about such adventure?

In truth, I don't know why they rejected my application. But the scholarships for the program were scarce, and my bitter hunch is that it was about submitting a resume of jobs—not extracurricular activities—and giving pedestrian interview responses. Lack of gusto for nature gigantism.[24] My biggest fear exhibited a low level of zest, and perhaps also evidence of a video game chest. I wanted to go to Ecuador to study Spanish. I had never been out of the country. Top-ish grades, I was a very good, but not outstanding, student with extensive work experience and church attendance. Whaddya want me to say? However integrated into the country suburbs, we weren't harmoniously polished in appearance and didn't play tennis and had relocated from a lower-echelon mix, and we were now in the sticks, with some social access, sitting on soft money.

And then. I scored a little above average on the SAT with a budget for one try and no preparation classes or study guides. I applied early decision to an aspirational, rankings-conscious southern private school (with an exciting Division I sports program) that, I figured, might generously accept and support a first-generation, public-school kid from the North as part of its neoliberal diversity vibe and goal of being nationwide. I got scholarships, merit- and need-based, and took out sizable loans, and I fell in love and found a major—one of the least popular on campus—and after graduating, I finally did it, my study abroad, living for stretches in Guatemala, hanging around expat lurks, and doing Spanish-language work, and, as part of a research project in the rural highlands, I did my first lengths of anthropological fieldwork.

---

24. Neset, *Arcadian Waters and Wanton Seas*, 17.

I never swim or go to beaches because of the bathing suit—and because of multispecies agency.

The Snack Bar

The Boys & Girls Club, the town's recreational facilities—baseball and softball fields, basketball courts, picnic tables—were located up the road from our house, from everyone's houses, and were the commons for adolescence.

A gravel trail wound around the property. It allowed access to the ballfields from the parking lot and main building and covered pavilions up front. One afternoon, near the end of the school year, two of my classmates scampered down the path, past manicured, chalk-laid diamonds and youngsters playing rounders, to the far end of the place, where one field was not, at that moment, in use, where there was, therefore, an empty dugout. After a while in the shadowy bunker, the boy sprinted back, out ahead of the girl, to the group of boys milling around the front facilities. He said she gave him a hand job. He said smell his fingers. Everyone yowled. I anxiously looked over my shoulder to see if my parents were monitoring me. I gazed across the buildings and pavilions to the rectangular shack, the long service window, the rec center's center of attention—that hole in the wall, the snack bar. Right there, like the cafeteria, coming of age, the wonder years, glances and holding hands, scores and lands, fitting in and being cool, afternoons and evenings after school, my mom and dad on the scene, quite the team, operating the canteen, where growing up was therefore cleaved in defining contradictions of living between and stretching across spheres of recreation and situation.

The snack bar technically belonged to the town, like the blacktop and the mounds. But you guys ran the joint. Everyone knew our surname. Everyone saw, through that cutout frame, public displays of industry and identity. No one else could make those delicious quarter pounders, handshaped and temped by a career restaurateur. Dad dropped tenders and fries into the gas fryer and flipped patties in the weeds. Twizzlers, Mountain Dew, Big League Chew—Mom at the window. Plastic sporks for sour cream-and-jalapeño-dabbed nachos and old-school Terlingua chili. A real deal wooden cashbox. Burgers in SCT 413 No. 100 Red Plaid

Disposable Paper Food Trays. Long summer days. I hung out with who-ever was hanging around. Made mixtapes in the backs of hatchbacks. Laid low in the back of the shack until night was drawn and it was time to return home. Snuck free candy for my friends—and for other kids to sweeten 'em and make more friends.

Whaddya want me to say? We were an extra-cash family working to make ends meet in a salaried, knowledge-economy Connecticut career center. The sun set as fathers in suits arrived from the City on the Metro-North to catch the last innings of Little League contests. Families at-the-bit chomping in line. Grilled chicken sandwiches hitting the counter on time. Ballpark food done well, nothing fancy, hot dogs and french fries under moonlight, parents respectfully accomplishing an economic life.

And then. The spotlights that shone down on the playing fields and unpaved amble went dark. The lone source of illumination was now a sin-gle bright floodlight on the shed. No one saw or tipped out the proud labor that proceeded. The operation had to be clean. Dad scrubbed the grill, the machine. Drained the goopy fryolator and poured the thick, dirty oil around the base of what came to be known as the "grease tree," which stood tragically close to the rear door of the building. The trunk accumu-lated layer upon layer, a gunk lamination, slowly being snuffed out. It reeked of burnt carbohydrates—overdone fries, submerged sludge chunks of mozzarella sticks, and blackened flour dust from fingers.

I helped now and then with the work and cleanup, maybe maintaining the condiment shelf on the building's exterior or, inside, in the back, man-ning the ice cream station, tubs of hard serve. But I was never a full-fledged employee. The kid who was hired—one of my friends from school—manically cleaned the kitchen. Set goals for himself. Did pull-ups, chinning the exposed rafters of the edifice's unfinished interior. A lotta moxie was great because, let's face it, we all wanted to get home as soon as possible to veg out.

Maybe you guys paid sportboy to defend me from the grease, under-standing the body as the site of incorporated history.[25] My hands, my own hands, guarded by a world, a sweet attention, would be different.[26]

---

25. Thompson, "Editor's Introduction" in *Language and Symbolic Power*, 13.
26. Kerouac, *Visions of Cody*, 368.

Like I'm veal. Because there weren't hyphens. The wages of whiteness had presumably been earned.[27] You guys let me dillydally and desert. You moved up to a town where it's impossible to see other houses from inside your own. A thing of principle perhaps—not to formally employ one's own. A matter of pride, independence, management, and threshold. This was your establishment and not part of paying dues or some older purview. Grandpa didn't work in a factory and Grandma at the checkout so that rungs of descendants would be wage earners, too. They ate because this is what's working hard, and they saw hard work as the path and premise of elsewhere. A stratum where work does not mean dependency or subservience.

Whaddya want me to say? Mine was as good as it gets.

27. Roediger, *The Wages of Whiteness.*

10 The Graduate

Mantel Culture

Manny's kindergarten portrait displays the dark spaces of lost teeth.

His newborn picture, snapped at, like, hour one, is a scrunched face. He's lying sideways in the crib in the birthing room, skull-cap cozy.

In his annual Little League photo, he strikes a proud, batter-up pose in front of tacky, graphical schooldays light rays. Not sure if he picked that background or if it's now an obligatory part of the package.

In Henry's first-year day care picture, he is propped up, wearing over-alls, clueless, mesmerized by the flash, smiling beside a Kids Only sign. That sign was either superimposed (as with Manny's light rays) or diegetically at day care. The hay bale beside him makes such materiality doubtful.

I'm seven, kicking hard at home plate in a game of kickball, wearing a dark-blue Don Mattingly tee, kicking so darn hard I am falling backward. The kilter of a bad swing.

I'm at my college graduation with a black robe and a yellow cord for honors.

I'm atop a pyramid at Tikal.

Kedron is gorgeous, dancing with her now-deceased father at our wedding.

The whole of us are sitting on a bench in the park behind Manny's elementary school, gleaming cheeses. A professional photo shoot gifted by a colleague as a congratulatory gesture for Henry's birth.

Our house.[1] Sills and stills. The gratifying, perfect images of a little life. Frames of standing and success. Satisfaction swells that conceal phoniness, unbearables, such shambles, fucking bullshit, innocence wreckages, the wearing down of sweetheart fondness, a "mix of ghostly memories."[2] Still remains.[3]

The white popular culture of the nineties is often stereotyped as apathetic, lighthearted nihilism. But there were countervailing concerns with "authentic emotionality and passionate relationships" and "escape from [. . . the] plasticized, televised world."[4] This is a book about a boy who grew up consuming wistful movies about "the hopes and the discontents" of white, middle-class life.[5] Movies about alienation and claustrophobia,[6] "conformity" and the "facade of respectability."[7] For example, *American Beauty*, a defining achievement of this category, looks at repressions and fragilities in marriage, family, and the everyday.[8] It aspires to breach pallid surfaces for bits and pieces of profundity. The noumena withdrawn in the flow of present-at-hand experience.[9] The magical metaphysics of what the movie calls "this entire life behind things." The hurried family breakfasts forfeited to the toothbrush and morning rush and genuinely missed in the afternoon . . . every afternoon . . . for decades. The low-hanging fruit of existence fulfillment, what the movie's director, Sam Mendes, calls the "little life."[10]

1. Crosby, Stills, Nash & Young, "Our House"; Madness, "Our House."
2. Stewart and Liftig, "Scenes of Life/Kentucky Mountains," 353.
3. Stone Temple Pilots, "Still Remains."
4. Dickinson, "The *Pleasantville* Effect," 222, 225.
5. Ibid., 213.
6. Hausmann, "Envisioning the (W)hole World 'Behind Things,'" 118.
7. Munt, "A Queer Undertaking," 265.
8. Mendes, *American Beauty*.
9. Harman, *Tool-Being*.
10. Mendes, introduction to *American Beauty*, viii.

Magnolia[11]

We dashed across campus—undergrads—to catch another emblematic movie at the Student Center when it came out.

(Cue "Fade into You" by Mazzy Star.)[12]

She liked the movie. I, like, loved it. Like, my favorite movie ever.

We strolled back to the dorm, holding hands, knowing that we moved and breathed in the same world.[13]

"Look how the leaves fall so delicately on the surface of the pond. It's so beautiful."

"Not as beautiful as you."[14]

("He could see, as though it were already happening, the pots of spicy pasta, the games of Yahtzee, endless talk. Bohemian friends dropping by. He liked the idea of looking for used furniture with her, joking about each other's bad taste. He could be buddies with her, with a woman. Why not? He could be a Nineties guy.")[15]

I, like, loved it. The drama. The suspense. The exceptional soundtrack. Man, oh man. Aimee Mann.[16] Melancholy, quirkiness, indie difference, that characteristic meld of irony, sincerity, and significance.[17] Entry into the decade's cinematic emo catalogue for nineties guy affiliations with assimilable, soft masculinity. The cool cinematography. The touch of reality, characters caught up in drugs and alcohol, random sex, compulsions, insecurities, deep needs, physical disease, regrets and deficiency, anxieties about looming ends, what the future portends.

Smoking cigarettes on the patio outside of the dorm afterward, we talked the phantasmagorical storm, frogs thumping down, splattering around, everyone reaching to fill the void, that "pre-consciousness" destroyed.[18]

Vanderbilt Hall. A couple of years earlier, the fall. They had driven me in the family's Chevy Suburban to Nashville for freshman orientation. On

11. Anderson, *Magnolia*.
12. Mazzy Star, "Fade into You."
13. Fitzgerald, "Benediction," 155.
14. *South Park*, "Starvin' Marvin."
15. Gaston, *The Good Body*, 219.
16. Mann, *Magnolia*.
17. MacDowell, "Quirky."
18. Gado, *The Passion of Ingmar Bergman*, 103.

the first day, I met a girl who had also grown up in church youth groups, worked high school jobs, made promises, and experienced spiritual and financial burdens. We had a lot to talk about.

Alternative

It is more efficient to forgo the drive and grab a sermon on television—phone in the tithe with a credit line. My brother and I begged. More time for playing war, video games, and watching the Giants. Piling in was leaving the playroom at home for coffee cake and Christian jam rock, a schlep across the county to a nondenominational evangelical church with an appealing yuppie feel and a vibrant youth group

With the rest of the church kids, we talked DC Talk and Newsboys—the Christian wing of the mall's music store. Meanwhile, the kids at our high school didn't have a clue. With them, we talked Pearl Jam, Red Hot Chili Peppers, and Dr. Dre—the featured frontline displays. And so, the CD collection in our playroom was ample and ambivalent, attempting appreciation for religious rock, and registering strong preferences for the varieties of popular culture that the televangelists were referring to as "the new pornography."[19]

At the evangelical sleepaway camp one summer, the charismatic pastor, twentysomething, a long-haired nineties guy, had the campers sit on the floor in the gym, legs crossed. He prayed into a handheld microphone and paced the room and beckoned us to stand to pray for personal salvation, impassioned, welcoming, and terribly leading. This was not multiple choice. It was true/false. I had already spent that spring immersed in the coverage of bombs over Baghdad.[20] I heard Whitney Houston sing the national anthem at the Super Bowl (which the Giants won). Amid a public culture of saturating and engendering loves of God and country, of alarming, normalizing, and entertaining relational forms and affiliations, twelve years old, I stood along with the other campers. The pastor spoke of a crucial decision and an "age of accountability"—the idea being that when a person reaches a certain age, and hears the good news about Jesus, they

19. Goldstein, "Jimmy Swaggart Blasts Rock Porn."
20. Outkast, "B.O.B."

are henceforth responsible for where their spirit goes after death, an age- and information-related, unconditional, heaven-or-hell theory of agency in being saved. The chronic falling into sin that every day reoccurs then requires petitioning God for forgiveness to sanctify the soul. Steadfast boundary maintenance.[21]

After two weeks of archery, basketball, swimming, arts and crafts, Bible study, cafeteria cleaning, dishwashing, late-night hands of hearts in bunk beds, and homesickness, they arrived. Pulled me and my brother aside. Grandpa died. The funeral was last week.

I have never understood why. Maybe a money thing, the inability to afford hurried airfare. Maybe a variety of care, wanting us to complete the stay there. Maybe an emotional protection thing, like the quietude around lots of things: food and eating, mortgage refinancing, an older cousin who ate turkey sandwiches and drank Tab like everyone else, who swam in the pool with everyone else, who died from the silent cause of the times. Some people who died were in principle damned because they were not saved and redeemed, not "born-again." This included Catholic kin, like Grandpa and my cousin. We didn't talk about difficult things.

We were asked to take rules and realities for granted. The other youth group kids and I led multiple, contrasting lives, working within an unre- marked, manipulated "formula of hyphenation," to quote Arjun Appadurai, where "the right-hand side of the hyphen can barely contain the unruli- ness of the left-hand side."[22] Coming up good Christian was interrupted by the impulses and moves of fitting in young American.[23] We were two- channel stereos, the Newsboys and new pornography side by side on the racks, with a flexible moral logic adapted for maintaining second lives and otherness across scripture readings, youth group meetings, bleacher seats, back seats, and house parties.

This suburban adolescence was lived through what Homi Bhabha describes as "a strategy for articulating contradictory and coeval state- ments of belief,"[24] doing different identities and inhabiting different domains at the same time. Methods for managing presence and piety

21. Barth, *Ethnic Groups and Boundaries.*
22. Appadurai, *Modernity at Large,* 172.
23. Bowie, "Young Americans."
24. Bhabha, *The Location of Culture,* 132.

in different lanes for multiple kinds of access—schooldays relationships, evolutions around alternativeness, and furtive, earnest attachments to a fundamentalist version of final love that was essentially unknown regionally yet a precondition for the afterlife. We didn't proselytize or publicly identify as born-again and sex-negative at school. At youth group, we hid high school happenings, were more muted in merriment, and kept faith in continual renewals for the inevitable lapsing given a dangerous cool.

Negative meanings of pleasure collided with the material culture and worldly living of the Connecticut woods and made for mixed messages and heterogeneous experiences of being and having.[25] It was all so wasteful! Boys clicked through pics, privately betraying promises, violating prayers, becoming mannish beneath old keyboard trays at the hutch. Look at him up there, above the garage after hours, playing things, praying immediately afterward out of panic about the chance of a sudden heart attack. ("Do you know I think there's a tape recorder in heaven for each of us? [. . . There] is that tape recorder taking it all down?")[26]

He was devastated by Grandpa going. The smile taller than wide. The best hugs. The same, shared name. Grandpa religiously attended his baseball games, driving from working-class Norwalk to the country for evenings under the lights. And now, Grandpa got to him from beyond Saint Pete, peering at Pete through that sticky sheet, a man who spent his whole life on a line working vices, cutting keys, sustaining gradual deafness, the gaze sometimes hit the kid so hard as to flaccidify. He felt ashamed and entitled in expenditure, betraying the ethnicized values of frugality and industry of a man who sacrificed for grandkid comforts and was now perched as panopticon.

God forbid. So the youth group crowd improvised. Thinking loosely about the depth and permanence of sinfulness, we dealt in practice theories of dabbling and double consciousness,[27] the premise being more or less reasonable transgressions, a sliding scale for rationalizing sexual and recreational behaviors against an intrinsically ambiguous theology, in which

25. Marcel, *Being and Having.*
26. Mailer, *Why Are We in Vietnam?*, 9.
27. Moreiras, "Hybridity and Double Consciousness."

questions might be raised about swear words, speed limits, stop signs, and *Seinfeld*, about fibbing, fooling around, fucking around, and saying "fuck," and against the knowledge that sins can be prayed and wiped away, always a reset button. ("I'm so horny, that's okay, my will is good.")[28] Stubbing a toe or having sex as occasions for reconfirming faith, testifying in a gymnasium or pew or simply inside you. It was a miraculous, confusing, and hypocritical proposition. Everyone was doing it upstairs and consistently sending apologies into the air. Slates cleaned every every day, hour, minute.

FADE IN:

INT. ST. LOUIS – PETER AND KEDRON'S HOUSE – BEDROOM – NIGHT

KEDRON lies still on her side, pretending to sleep, staring into the window dimness. Attuned to something suspicious. CAMERA ZOOMS IN on her face — a mild grimace. A beat. Feels like minutes.

She hears the dampened, light ruffle of PETER masturbating under the comforter. She flips over to square up. Switches on the bedside LIGHT. Busting this up. Then, he leans up.[29]

> KEDRON
>
> I wasn't asleep, you know.

CAMERA ZOOMS IN on him.

> PETER
>
> (red-handed)
> Okay . . .

He rolls over slowly to face the wall. Stalling for a moment. Something to say.

---

28. Nirvana, "Lithium."
29. Ball, *American Beauty*, 41.

PETER (CONT'D)

(combative)

Yeah, okay. That's not cool, Kedron. What the
hell? I don't know what you think is going on. . . .
I'm really frustrated. Our life is so mundane.
Chicken breasts. Brussels sprouts. Rice. What
else? Let's see . . . I can't stand being part of
the exact same day, every day. It literally feels
like an eternity. It literally is. I want more us-
actuality.

KEDRON

I'm frustrated, too. I'm carrying the weight and
you're the one complaining. Days are hard. Nights
are hard. Weekends are hard. The end of the
semester is hard. Your life is always hard. Call
your therapist. Call your psychiatrist. Call your
mom.

PETER eases out of bed. Leans diagonally against the wall, picking at the
bedside lamp's brass finial.

PETER

If rhinos could scream, this is what they would
say: "Let's go get Thai food, just you and me.
Drunken noodle, please! Tom yum!"

KEDRON

I don't know how to talk to you. You don't make
any sense.

PETER

Okay, I get it. Don't mind that we've constructed a
domesticated zoo environment where there aren't
any corners, crevices, or discontinuities. I guess

what I'm experiencing has a name. It's called
"wrongthink." [30]

KEDRON

I'm frustrated, too. Do I stick with a lonely life
apart together? Do I continue with the rescue
attempts and relief efforts?

PETER

Don't you see? That's precisely the problem. It's
medical anthropology! These are structural
disasters. Humanitarianism is a Band-Aid.

KEDRON

Just pull it together. I'm a mom. And a professor.
And a wife. And a caretaker. Dishes. Diapers.
Detergent. Depression. Durations.

He is slow in responding.

PETER

Don't dream it's over.[31] Feel it still.[32]

A few moments of quiet.

KEDRON moves to a seat in the upholstered armchair. Straightens out
the bunches in her pajama bottoms. Glances out the window as she offers
a rejoinder.

KEDRON

Everything falls apart.[33]

---

30. Didion, *The White Album, 168.*
31. Crowded House, "Don't Dream It's Over."
32. Portugal. The Man, "Feel It Still."
33. Dog's Eye View, "Everything Falls Apart."

A short beat.

> KEDRON (CONT'D)
>
> (turns to him)
> Oh baby, I feel so down. . . . Oh, maybe I don't care
> no more. I know this for sure, I'm walking out that
> door.[34]

> PETER
>
> If I hadn't blown the whole thing years ago. . . .
> You can trust me not to think and not to sleep
> around. If you don't expect too much from me,
> you might not be let down.[35]

PETER pauses and sighs. Plops back on the wadded-up bedspread and replies.

> PETER (CONT'D)
>
> Sturdy brick house in the middle of America. I
> want to be that, what I promised and set out to be
> back at Vanderbilt. My aim is true.[36]

> KEDRON
>
> Yeah, and so is the division of labor. You're always
> stalling out. At best, you help with Manny's
> homework. Once in a while. No help with folding
> the clothes, changing beds, loading and unloading
> the dishwasher . . .

> PETER
>
> Dinner once in a while.

34. The Strokes, "Last Nite."
35. Gin Blossoms, "Hey Jealousy."
36. Costello, *My Aim Is True.*

KEDRON

But your mind is in your inbox, or it's spaced, and
in constant haste, and the pork comes out pink,
the pasta al dente, even for our refined tastes.

PETER

I've studied the social determinants of health. The
thing is, these are disasters of civilizational
proportions. Maladies, not moral failures. Not a
mode of masculinity that is molding, setting in
ways. This conjunctive synthesis of college
sweethearts isn't roped around problematic
domesticities like some commingle of sweetness
and power.[37] It's not a marriage of plain old dirty
laundry. Because generously speaking, the lines
between crazies, lazies, excuses, accumulates,
effects, willpower, wider culture, and debility are
so fucking hard to understand and unravel.

FADE OUT.

The Wedding

A picture of the first dance hangs in our bedroom in St. Louis. The vows
were said in an oven of a community church on a one-hundred-degree
August afternoon in Appalachia. The family farm was the setting for a
homely, pastoral reception. We worked on a shoestring to ensure that everyone was eating and drinking and dancing. Dad made a buffet of food
and a towering cake. A local bluegrass band was spot on, the perfect fit,
her choice. The "Tennessee Waltz" was our dance, solemn sounding, slow
swinging. We broke with the conventions of a tacitly dry community
in having coolers of beer for friends from college and grad school. And
for me.

---

37. Mintz, *Sweetness and Power.*

The Clown[38]

Do the students know what it takes for me to be fungible liveness?[39] At once dynamic and rehearsed, compelling and moderately challenging, and essentially a salesman. "Structural violence." "Cultural competence." These are some premium-grade credits. Working the room without breaking the news that in teaching and learning about social inequalities, we are problematically absorbing and reproducing them. And without breaking the news that, for over a decade, it has been soul-crushing for me to stand at the podium and work the front of the hall like a stand-up comedian. There is a reason comics suffer offstage lives of depression and addiction and find relief and abjection in performance, living a cycle of clowning and crashing.[40]

Without breaking out of the PowerPoint presentation and confiding in the students that right after class, I was gonna go home to my couch and smoke a bowl, and that my role as recruiter and revenue generator for the acclaimed institution was a major part of why I was addicted to drugs.

My Morning Jacket[41]

They classify it as "bipolar disorder." The term "manic depression" is accurate. Phenomenology: caught between depression-pillowing and pseudoephedrine-surging, intense-torn suspended, jammed and stretched simultaneously, not knowing how or being able to evade or escape, incessant thought inundation, irritability, extreme anxiety, no good sleep, needing something, anything, to calm the maddening freak-out. Hence, high correlations with addiction. It's a brain running as fast as it can in place, in a grim place of staggering depression. A cul-de-sac of despair (IMHO the DSM should name this rapid-cycling, mixed-episode affliction "stuck moving"). Mental illness and mood disorder shape all aspects of my life. Substance abuse. Kids and wife. Hardships in marriage. Hospitalizations. The dilemma of pushing or scaring people away. Losing

38. Mingus, *The Clown*.
39. Ong, *Fungible Life*.
40. Limon, *Stand-Up Comedy in Theory, or, Abjection in America*.
41. My Morning Jacket, *Z*.

them in description. Being too much, too expensive. A wicked hard come-down at every semester's end. And just, like, ordinary quirks. Insane capacity for work. Mortgage dependent on meds and a momentum that's the flip side of a sometimes devastating behind-the-scenes. There are no publications or peppy lectures without a nonlinear, endeavoring, and epi-sodically faltering functionality in a workplace where I have been dispar-aged and felt injury. My personality is dynamic, touched especially, a bit much, maybe, brainy, a little loony, at times edgy, flashes of belligerence. And my colleagues at the university, such prestige, some of them, the irregularities of an expressive and moody masculinity, they've stigmatized or cast aspersions on me. A few times, I have lashed out at colleagues and graduate students in St. Louis. I hurt people. I feel bad about it. They didn't know, couldn't know, why that happened. I don't set out to lash out. I don't defend it. I'm not a mean person. There's this thing, the thing that I am, what I sometimes can't dam. Sometimes I suddenly feel very strongly about something. Or I anger in an instant. Like when I impetuously send an email to the chair. Or when I take something out on someone in a way that isn't fair. There are factors there. Things that aren't in the open air. Social, biographical, medical, and contextual factors of which people are not aware. I feel bad about it. For me, bipolar disorder is an ableism pre-dicament because institutions are organized around surface perceptions, selfhood stability, and limited space to share. The effort, brilliance, and creativity—what me brings to anthropology—is made possible by disabil-ity and disease, just like that anger that can also percolate in there. That's partly why I titled this book *Stuck Moving*. I did study with Arthur, after all. It's a covert illness narrative.[42]

Cocoon[43]

Psychology tells a story about the arcing growth-geometry of boys to men:[44] the interiorities and desires of me (Moi) are progressively super-seded by the "values," "ideas," "choices," "conduct," and "social roles and

42. Kleinman, *The Illness Narratives*.
43. Howard, *Cocoon*.
44. Boyz II Men, *Cooleyhighharmony*.

professions" of a normalized self (Soi), an "identity," "a certain kind of stability."⁴⁵ But boy, man. That isn't how me works. I took Bhabha's class in grad school. Learned his critique of the liberal subject and "normative expectations of development and progress."⁴⁶ His attention to "in-between states and moments of hybridity."⁴⁷ Subjects formed within "the ambivalent world."⁴⁸ The "strategy of ambivalence in the structure of identification that occurs precisely in the elliptical *in-between*."⁴⁹ He writes of "a sense of disorientation, a disturbance of direction [...] an exploratory, restless movement caught [...] here and there, on all sides, *fort/da*, hither and thither, back and forth."⁵⁰

This book is being written on the couch where I used to smoke pot. There is a Diet Coke on the table instead of a glass pipe. Not as intense as the unyielding grip of the chronic, the couch's hold is not tenaciously immobilizing like the contoured biochemical clutch. But no fucking way, there is no breakthrough accumulation of an ironed-out improvement person, no finally straightened-out scenario of sharply focused, economic productivity, no switched-on domesticity, no altogether aggrandizing agency.⁵¹ I am languid and lateral in a writing project that is at once productive and combative of reclusiveness, and yet inductive of cocooning and closing down, a "regularized infolding,"⁵² solipsism as a "fitting response to a stressful environment," like a professional field, or "like a family."⁵³

"Look, Mom. This is Dad. Look." Manny mock-types at an imaginary keyboard. "Oh, look at me, I'm just gonna lay here. Tobacco is bad! Tobacco is bad!"

Self lies on the couch, and mental me is blinkered by the laptop.

Self stands up from the couch, and motley me comes along, too. Sometimes sullen. Sometimes too animated and self-expressive. Anecdotes

45. Tarasti, "Existential Semiotics and Cultural Psychology," 328–29.
46. Bhabha, *The Location of Culture*, 2.
47. Ibid., 208.
48. Ibid., 92.
49. Ibid., 60.
50. Ibid., 1.
51. Berlant, "Slow Death."
52. Massumi, *A User's Guide to Capitalism and Schizophrenia*, 58.
53. Berlant, "Slow Death," 777.

and wisecracks wrong for the kids. Songs on the playlist vulgar for little ears. Loose speaking in front of Manny about the overpolicing of Blackness in front of Blueberry Hill. And my blue insideness.

"What do you want to eat tonight?" she asks.

"You," I text back.

Sometimes we go to Blue Hill for burgers and fries. Sometimes Mi Ranchito for enchiladas. The weekdays are pasta, tacos, bistro night (i.e., medium rare steak with a bleu cheese salad for me and Kedron, hot dogs for Henry and Manny), and mac and cheese with a meat and veggie.

In verbalizing and writing about recovery, maybe I'm talking about "becoming and being ordinary."[54] Stuffing flimsy corn tortillas with shredded cheese, sour cream, and sautéed peppers, rousing excitement in the kids in enunciating "cheese" in the vein of a dragged-out, vowel-accented *please.* Lateral agency indicative of low-key everydayness, every day.[55] Taco night is a sign of something, right?

The Asshole Years

He held court around a hefty flotilla of a table that seated a couple dozen students, fine upholstered dining-style chairs in a room with ornate crown molding and half-wrapped with built-in bookcases containing uniform-colored collections of canonical volumes, a realm that austerely intoned: "Literature." We hung on words.

He opened one session with a contest. "Who knows the author?" Then he read from a piece of paper. "Just as a tangent touches a circle lightly and at but one point, a translation touches the original lightly and only at the infinitely small point of the sense, thereupon pursuing its own course according to the laws of fidelity in the freedom of linguistic flux."[56]

I was reading that masterpiece on the side anyhow. I won a bottle of wine.

54. Shinebourne and Smith, "'It Is Just Habitual,'" 293.
55. Berlant, "Slow Death."
56. Benjamin, "The Task of the Translator," 261.

A handful of us routinely hung out at Grafton Street Pub across from the Humanities Center after classes. We argued poststructuralism and shit like that. One night a cohort mate, burned out from a typical, ridiculously heated debate about critical theory and politics, and the war—such spats frequent and inevitable facets of our time at the bar—anyway, one night, definitely right, she told me, "Go home to your wife."

(Cue "The Man in Me" by Bob Dylan.)[57]

Grafton Street. Grendel's Den. Daedalus. Middlesex Lounge. The People's Republik. The Middle East. Charlie's Kitchen. Noir Bar. I was a tangent pursuing its own course according to the freedom of linguistic flux.

"Okay, see. What I mean is, the soul is the prison of the body.[58] And power is everywhere; not because it embraces everything, but because it comes from everywhere.[59] And so . . . power is also nowhere—a multiplicity of force relations.[60] And so . . . I mean . . . here comes the bartender. Yes, please, White Russian. . . . I mean, I think, that's the key—it's always already both/and. I'm obviously thinking Derrida. Bhabha. If identity is only a game, if it is only a procedure to have relations, social and sexual—pleasure relationships that create friendships, it is useful. But if people think that they have to (scare quotes) uncover their (scare quotes) own identity, and that their own identity has to become the law, the principle, the code of their existence.[61] I mean . . . the relationships we have to have are not ones of identity . . . they must be relationships of differentiation, of creation, of innovation.[62] They are a part of our world freedom.[63] The discovery of a secret side of our desire.[64] Because . . . I mean . . . to be the same is really boring.[65] I'm thinking Nietzsche. Massumi. And like. Do not ask me who I am and do not ask me to remain the same: leave it to our

57. Dylan, "The Man in Me."
58. Foucault, *Discipline and Punish*, 30.
59. Foucault, *The History of Sexuality*, 93.
60. Ibid.
61. Foucault, "Sex, Power, and the Politics of Identity," 166.
62. Ibid.
63. Ibid., 163.
64. Ibid.
65. Ibid., 166.

29. Jack Nicholson as Jack Torrance in *The Shining* by Stanley Kubrick, 1980 (PictureLux/Alamy Stock Photo).

bureaucrats and our police to see that our papers are in order.[66] Everything is so overcoded, you know. I'm thinking Deleuze. So, I mean. It's weird . . . and I'm like. Bhabha. Blah blah. The problem is not to discover in oneself the truth of one's sex, but, rather, to use one's sexuality to arrive at a multiplicity of relationships.[67] And, I mean . . . it's not either/or. Asymmetrical lines of flight.[68] Intensities, not identities. Ha ha, that would be such a sweet poststructuralist bumper sticker. It's like. The game is worthwhile insofar as we don't know what will be the end.[69] Because inventing new possibilities of pleasure . . . I think it's a kind of creation,

66. Foucault, *The Archaeology of Knowledge*, 17.
67. Foucault, "Friendship as a Way of Life," 135.
68. Deleuze and Guattari, *A Thousand Plateaus*, 9.
69. Foucault, "Truth, Power, Self," 9.

a creative enterprise.[70] A microphysics of experimentality. I'm thinking Nietzsche. Bergson. I mean . . . I'm like. What strikes me is the fact that, in our society, art has become something which is specialized. . . . But couldn't everyone's life become a work of art?[71] . . . We have to create ourselves as a work of art.[72] I'm thinking Foucault. . . . What do you think?"

Manic stew of a circus, a military campaign, a nightmare, an orgy, and a high.[73] Foucault on the rocks. Eroticized, intellectualized evocations of posts propaganda. Adoptions, appropriations of queer theory for an alternative, open, progressive styling on the stage of nineties-guy screen sap. Wartime libertinism fashioned as radical politics in opposition to militarism and metaculture. Enticements of action in a twentysomething scene of blended intellectual, social, and sexual energies. Rebellion against the prohibitions and regimentations of a strict religious upbringing and sexual culture. And id-ish, stirred and shaken, me stuff—stagnations in puberty and new pornography. Call this cocktail "the prisoner of the soul."[74]

("You can plan a pretty picnic, but you can't predict the weather.")[75]

I did not want to or could not at that point in my life summon the courage or decency to confidently, plainly abide. I did not have the self-esteem or good thinking or moral qualms to live the dynamics of marriage authentically and forthrightly. It was fantastical lines of flight, pretending to not, in fact, have or enjoy groundings or entitlements, playing scenario to obscure a hegemonic usualness and normalcy and the privileges, anxious to fit into and even radically stand out within an early-aughts academic milieu of theory—Cambridge—where I was a category and afraid that a location of culture would diminish my social life, intellectual cred, and access and involvement in a smart life.[76]

70. Foucault, "Sex, Power, and the Politics of Identity," 165.
71. Foucault, "On the Genealogy of Ethics," 261.
72. Ibid., 262.
73. Norman Mailer, quoted in Goodell, *Independent Feature Film Production*, 389.
74. Foucault, *Discipline and Punish*, 30.
75. Outkast, "Ms. Jackson."
76. Bhabha, *The Location of Culture*.

30. Jeff Bridges as the Dude in *The Big Lebowski* by Joel Coen and Ethan Coen, 1998 (Pictorial Press/Alamy Stock Photo).

The body does not happen as an accident to the soul.[77] I thought love-making was passé before I ever knew what it was. I got drunk on disavowing meaningfulness, refusing a bona fide little life, confusing Foucault and laissez-faire, and masking the "mundane pursuit of self-aggrandizement" in performances of a "self-styled political vanguardism."[78] I gained a reputation as a heavy drinker in a self-concocted carousel scene. I was a creep, coming on to women in ways that surely hurt them and made them feel uncomfortable. It is something that I forever regret.

FADE IN:

EXT. BOSTON – ALLSTON-BRIGHTON – PETER AND KEDRON'S APARTMENT BUILDING – NIGHT

Before entering graduate school, KEDRON works at an advertising agency downtown. Each day, PETER is across the river in Cambridge for classes. He has a habit of staying out very, very late. He takes the last bus on the 86 line home to their teeny apartment. Sometimes he stays out all night.

PETER lumbers up the stoop, slowly. Jangles keys in blue jeans, a bit loopy.

INT. PETER AND KEDRON'S APARTMENT – LIVING ROOM

KEDRON on the couch. Waiting, watching the clock, it is four o'clock, it has got to stop. Tell him, take no more. She practices her speech as he opens the door. She rolls over, pretends to sleep as he looks her over.[79]

A few hundred square feet made even more incommodious by the circumstances. CAMERA is HANDHELD and MOVES with PETER at the threshold, revealing the compact living space as he advances. A homecoming arrival premised upon the assumption of second chances.

---

77. Levinas, *Totality and Infinity*, 168.
78. Murray, *The Revolution Deferred*, 54.
79. Pearl Jam, "Better Man."

KEDRON

> The waiting drove me mad. You're finally here and
> I'm a mess.[80]

She is speaking to someone dense and once again declares his behavior nonsense. There would be fireworks were this genre of meeting not a tedious chore. They have had this discussion before. The talk of why and wherefore.[81]

KEDRON (CONT'D)

> In case you don't recall, I was yours and you were
> mine. Forget it all. Is there a line that I could write
> that's sad enough to make you cry? And all the
> lines you wrote to me were lies.[82]

Her upsetness, her ire, more and more phrased. She is worn out, frustrated, deep-blue amazed . . . deep blue something.[83]

KEDRON (CONT'D)

> It's too late.[84] I'm burnt out on some empty
> reasons.[85]
>> (staccato)
> You wreck me.[86] You don't know how it feels.[87] See
> these bones.[88] Un-break my heart.[89] Where did you
> sleep last night?[90] Will you love me tomorrow?[91]

80. Pearl Jam, "Corduroy."
81. Shakespeare, *King Henry V*, 337.
82. Gin Blossoms, "Found Out about You."
83. Deep Blue Something, *Home*.
84. King, "It's Too Late."
85. Goo Goo Dolls, "Ain't That Unusual."
86. Petty, "You Wreck Me."
87. Petty, "You Don't Know How It Feels."
88. Nada Surf, "See These Bones."
89. Braxton, "Un-Break My Heart."
90. Nirvana, "Where Did You Sleep Last Night."
91. The Shirelles, "Will You Love Me Tomorrow."

For his part, PETER feels caught between. Compelled by the night, another scene, and the sorry prospect of losing everything. CAMERA ZOOMS IN on him.

> PETER
>
> Don't fade on me.[92] It ain't over 'til it's over.[93] Talk about the passion.[94]

He is an impossible refrain of please, please, please let me get what I want.[95] He continues with fraught, tender moonshots.

> PETER (CONT'D)
>
> I can hear the heart beating as one.[96] Nearly lost you.[97]

He suffers hereditary discomfort with the emotionally laden. KEDRON on sofa in b.g. half-reaches out in concern but swiftly pulls back — straightened. Tired of the pain, tired of taking care of him. Tired of asking are you alright.[98] Withdrawing in disgust is not the same as apathy.[99]

> KEDRON
>
> It's tearing me apart. It's ruining everything. And I swore, I swore I would be true and, honey, so did you. . . . Was it just a game to you? . . . Oh, I thought the world of you. I thought nothing could go wrong. But I was wrong, I was wrong.[100]

92. Petty, "Don't Fade on Me."
93. Kravitz, "It Ain't Over 'Til It's Over."
94. R.E.M., "Talk about the Passion."
95. The Smiths, "Please Please Please Let Me Get What I Want."
96. Yo La Tengo, *I Can Hear the Heart Beating as One.*
97. Screaming Trees, "Nearly Lost You."
98. Williams, "Are You Alright?"
99. Linklater, *Slacker.*
100. The Cranberries, "Linger."

PETER

Tell you I'm sorry. You don't know how lovely you
are. Tell you I set you apart. Oh, let's go back to
the start. Oh, take me back to the start. But tell
me you love me.[101]

KEDRON

Well, you couldn't be that man I adored. You don't
seem to know, or seem to care, what your heart is
for. But I don't know him anymore. . . . I'm all out
of faith. This is how I feel. . . . You're a little late.
I'm already torn.[102]

FADE OUT.

Gateway Drug

We couldn't afford the flush résumés of unpaid internships and vocational
volunteer activities. RAs. Work-studies. Summer jobs. My isolated extracurricular was a scholarshipped alternative-spring-break trip, a location-
based medical anthropology course on health-care delivery on the Navajo
Reservation in New Mexico where an alcohol treatment program was incor-
porating cultural meanings and practices. One day, students and faculty sat
around the perimeter of a hogan with program administrators and clients.
One of them lit a cigar rolled in a corn husk. Students who regularly smoked
cigarettes at campus parties and downtown honkytonks were skittish here.
This is where it started for me. I now teach a course on tobacco history and
anthropology. The real tragedy of tobacco, I tell the students, is not that
cigarettes have killed so many people. It's that industrialism transformed
the most sacred substance into the most profane thing. Back in the hogan,
the facility administrators explained that tobacco is of particular importance for Native peoples. The clients were not allowed to casually smoke
cigarettes; tobacco was reserved solely for ritual and medicinal purposes. As

101. Coldplay, "The Scientist."
102. Imbruglia, "Torn."

it came around to me, I lightly puffed the cigar. It was spring break in the Great American Desert and a gateway drug into anthropology.

Goodbye to All That[103]

Deloitte & Touche was offering signing bonuses and promises to comp business school. On the way to the campus Career Center, I got stuck. Needed a suit: didn't have one; didn't want one; didn't have a car to go to the store for one; didn't want to wear one every day; didn't want every day; didn't want to take finance and stats; didn't care if it pays. Alas, there was a class on pop music, and I knew a lot about the Beatles, and a few of us were already in the habit of taking off early in the afternoon across campus to a bar on Twenty-First Avenue, sitting on a terrace, drinking beer, sipping smoky scotches, and smoking Marlboro Lights.

A famous Italian American ballplayer, improbably great, once advised, "When you come to a fork in the road, take it!"[104]

That was the epigraph for my high school yearbook entry.

Option one: work out of Buckhead, wearing advanced capitalist prep, weeklong living in airports and hotels, canvassing the country as part of profitably useless consulting teams.

Option two: reading, writing, no arithmetic.

There were worries about liberal academia and anthro-what, for what, what's that? But what did they expect? It was kinda in the deck. An upbringing of encyclopedias and almanacs laid out before snacks. My diploma didn't say "psych" or "sosh." I chose the pagan discipline. The discipline of cultural relativism. Sensibilities and permissibilities for perversions, witchcraft, and sorcery.[105] The go-native discipline. The Samoans-do-it-better-(and-so-do-the-bonobos) discipline.[106] The Hopi-is-more-accurate-and-ample-than-English discipline.[107] The discipline of God-is-dead.[108]

103. Didion, *Slouching towards Bethlehem*, 225–38; Graves, *Good-Bye to All That*.
104. Berra, *When You Come to a Fork in the Road, Take It!*
105. Herdt, *Guardians of the Flutes*.
106. Mead, *Coming of Age in Samoa*; de Waal, "Bonobo Sex and Society."
107. Whorf, *Language, Thought, and Reality*.
108. Nietzsche, *The Gay Science*, 343.

31. Dustin Hoffman and Katharine Ross as reluctant grown-ups in *The Graduate* by Mike Nichols, 1967 (Allstar Picture Library/Alamy Stock Photo).

The graduate went straight to graduate school. One year later, marriage. And so, despite the repudiation rambles, the academic and spiritual craving for otherness, there was a prescribed personal arrangement. And that—the abrupt annulment of potential for independent growth—is also part of the cocktail, senioritis stuck, never starting adult life, never experiencing a semistructured individuality stretch, always hooked to support systems of family, university, and conjugality, the privileges of consistent buoyancy without much uncertainty or contingency with regard to employment, housing, insurance, health care, isolation, and domesticity, not needing to tolerate things on my own. A lecher, habit-lingering, lurching late nights, palling around with mates and dates, making acquaintances with anything strange, soaking in sauce, the sweet promise shattering like a cell phone thrown against a wall, the relationship of campus walks and starry nights. A godless nineties guy drifting, madman captured by chemicals, sliding into stone rolling. And taking it on tour—New Haven and the

Midwest—where any positive valences of the recreations and inebriations disappeared, the hook now nothing more than circularity, object-relations kinship ("Ceci n'est pas une pipe"),[109] like a rat tat-tapping the dispenser for the assurance and maintenance of repetition, a metaphysics of presence, the unconditional and unmitigated "there, there." The lonely stuckness of a couch from which I am now only somewhat freed.

Little Life

Manny's school assemblies begin with the national anthem. I think of Radiohead's heady jazz jam with that name.[110] Across the cafeteria, Manny stands hand over heart. With everything going on in the world, I wanna tell Kid A that life truly is sugar magnolias.[111]

This entire life behind things. Sturdy brick house in the middle of America. Photographs on the mantel. Graduation. Wedding. First-born. Second-born. The whole of us.

Kedron is the only person who knows me, inside self. ("This is the girl.")[112] The one who accompanied me that night on campus for a phenomenal movie about littleness. So much has changed since college—that promise. Sometimes more than we want to acknowledge. Not the life of our dreams, something like solace.[113] ("Life might prove difficult—was evidently going to; but meanwhile they had each other, and that was everything.")[114]

109. René Magritte, *The Treachery of Images*, 1929, oil on canvas, 23.75 × 31.94 in., Los Angeles County Museum of Art.
110. Radiohead, "The National Anthem."
111. Radiohead, *Kid A;* Grateful Dead, "Sugar Magnolia."
112. Lynch, *Mulholland Drive.*
113. Browning, "Nature's Remorses," 100.
114. James, *The Wings of the Dove*, 67.

11 My Own Private Idaho

FADE IN:

INT. ST. LOUIS – UNIVERSITY – STUDENT CENTER – DAY

PETER and KEDRON are lunching at the sprucy Student Center. She is having her usual: the alternating daily from the lunch special station. For him, it is also the usual: salad, side of fries, Diet Coke.

SUPERIMPOSE: "Small Potatoes."

PETER checks the online course calendar for the upcoming semester. "Introduction" has been scheduled for 9:00 a.m., rather than its usual midday slot.

His first impulse. Shrug and a fry. Give early morning teaching a try. But his backbone course has now been modified in a way that he knows will negatively impact its effectiveness. The online course checker-outer app triggers a snap. And for PETER, noshing on romaine tossed, stewing about a course he had well wrought and passionately taught, the decision feels greater than small potatoes.

INT. ANTHROPOLOGY BUILDING – MAIN CORRIDOR – DAY

A normal afternoon in the old dorm. PETER and KEDRON enter the Gothic archway. As she heads to her office, he ascends a winding stairwell to his. CAMERA TRACKS after him.

This is the psychological and emotional milieu where impulsivity gets coaxed. The torpid procession up the old oaks. It is remarkable how readily the melancholy of ketchup dips and a lethargic soda fountain trip morphs and combines with a manic skip.[1]

INT. PETER'S OFFICE

PETER looks at the computer stressfully. Angers at the interface. CAMERA ZOOMS IN on this personal workspace.

EXTREME CLOSE-UP SHOT – BLANK COMPUTER SCREEN

Flashing cursor.

PETER types: "Hi you. I just looked at the course listings for the fall semester . . . "

This is the angry email to the department CHAIR.

DISSOLVE TO:

INT. ST. LOUIS – PETER AND KEDRON'S HOUSE – LIVING ROOM – DAY (MONTHS LATER)

---

1. Freud, "Mourning and Melancholia."

PETER is vegging out. Sprawled out on the worn-in, coffee-colored leather couch. Laptop on lap. He is scripting his biopic.

> NARRATOR (V.O.)
>
> In one version of a plot, this diary-study pieces together a kilobyte blow-up. A scenario of emotion and action analyzed in the wider frames of moral biographies and affective histories.[2] How the hasty email reflects a genealogy of a Moi.

DISSOLVE TO:

DREAM SEQUENCE – EXT./INT. CONNECTICUT – HARBOR VIEW – NANNY AND POPPY'S HOUSE (HOME VIDEO)

PETER's DAD has shaggy hair and Allman Brothers vinyls. DAD's parents, whom all the grandkids call NANNY and POPPY, sit in rope-seat rockers in the parlor of a Cape Cod–style house in an exclusive area on Long Island Sound. Tennis courts and docks and, it seems, an amateur marching band for every block. Comforting mix of bohemian and midcentury modernist materialities of kidney-shaped glass-top coffee tables; ashtrays, tumblers, coasters, credenzas; pleated round throw pillows; and velvet, tufted throne lounge chairs. TELEPHONE RINGING. Rum raisin in the freezer. Hermit cookies in the cupboard. Salads and sandwiches. Meatloaf on Mondays. Fish on Fridays. Honey ham at the holidays. Commuter rail from Norwalk to Grand Central and back for dinner and, after dinner, revelries of SLOSHED NOISE, a gay charade of CHICO MARX on stride, BUNNY BERIGAN burning brass, BENNY GOODMAN and ARTIE SHAW roaring on the reeds, and GENE KRUPA driving the beat. A village of bridge clubs and weekend dinners at the club. Fantastic Fourth of July parades. Easter egg hunts. Sack races. Christmas dinners with POPPY dressed as Santa, making good use of his own belly and purple-red, bulbous nose.

---

2. Dave, "Witness," 435.

MUSIC CUE: "When the Saints Go Marching In" by Louis Armstrong and His Orchestra.[3]

> NARRATOR (V.O.)
>
> Poppy died of a heart attack on a tarmac in the
> City in the nineties. A traditional jazz band
> celebrated, moaned, and marched farewell down
> the central aisle of a historic church near his
> Connecticut home, belting "When the Saints Go
> Marching In," an apocalyptic standard performed
> as a nod to Poppy's merriment and a tribute to his
> love of jazz, his preference for horn swirls and
> gaiety, and maybe an appeal, too, for this man to
> be included in the number.

END MUSIC CUE

END DREAM SEQUENCE.

DISSOLVE TO:

INT. LIVING ROOM (BACK TO SCENE)

PETER's typing bears the quality of a pursuit: to understand how the things which seem most evident are always formed in the confluence of encounters and chances.[4]

> PETER (V.O.)
>
> I don't remember or know much about the man,
> like most of my predecessors, only tidbits, jobs,
> drinking, and died. I wish I knew that whole side,
> where I have a bare mythology about fanciful,
> ubiquitous alcohol, and a lively musicology.

3. Louis Armstrong and His Orchestra, "When the Saints Go Marching In."
4. Foucault, "Structuralism and Post-Structuralism," 450.

CAMERA PANS ACROSS and ZOOMS IN on a layout arrangement of old photographs of PETER's relatives — as in a Ken Burns documentary.

> PETER (V.O.) (CONT'D)
>
> Because I'm missing a big part of me: buried
> details of difficult and contradictory realities. That
> email — the one I sent the chair, the one we're
> exploring here — when I hit "send," I don't know,
> maybe it was driven by unknowns and bitter ends.
> Spotty evidence of what feels close, something
> diagnosed. . . . Because I can't merely concede my
> mistakes. I must decipher the morass for the
> reasoning.[5] . . . I just knew the moral of the story
> was plumbing. From the Latin, plumbum, or lead,
> that's me, my initials, Pb, up on that table.
> Meaning to measure the depth and find the
> bottom.

MONTAGE: AT HOME

Home movies and photographs of NANNY and POPPY's house. The parlor — with furnishings and decorative arts — represents a family's cultivated facade, an image of white middle-class habitation.[6] In particular, the coffee table is an integral part of the functional modernism of a social space focused on the television.[7]

NANNY avidly watches pro tennis.

> NARRATOR (V.O.)
>
> Whereas Poppy had a strict preference for rye
> whiskey, Nanny drank capaciously — the Tom
> Collins and Cape Codders — and smoked
> Chesterfields, which were niche-marketed to

---

5. Foucault, *Wrong-Doing, Truth-Telling.*
6. Grier, *Culture and Comfort*, 3.
7. Attfield, "Design as a Practice of Modernity," 281.

women in midcentury as a romantic, stylish, and
glamorous brand. She succumbed to lung cancer
some years after Poppy died.

CAMERA MOVES across interior photographs. Pastel walls and cabinets.
Ceramic vases.

> PETER (V.O.)
>
> So many funerals, all of my elders dying of
> structural causes, while I was reading Foucault —
> in hindsight, too faithfully, or mistakenly — and
> studying hypocrisies, doing a dissertation of
> tobacco farm vignettes, while drinking White
> Russians and smoking cigarettes. The clock of
> academia and inescapable regret. Time with loved
> ones lost to the field and the field and social fields.

END MONTAGE.

DISSOLVE TO:

**DREAM SEQUENCE – EXT./INT. CONNECTICUT – SPRING HILL
– GRANDMA AND GRANDPA'S HOUSE (HOME VIDEO)**

As the tour of the sinews of PETER's cultural and psychological heritage
continues, the documentary enters the wing of the legendary backyard
revues.

PETER's DAD marries across town and, socioeconomically speaking,
down. Dark-haired, fun-loving, MOM never does anything like drink or
do drugs, because she is afraid she will hurt her parents' feelings.

Her family's house is small, one-story, a few rooms only. Vinyl couch and
recliner. Weathered, olive-button, tufted hassock. Grain-finish hardboard
console television unit. Sewing machine, the HUM of a habitat's
filament.

Every year, GRANDPA dresses like Santa at the VFW, factory-line sturdy, and bashful, in an oversized costume, droopy, and a wispy white beard barely covering a baby face completely recognizable to the kids, chubby-cheeked like Capone, and like his first-born grandson.

MOM's side, mergers of second-generation ethnics from Old World fascist countries, gather out back for cookouts. GRANDPA and GRANDMA. UNCLE JOE and AUNT BETTY. UNCLE JIM and AUNT LOU. The Italian men, it seems, have a thing for Hungarian women, a New World nexus. They bowl the bocce ball. Talk Yankees and Mets around the waft of smoldering charcoal from barrel grills loaded with burgers and dogs and varieties of Italian, German, and Polish sausages. Metal folding tables uphold an assortment of homemade antipastos, fruit salads (with melon balls), and baked pastas, kept warm under hand towels — a Napoleonic spread. Aluminum webbed lawn chairs. High-fidelity WHIRLS of Frankie Valli and Elvis Presley. Polynesian skirts and hula-hooping contests. Chocolate biscotti and apricot–cream cheese pastry cookies battling it out and making love.

A squat half back door putting off paint bark and splinters, the passage to the basement, GRANDPA's dim, dust-covered workshop. And then, beyond that, aft, a trove of shelves of classic board games reclaimed by grandkids and cousins and neighborhood kids. Yellowed rulebooks, brittle. Game boards eroded around the edges. The smell of stale cardboard. The must of amusement. BUCKET OF FUN. CANDY LAND. TROUBLE. THE GAME OF LIFE. And then, up an unfinished plank staircase, rickety with one railing, itself a kind of CHUTES AND LADDERS game, to the living room's scratchy-rough polyester carpet, rug rats kneeling or sitting cross-legged, tumbling dice and getting carded.[8]

> NARRATOR (V.O.)
>
> In her heyday, Peter's mother won the regional
> Stratego championship, Stratego being a
> Napoleonic-themed military strategy board game

8. The Rolling Stones, "Tumbling Dice."

marketed in the sixties. Peter wonders what
happened to that aspect of American sporting life
— the Stratego championship — or whether it
ever existed beyond the immigrant, war-veteran
world of her northeastern adolescence. Maybe it
lives on as a personal heritage between mother
and son, an inherited impulsivity theater of
making setups, orchestrating fields of objects for
strongholds.

END DREAM SEQUENCE.

DISSOLVE TO:

INT. LIVING ROOM (BACK TO SCENE)

PETER continues typing at laptop. Ponders roots and limbs. CAMERA
TRACKS FORWARD onto him.

> PETER (V.O.)
>
> This boil isn't random. The email was the product
> of civilization, like a sense of humor that is shared
> by people from a common background.[9]

He leans up. Sets laptop on table temporarily. Sips Diet Coke. Then
returns to typing contentedly.

> PETER (V.O.) (CONT'D)
>
> Here are the reports from 23andMe. Haplogroup
> with Neanderthal ancestry. Risks for caffeine
> consumption and misery. Baked manigot with
> cheese. Family disease. Desperate need. Dimple
> on cheek. It's all simple. Hair is both light and
> dark. The report is gray on that matter. Grandpa's

---

9. Critchley, *On Humour*, 73.

stockiness. Grandma's shegg. Brillo-thick hair. But
fair skin, greenish eyes, and a last name that's
sorta round and sorta square. Taking all the (scare
quotes) data into account, it's an expert matter for
the doctors of anthropology. The email has
something like its own archaeology.

He looks at these prehistorical findings. Jango of ethnicized and deethnicized whitenesses, northern and southern climes. Smoosh of parlor comforts and gentility soundtracked by Waller; an afterhours, drunken circus
of woodwinds and jazz goes to college;[10] the hungry of the Huns, an unin-
telligible, warlike people revered as conquerors; and the heated, intem-
perate Mediterranean.[11] The Italians, it has been said, made their world
and insisted, "Who's better than me?"[12]

DISSOLVE TO:

**DREAM SEQUENCE – INT. CONNECTICUT – BENSON HOUSE –
DINING ROOM – NIGHT**

The OVERHEAD LIGHT fills the room. PETER's MOM is dressed for a
day of cooking. She is overjoyed about her son, who is headed to college in
a few weeks.

MOM

Okay, let's go, guys. Dinner's ready! Gavadeels
everybody! Tossed salad. Italian dressing. Take as
much as you want.

PETER

What's the matter, Ma? I thought you said calamad.

10. The Dave Brubeck Quartet, *Jazz Goes to College.*
11. Horden and Purcell, "The Mediterranean and 'the New Thalassology.'"
12. DeLillo, *Underworld,* 207.

MOM

Take it easy, wouldya? And sit next to your Aunt
Rose. Salad's on the table, Pete. Here comes the
chicken marsala. Your garlic bread. Go ahead.

Dining room wrapped in meadow-flower wallpaper. PETER's MOM
moves about the oblong table with a ceramic serving dish discolored from
long-term use, forking sauced cutlets onto individual plates.

PETER

Honest to God, Mom, you're the best. We've been
fighting a lot . . . and I'm sorry. Me moving out, I
don't want you to worry. You know I miss this
house already.

MOM

You too, my love. Don't you worry, either.
Everything is fine . . . everything is fine . . .

She repeats the line. Her classic refrain, like God's name. Her voice trails
off before she turns again to the task at hand.

MOM (CONT'D)

Make some room. Here comes the brajole. Pour
some gravy on the meat so it stays very tender.[13]

PETER wears a Patagonia fleece and retro Yankees ballcap. He eats at a
healthy clip.

PETER

Delicious.

13. Scorsese, *Italianamerican*.

>   MOM
>
> I'm glad. Enjoy it, Pete. Aunt Anna and Antonietta
> are on their way, you know, with Ralphie. Mind
> your manners. But I don't have to tell you that,
> Peter . . .

Her voice softens as she scoots back to the cookroom. Moments later she reemerges with hands full, urging the family to consume.

>   MOM (CONT'D)
>
> . . . and here comes the antipasto, with the
> gabagool and fresh moozadell. Take whatcha want
> and pass it around.

Meatballs delicately browned. The back and forth a VOLUME OF SOUND. Like the chaos of cocktails and jazz, that drowning-out surround.

>   DAD
>
> Oofah! Stanna mabaych! Enough already. Take it
> easy, wouldya?

>   PETER
>
> Leave it alone, ya gidrul. And pass the proshoot.

At the end of the table, AUNT ROSE mumbles about Babe Ruth's stat line. Lost in her own epochal time.[14]

>   MOM
>
> Who wants more crusty Italian bread?

>   PETER
>
> Oh marone!

14. Whitehead, *Process and Reality*.

MOM

Peter, what's the matter? Is everything all right?

PETER

Ma, you know what I like. Where's the squingeel?
I'm confused.

DAD

Hey kid, give your mother a break. Stop acting like
such a chooch.

PETER

Relax, relax. I'm joshing. I'm taking manners
with me to college, 'cause you guys taught me
right.

MOM

We're gonna miss you, son. Don't you forget the
hard work where you're from. Your grandfather
loved to see you play ball. He would be so proud of
you going to college, doing what you're doing.

A beat.

MOM (CONT'D)

The neighborhood where I grew up, a man
would come around on Sunday morning selling
dry beans, yelling up and down the block. He
used to be so loud. You would bring out your
dish, everybody would come down with their
dish.[15]

PETER's MOM darts into the kitchen to grab another round of platters of
food, as she continues . . .

15. Riccio, *The Italian American Experience in New Haven*, 363.

MOM (O.S.)

(forte, toward the dining room)
. . . and the newspaper man used to yell from the
corner, "Extra, extra." But there never was
anything extra in the paper.[16]

PETER

(turns to kitchen)
Whaddya want me to say? My heart aches. I'm
going away. But nothing is gonna come between
this family. You know I'm gonna miss your gravy.
Ravioli and eggplant parm — can you ship 'em to
me, Mom? Overnight, to keep 'em warm.

DAD

Both of you, cut it out and eat, capeesh? You know
what they say: "Too much eggplant for one person
is too much eggplant for everybody." That's what
the old-timers used to say.

PETER

(while chewing)
What does it mean?

DAD

Just that everybody used to grow zucchini and
eggplant in their garden. And you would go to your
neighbor to ask if they could use some eggplants,
and the goombah would say, "Nah, we've got a
bunch of eggplants, you've got a bunch of eggplants,
whaddya want from me, it's a good year."

16. Scorsese, *Italianamerican.*

PETER mechanically nods. Not sure about the word of God. Stands up from the table and plods. He eyes the recliner in the TV room to relax the bipod.

> PETER
>
> (looking over his shoulder)
> If it's all the same, I'm gonna check out the Yankee
> game.

Agitated by his son's defiance, DAD appeals to the platters of meat and pasta that remain to be eaten. PETER pauses at the table's edge. MOM hurries into the room, hand towel draped over her shoulder, crusty from caked flour and spotted red from marinara.

> MOM
>
> Holy mackerel, Andy![17] What's the matter, Pete?
> Have some more macaroni. Gotta put meat on
> your bones, ya gavone. Here comes the salseech.
> And the country ribs with the tomato sauce you
> like. This towel has been in my hands all day
> because I've been cooking for you.[18]

PETER and MOM stand off several feet from each other, like two gunslingers in front of a saloon.

SFX: Spaghetti western whistling trill, castanets, distorted guitar twang.

In the months leading up to his departure, this mundane clashing is the norm. She is perhaps anxious about the dorm. He is no doubt psyched for it. Both having a structured interdependence torn. Everyday quarrels, even screaming bouts — a distinctly temperamental, ethnicized way to mourn.

---

17. The Treniers, "Holy Mackerel, Andy!"
18. Scorsese, *Italianamerican.*

SERIES OF SHOTS inside the dining room as PETER backs away, inching closer to its bourn.

> PETER
>
> Panzagin! You know I love you, but I said I'm full.

> MOM
>
> Oh, marone! Get over here. Say goodnight to your Aunt Rose.

> PETER
>
> Hey, Aunt Rose, how's Phil Rizzuto this year? She can't even hear, the skutch.

> MOM
>
> Nem yo. Don't talk like that.

> DAD
>
> Show some respect, ya jamoke. It will be easier if you do what you're told.

> MOM
>
> Peter, look what you're doing. You're giving your father agita.

> PETER
>
> Whaddya want from me? Take a Tums. Have a seltzer, ya stunad.

> DAD
>
> Serenity now![19] Make it stop, hon. Hon, make it stop. Make it stop, you two.

---

19. *Seinfeld,* "The Serenity Now."

>MOM
>
>You've got your father upset. Is this what he
>deserves?

PETER's DAD is perturbed. He elevates his fork from the plate. Tilts it at the soon-to-be high school graduate.

>DAD
>
>Show some respect for authority, ya scustumad.
>When I was your age, we got our legs broke
>mouthing off like that.[20]

>PETER
>
>Come on. This boil isn't random. She's literally a
>Hun. And the reigning Stratego champ. And I'm
>G. I. Joe in the desert encamped.

>MOM
>
>Fuhgeddaboudit, both of you. Pete, go watch TV. I
>want you to leave it to me, Pete. Go to the living
>room, watch a movie, watch the game, honey.

INT. TV ROOM

Recliner and sofas angled on the far corner. Tube television situated on the entertainment center. Shelves embarrassingly full of VHS tapes. PETER grabs the clicker.

INT. DINING ROOM/KITCHEN

PETER's MOM heads to the kitchen, proud of her cooking, and proud of her son, if also enduring the growing pains of separation. She wraps leftovers in foil for a shelf in the refrigerator. Additional days of alimentation.

---

20. Scorsese, *Goodfellas*.

MOM

Oh, where are you going, my darling one?[21] Don't
you forget, you will always be my son. There is
panettone on the kitchen counter for later. My
rock, named after my father, my shining star, I
love you, dear Peter.

END DREAM SEQUENCE.

DISSOLVE TO:

INT. LIVING ROOM (BACK TO SCENE)

FAST MOTION SHOT of PETER bouncing around the room.[22] An up-
and-down circuitry. Alternating between keyboarding horizontally outstretched and pacing perpendicular obsessed. Pontificating to himself and
gesticulating. Like a director on the set . . . or a feverish academic.

PETER (V.O.)

Please understand that it wasn't a simple tantrum;
straight man is congenitally primed for such a
send. Infilled coagulations, admixtures of
dissidence, recalcitrance, and irritability. The
affective imprints and residues of wondrous and
multifarious pasts.[23] The forms and discord and
structures of the lifeworld.[24] Man, this boy's
beautiful.

Old rope-and-pulley windows. White paint chipped. PETER contemplates the neighborhood collegiate. Dogwoods in front yard. Prius car.
Setting for the anthropological memoir.

21. Dylan, "A Hard Rain's A-Gonna Fall."
22. Phish, "Bouncing around the Room."
23. Chakrabarty, "Reviews: History and Historicality," 125.
24. Schütz and Luckmann, *Structures of the Life-World.*

PETER (V.O.) (CONT'D)

This pearl, this gem, cute as a button. A pressure-
formed, gelled me, like anybody, a real cooker,
goulash, expressive modes that I don't want to
repress as shame or grief because that is hiding
my face. But the spirits and passions can get me
into trouble in a cortex and comportment
superconscious professional space.

PETER circles back to the couch listlessly. Feels distant in his soul from
what academia extols. But fondly senses the special pull that initially drew
him to anthro. And that propels him to continue at the cathode.

NARRATOR (V.O.)

He heard the news. Churchgoing and the daily
disciplinary refrain to "strive for normalcy," heads
down in this family (we're part of the flock) as
much as Aunt Rose gets her pork chops. The
demand to abide. The great divide. Feeling
terrified. That stuff got inside. But the belief
system mightily impressed, over time, it became
difficult to fathom. Such a chasm. Real-life
secularism: pop culture, parties . . . anthropology
studies.

MONTAGE: PETER AND KEDRON IN GUATEMALA

– Adventuresome treks up Maya pyramids overlooking the jungles of the
Petén.

NARRATOR (V.O.)

Year after year following college, the sweethearts
traveled to Guatemala to learn Spanish . . .

– Anthropological fieldwork (e.g., interviews, digital recorders, shared
meals).

> NARRATOR (V.O.) (CONT'D)
>
> . . . and reside in communities long seen as
> convertible and targeted by American
> imperialism.

– Hunting for textiles in street markets.

> NARRATOR (V.O.) (CONT'D)
>
> They backpacked, studied, and spent lots of time
> dwelling, losing religion in search of different
> truths, friends, and selves.[25]

– Making lasagna with a Maya family, close friends, in their concrete block
house.

END MONTAGE.

DISSOLVE TO:

**FLASHBACK – INT. CONNECTICUT – PETER'S FRIEND'S
HOUSE – BASEMENT – DAY? NIGHT?**

Finished room with carpeting and warm wood paneling. White sectional
sofa.

> PETER (V.O.)
>
> I grew up thinking sex before marriage is a
> grievous sin. And in this context of stringent
> religiosity, imagine . . . the emotional and spiritual
> gravity, and relief, of the soda jerk. The liberating
> occasion of confidential, clandestine joy, making it
> with a boy. Not just some quirk, the secluded
> basement dates were about being ordinary,
> because everything was made to seem exceptional

25. R.E.M., "Losing My Religion."

and stark. And maybe I'm still caught up or
whatever, I never arrived, I never embarked. No
handle on the internal amusement park. No
snorkeling around with sharks. I've never been the
self of personal-growth benchmarks.

END FLASHBACK.

DISSOLVE TO:

INT. LIVING ROOM (BACK TO SCENE)

PETER cracks fingers and nibbles on nails. Thinks about humongous
whales. And a diary-study of layers and scales.

MUSIC CUE: "Ashokan Farewell" by Jay Ungar, main theme of Ken
Burns's "THE CIVIL WAR."[26]

> PETER (V.O.)
> Road trips and ballgames with Dad. The paternal
> companionship of tobacco country. The
> adolescent friendship and freedom of cellar
> secrecy. Fixations on combat and sport and a
> knack for playing fort. The bosom warmth of
> setups and childhood sick days. Setups and, later,
> term papers and essays. The mania of
> diagramming and organizing things. These
> registers of stuckness in a space-time of linger and
> cling.

CAMERA PUSHES IN on PETER across a living room cluttered with
piles of books, yellow legal pads, and crumpled papers. Hammering away.
The gratification of an academic making headway.

---

26. Ungar, "Ashokan Farewell"; Burns, *The Civil War.*

PETER (V.O.) (CONT'D)

I grew up believing that God himself was sent,
and there's like a ledger and these personal scores,
and in sum there is either straight or bent. And
warp is me, that email was an irritated sent. I was
talking about taxation without representation, as
in, feeling exploited at work, and like even
minimal acknowledgment is a well-deserved perk.

PETER works at laptop as though he is jumping around a ditch. Alternating between multiple open Word documents. The chapters of the flick. The story of the overdetermined email glitch, a woven narrative, a litany of reticulated factors, the threads of a stitch.

NARRATOR (V.O.)

First-born devotion. The maternalism of non-
centric immigration. The smother and goof of the
Italian American "mammone," the mama's boy, a
curious mix of spoiled, defensive, combative,
overreliant, and overcompensating features.[27]

PETER regularly reaches for caramel-colored, carbonated refreshment. Typing through the headache, low blood sugar, dehydration, and mental fog that all scholars experience, searching for a rhizomatic sense of things amid the epistemological pull toward arborescence.[28]

PETER (V.O.)

It's because of factors, there are factors.
Headspace where it's either family style or go fuck
yourself. And in the living room, that front row
floorspace where the kid knelt. Because the good
wars make for good TV. Everything a fight or
battle of the century. The spectacle as pulse of

27. Tamburri, "Italian Americans and Television," 461.
28. Deleuze and Guattari, *A Thousand Plateaus*, 3–25.

society.[29] As in compulsion. Do you get it? The
structured alcoholic habit-world of tube and food
and use, sedating releases, jouissance leases,
pleasant decorative pieces. Rhetorics of fine, snug,
and yes, inhibited capacities for expressive
relationships.

> NARRATOR (V.O.)
>
> How many fingers are on the nuclear button?[30]
> These are chicken feet — the bullet points, the
> supporting evidence for explaining the email. Like
> a PowerPoint.

END MUSIC CUE

PETER rolls his neck backward and around for a stretch . . . before returning to the kvetch.

> PETER (V.O.)
>
> Yes, I work for the company. I'm a salesman of the
> highest degree. And yet I was not extended a chat
> in a spirit of collegiality, you know what I mean?
> The boss picked the wrong soldier to routine.

A beat.

> PETER (V.O.) (CONT'D)
>
> This professor has read Foucault on fearless
> speech and Nancy on anger.[31] Back in grad
> school, I foolishly and woundingly styled myself a
> philanderer. I also have a severe mental disorder. I
> come from people who were employees and
> functionaries. That was a context for me to be the

29. Debord, *The Society of the Spectacle.*
30. Ellsberg, *The Doomsday Machine,* 297.
31. Foucault, *Fearless Speech;* Nancy, *"La Comparution*/The Compearance."

first to make university. Smart, and achieved, with
persistent anxieties. And, um, let's see . . .

Books and beverage ready-to-hand. He is trying to make sense of himself
as an instantiation of human.

> PETER (V.O.) (CONT'D)
> Shoulder chip. All the bullshit. Sure, you can plan
> a pretty picnic. But you don't anticipate the
> problematics.[32] Substances. Attachments.
> Inpatient psychiatric. The susceptibility of
> pregnancy precarity . . . fucking traumatic. The
> traumas of what my colleague, what she did to me.
> These things suffused in the nuclear decree. It's
> like . . . the self is the prisoner of me. I'm talking
> about chicken feet. Or Sunday gravy . . . the slow
> reduction sauce of meats, a Napoleonic feast. This
> is my ethnology, a compendium of facets, aspects
> of a problematique.

PETER is plotting personhood as thingamajig. He takes another swig.

> PETER (V.O.) (CONT'D)
> Yeah, he picked the wrong classroom to reorder. I
> don't care to belong to any club that will have me
> as a member. . . . Marx said that.[33]

DISSOLVE TO:

FLASHBACK – INT. ST. LOUIS – UNIVERSITY – STUDENT CENTER – DAY

Back in the dining hall. The cathedral ceiling echoes LAUGHTER and
VOICES.

32. Berlant, "Intimacy," 1.
33. Groucho Marx, quoted in Sheekman, introduction to *The Groucho Letters*, 8.

SUPERIMPOSE: "Small Potatoes."

An undergraduate holding a food container bides time beside PETER and KEDRON, waiting for them to finish eating and move along.

MED. CLOSE-UP SHOT of PETER grazing on fries. Napkin dispenser in f.g. on table.

> PETER
> (looking straight ahead)
> I know, I know. Small potatoes. But they want
> enrollments, and I put butts in seats. And guess
> what? The students aren't going to show up at the
> crack of dawn. I mean they will enroll, but . . .

> KEDRON (O.S.)
> They won't show up.

> PETER
> And that impacts course prep and assignments
> and grade inflation and yada yada. And nobody
> talked to me about it.

PETER mutters under his breath. Slightly weeping as he speaks.

> PETER (CONT'D)
> The chair never invites me to his office for a cup of
> coffee. But he asks me to sing and dance in the
> morning with glee. But he didn't ask with
> respect.[34] I found out the same way as the
> students: online.

PETER picks at his salad.

---

34. Puzo and Coppola, *The Annotated Godfather*, 27.

PETER (CONT'D)

Someday I'll give him a piece of my mind.

EXT. STUDENT CENTER

PETER and KEDRON swing open the building's cumbersome solid wood doors.

HIGH ANGLE LONG SHOT of the quad.

Clear blue skies. A spacious, manicured field. Hundreds of students. FRISBEE. Hammocks drawn at intervals across trees lining the perimeter of the green. Loud party MUSIC BOOMS from tables where student groups promote their activities. PETER and KEDRON navigate this setup and perambulate, sightsee back to anthropology, holding hands.

END FLASHBACK.

FADE OUT.

12 Boyhood

<u>Horsing Around</u>

I call my son "cheddar." It started as a tickle game. He was about four years old. I was just getting sober. We'd roll around on his bed, and I'd tickle him high on his body, near his chin, and I'd ask, while tickling, "Manny, do you want Gorgonzola?" Belly laughing, writhing, he'd go, "No, no." And I'd persist: "Okay, how about a different cheese?" The idea of the game was that each cheese was linked to a different tickle region of the body.

Knismesis is light spidery tickling. Gargalesis is an intense attack.[1]

"How about Swiss, do you want some Swiss?" I'd keep at it, tickling around his chest. And he'd contort: "No, Daddy, no," beneath carried-away giggles and unmistakable, joyous pleasures. Dopamine pouring down the mesolimbic pathway.[2] Neurogenesis amping in the hippocampus.[3] I'd pause for a second, letting him catch his breath, and then announce, "Okay, American," tickling the torso and moving further downward into

1. Leavens and Bard, "Tickling," R91.
2. Panksepp, "Neuroevolutionary Sources of Laughter and Social Joy."
3. Yamamuro et al., "Neurogenesis . . . of the Rat Hippocampus."

the mozzarella region, the midsection. I asked if he wanted mozz or mozzie sticks or Bosco sticks (the brand served at his preschool).

I'd tickle his back as he wriggled over, and then I'd tickle the anterior again, and I'd go a little lower, saying Muenster, telling him that Muenster is the yellowish one. And he'd squirm and worm: "I know, Daddy, I know." And I'd pause. And he'd breathe—sigh, relief, game over.

"But not as yellow as Colby!" I'd crescendo, diving down onto his help-less body, tickling around the belly button. "No, Daddy, no." His knees would buckle, and legs kick out, one tickle spasm after another. I'd move around the pits and neck, and then down again, maybe tickling behind knees and under feet and saying feta, and then tickling thighs, humoring: "Look what I found down here; I found cheddar."

The fun of tickling merges key components of physical and temporal play. The sense that it might never end. The wanton up-and-down and all-around of dodgy, elusive hands and limbs. And the induced inability to withstand culminating joys and pleasures. It is, in some ways, like sex. There are crucial pauses for delight, relaxation, catching breath, and effect, and there are buildups of intensification.

Playful tickling—and sometimes sex—has no purpose.

"[T]he caress does not know what it seeks," Emmanuel Levinas writes. "This 'not knowing,' this fundamental disorder, is the essential."[4]

Playful tickling is not functional or instrumental unless pleasure, trust, and bonding are crassly considered utilities. Nor is it a generic playfulness or touching. Fingers merely graced across the epidermis are not generative of intense tickle effects.[5] One cannot tickle oneself. Tickling requires the separation and spontaneity of another agency.[6] There needs to be an ele-ment of powerlessness, at once simulated, so as to be withdrawn at any moment, and felt, so as to induce the horror of infinity. To be tickled is to be in someone else's hands, and the mirthful laughter is thus a kind of ecstasy, as in the Greek word "ex-stasis," meaning to be or stand outside of oneself. Playful tickling stimulates a body into throes by using an uneven and mer-ciful power relation to impart intensities and senses of uncontrollability

4. Levinas, *Time and the Other,* 89.
5. Leavens and Bard, "Tickling," R91.
6. Ibid., R92.

that are understood as safe.[7] It is an "absolute of calculation and innocence [...] an obviously acceptable form of sensuous excitement [... that] require[s] the enacted recognition of the other."[8] The "intention," to quote Roland Barthes, is "utterly obvious," for if not, it would be cruelty and violate morality.[9]

Tickling can indeed be torturous. A nineteenth-century article from the *New York Times* entitled "England in Old Times" states, "Gone, too, are the parish stocks, in which offenders against public morality formerly sat imprisoned, with their legs held fast beneath a heavy wooden yoke, while sundry small but fiendish boys improved the occasion by deliberately pulling off their shoes and tickling the soles of their defenseless feet."[10] In medieval Europe, tickling was a distinct technique of torture. With the victim bound on a rack, feet were dipped in saltwater for a goat to lick. This was reckoned a "very hard torture."[11]

The language of cheese is a vocabulary of love, trust, and care. Manny knows that the tickle game is all in good fun, horsing around.

These Are Days

Animals are scripted in zoos and cartoons in terms of human characteristics and personas. But it works the other way, too. When humans make love, they make love with the horse in the field, implicating surges assimilated in adolescence.[12] They make love with the dolphin at the theme park and the calf on the farm, having internalized the gentleness of strokes given as little ones.[13] They make love with the kitten, whose underside they have caressed and tickled.[14] They make love with the "[c]rickets in the meadows [...] coyotes in the night hills [...] birds and bats in the

7. Panksepp, "Neuroevolutionary Sources of Laughter and Social Joy," 240.
8. Phillips, *On Kissing, Tickling, and Being Bored*, 9.
9. Barthes, *Mythologies*, 18–20.
10. Ker, "England in Old Times."
11. Cohen, *The Modulated Scream*, 76.
12. Lingis, *Dangerous Emotions*, 31, 37.
13. Ibid., 31.
14. Ibid., 37.

skies," familiarities known not from scientific study but from walkabouts, scampering-abouts, and campouts.[15]

Most sexuality research frames adult human sexuality as a "qualitatively [. . .] distinct and discontinuous developmental entit[y]" vis-à-vis adolescence.[16] Intercourse is described as the defining "status boundary."[17] But teases, elations, and spasms are also embodied in rounds of hide-and-seek, antsy, in nonutilitarian ludic play, frisky, kids dangling from trees like spider monkeys, in waves of sharks and minnows, in horsing around, kids pulling each other's pants down, sometimes peeing on themselves, in what Alphonso Lingis calls "the challenge and purely imaginary stakes of games."[18]

Cheddar is the most insufferable and treacherous of the cheeses. Furthest down on the body, down where there are pressure points, the inner thigh, super ticklish. Manny withstands cheddar for a few seconds and then we stop. I let him tickle me. His small hands on my big body do not produce ecstatic effects.

I have no idea where the metaphor came from. One day, I randomly said, "You're my cheddar." It became an affectionate idiom.

"Cheddar," he corroborates.

No other family has this vernacular. We talk about school days. I check in: "Everything okay? You're my ched, and nothing you tell me is going to change that."

He hides his stuffed animal (I won't say where) when Kwame comes over to play. And cheddar has become an embarrassing thing for him.

"Hey, cheddar." I waved him over to the shopping cart the other day at Schnucks.

He sheepishly answered, "Dad, I told you: not in public."

As intimate recesses and discretions develop, I'm asked to heed boundaries of disclosure, enclosure, and emergence.

I'm lying next to him on an assortment of Star Wars, Spider-Man, and sports-themed blankets and pillows.

15. Ibid., 34.
16. Fortenberry, "Puberty and Adolescent Sexuality," 281.
17. Ibid.
18. Lingis, *Dangerous Emotions*, 39.

"Lucas joned on Jeffrey, and Jeffrey said I'm gonna throw your *uh-oh,*" he crescendos, "cuss word, on the ground."

"Which 'uh-oh cuss word?'"

This us-space, unnerving for him, is sadly, shamelessly, amusing for me. He doesn't have a clue that grown-ups swear all the time.

"A."

"What's A?"

He verbalizes it. I feel like I should congratulate him—well done. I also feel guilty about the jocularity of cheddar banter.

"Don't ever say that word. A is one of the really bad ones."

"Not as bad as F," he supposes, not entirely sure.

"That's right. And do you know what F is?" Jesus, Mary forgive me. I want to hear that word come out of the kid's mouth.

We wince as he nails it.

"What about C?" he asks.

I cringe. There's a caboodle of Cs. I don't know which one he has in mind. I hazard a go-ahead, like an act of drawing straws.

He selects the least bad one. Phew. "Good night, cheddar."

("These are days you'll remember. Never before and never since, I promise, will the whole world be warm as this. And as you feel it, you'll know it's true, that you are blessed and lucky. It's true that you are touched by something that will grow and bloom in you.")[19]

Special Parts

"I'm like the kind of person who people don't like."

"You don't even."

"On the bleachers with Lucas."

"Yeah, and that's why Aaron."

"I was the one kid who wanted to go in the water so bad."

"Sitting on the side where those mattress things are."

"There's like this season where I have no friends."

19. 10,000 Maniacs, "These Are Days."

Trust me, Manny, I know. It's not straight lines, no standard time. School days or days at camp that seem like seasons. These are the days that must happen to you.[20]

"Yeah, with Lucas."

"Kind of good, kind of not good with Aaron."

"One of the counselors threw a pass to some fourth graders, and I caught an interception."

Parent-teacher conferences. Doctor's office visits. Dinner-table chit-chat. Bedtime tuck-ins. Boyhood glimpsed as snippets, reported speech, highlights, homecomings. Everything is "what else?" We surrender, barely grasp, intuit, and surely miss so much of the blacktop, cafeteria, classroom, and movie days.

Manny and I were in the car the other day, and he mentioned an impossible piece of trivia. I forget what it was. The factoid doesn't matter. The point is that the data was, according to him, stored in his hippocampus. He evidently learned that big science term when his class completed a lesson about memory and the brain several months earlier—*months*, a season.

LOL. If he yada yadas the hippocampus, what else goes unmentioned?

He has a part that is regularly euphemized in society. The doctor refers to it as "boy parts" and annually instructs and reminds him that only Mommy and Daddy can touch boy parts. For his part, Manny has several words, presumably learned on the blacktop, such as "nuts," "goodies," and "balls."

I do not remember seeing my father's penis, or my brother's, or my cousin's. There are no lasting memories of these penises, although I must have seen them. The first other penis that I remember was a cliché penis. Schoolmates were flaunting early onset pubes in a middle school locker room. Then penises proliferated in porn. And there were basement scenarios. A friend and I would take off our pants and underwear, rub our dicks on pillows, jack off with each other, and jizz. That was the word we used. This was before I had done anything sexual with a girl. It was something I felt that I could not tell anyone else. I was scared and nervous. And into it. Down the stairs in a secure, finished room with carpeting and

20. Whitman, *Leaves of Grass*, 233.

warm wood paneling, the door leading to the ground floor locked from the inside.

Society does not acknowledge things. Most things. But I don't experience those days as having disappeared and been sublimated into a Hegelian higher identity. I never did anything like that again—getting with a guy. I do not have a solid explanation for why. Internalizations of shame run deep. But lingers live inside and underneath. Formations are knotted and not neat for me. The affects and desires of something that is mine, cherished, longed for, and genuine, a historical part of me stuck in the pines. Sometimes I wake up down in that basement. I never dream of the ballfields of my youth.

Not Knowing

I wanted a Little Leaguer.

We didn't do the demonstrative ultrasound or blood test. We wanted to find out the old-fashioned way. But I had a preference. And we had guesstimates.

"I don't know. I'm like 60/40."

"I'm like 80/20."

"I don't know, maybe like 70/30." (Always round numbers.)

"What do you want to name it?"

A name is a tribute—a eulogy, always already a chiseling on a gravestone. It is also a signature, an imprint on the soul.[21] There are lots of people named Emmanuel. But when Emmanuel Levinas died, that Emmanuel took the whole of creation with him, as everyone does in death. The end of a singularity, an individual that cannot be replaced.[22] The end of everything—everything for the deceased individual and everything in the deceased individual for everyone else.[23] The death of what Jacques Derrida enigmatically writes about in terms of God. The death of a single human is also the death of God.[24]

21. Derrida, *On the Name.*
22. Levinas, "The Philosopher and Death."
23. Lingis, "To Die with Others."
24. Derrida, *The Gift of Death,* 108–9.

People say they have a feeling. We went into the birthing room with one ready name. And, if needed, an esoteric Hungarian girl's name from my mom's side that we weren't fully settled on. We were banking on 90/10, maybe more.

The thing is, I would have loved that baby no matter what. But I honestly had a preference. An "at some point." I wanted to get it out of the way. If the first one was a girl, we would have to give it another go, and then after the second girl, a third attempt, and I was drinking and using drugs and who knows.

Natural Beauty

In the cold, snowy wintertime, her daddy and granddaddy went up in the fields below the knob and castrated the newborn calves with razor-sharp pocket knives, tossing spindly testicles to hungry, trailing farm dogs. She rode the rumbling four-wheeler, bouncing over ridges, separating out the newborns from the herd. With calloused hands, coughing, inhaling moldy hay and straw dust, she threw eighty-pound bales from wobbly trailers to the herd every day over winter break, while other kids were on ski trips or playing Nintendo. She developed a firm grip and hard body, shouldered the chores of a patriarchal agrarian upbringing, worked in the cattle chute—a narrow corridor into which the cattle are funneled so the animals cannot turn around or escape, so they can be branded, examined, or injected with medicines and growth hormones. Daddy and Granddaddy worked the herd wearing plastic coveralls, mucking around in piss and shit, excretions, filth, the cows thrashing about.

She was the most amazing person there could ever be—and way smarter than me. First-year orientation. She was taking social sciences and humanities—great registration. She was confident and charismatic—went on to campus leadership positions. She had a killer music collection (The Cranberries, Stone Temple Pilots). Shared lyrics and late-night listening cultured connections and cohabitation and valences of contact amid "the aura of outrage, the feeling of alternativeness."[25]

---

25. Marche, *"Dazed and Confused* Was the Definitive Movie about the '90s."

I started visiting the farm in college. I saw chiseled muscles, veins popping out from forearms and biceps and neck. She wore only sports bras. Her chest was solid and muscular, and she kicked the cows to get in line, sloshed around in the chute, and then washed her grubby hands like some violent shedding, forcefully scrubbing up to elbows. All of this turned me on so much—a farm girl, kind of, sort of masculine.

(Cue "Then He Kissed Me" by the Crystals.)[26]

She runs the show in our house. She sits at the head of the table. When we fell in love in college, I was a bookish loner, and she was the vice president of the student government. Everybody asked why she was dating me. Even I asked that. I still don't get it. Now she is active in the Association of Women Faculty and efforts to improve reproductive health and family resources and policies at the university. Seeing the chocolate milk and sugary cereals at Manny's elementary school, she helped initiate a task force to improve food and nutrition services in our school district.

Socialities and agencies are enmeshed with the edge and style of gendered and eroticized presence. She prefers vintage clothing for ethical and aesthetic purposes, mostly marked-down designer wear from the seventies and eighties (a plush Armani blazer to impress at a women's studies faculty meeting). She rocks leather jackets (some studded) and tight jeans, and it's a particular and cultivated androgynous look and feel. She experiences herself in relation to a hard femme situation. Entangled lingerings and intricacies are part of our enduring love, harvest moon.[27]

Granddaddy is in the back end of the chute with a cattle prod, smacking cows on their backsides, shouting "ya ya" and "soo cow soo," a phrase popularized in a country-blues song by Memphis Minnie.[28] Daddy's up front in the chute injecting pharmaceuticals. In the early spring, the chute is used for breeding. Daddy or a veterinarian applies lube, lifts the cow's tail, and inserts his hand through the rectum. "Come on, darling, let me in," feeling around for the uterus and the shape of the calf's head.[29]

26. The Crystals, "Then He Kissed Me."
27. Young, "Harvest Moon."
28. Memphis Minnie, "Soo Cow Soo."
29. Conover, "Cattle Calls."

She rode horses throughout her childhood and teenage years. (Cue "Unknown Legend" by Neil Young.)[30] Whenever we visit the farm, she rides. She's graceful, unintimidated, and fast. She's a natural beauty.[31] Her hair, pulled back in a ponytail, flaps about as she cues the horse. She wears a flannel shirt and distressed jeans. Flies swarm about the horse's mane. She brushes the horse gently, whispers its name, and gallops into the grassy field. The ride, like the caress, does not know what it seeks.

In horseback riding, she came to assimilate sweaty caking as a no-sweat condition of possibility, toughening to bruises and soreness and exposure to hazardous animal instincts like spooking, bucking, kicking, and bolting. She learned to find a stride, to pump up and down into careens of pleasure, to go with surges and pulsations. She learned "the thrill of speed and the soothing decompression of slowing down."[32] She internalized purposeless carnalities of play, thrownness, and danger as accumulating propensities of power, identity, and repertoire.

induction

the ward radiates happy baby birth. bright splashes. pastel swaddles. beanies. teddies. balloons. soothing murals and spirituals. the beeps and blinks of a hypertechnological apparatus. it's-all-good institutions. no-worries modernity.

what god did to eve was evil.

laboring women in the tamil nadu region of south india commonly reject anesthesia. in fact, they request labor-inducing hormones that markedly intensify the frequency and force of contractions, making labor more painful. there is an anthropological explanation. pain in childbirth is there associated with salient meanings of gender, strength, and power.[33]

she wants a natural birth. no c-section. no anesthesia or epidural. she wants to feel her body and feel in control of her body. natural childbirth

---

30. Young, "Unknown Legend."
31. Young, "Natural Beauty."
32. Lingis, *Dangerous Emotions*, 31.
33. Van Hollen, "Invoking *Vali*."

leaves babies alert, better able to begin breastfeeding, not zonked by the sprawl of numbing agents.

diagnosis: severe preeclampsia. high blood pressure. life-threatening. crisis.

treatment: magnesium sulfate, an anticonvulsant to prevent seizures, plus emergency induction with pitocin, a hormone to assertively stimulate, generate faster, more agonizing paroxysms of impossible, impelling pressure. the pain of being riveted to oneself, unable to distract oneself by turning to the outside, unable to retreat behind the pain to observe it and deal with it.[34]

no. a short word; a snap.[35] farm girl refuses. she's adamant. rejects the anesthesia offers. no to palliation. no over unfolding thresholds of deliverance. one must become animal—shed conventions and culture—to do this.[36] endurance here another sense. eyes not agonizing are gathered to care and caress.

"i am here, give me the pain." a guy, intensifying, too, wanting to do, leaning, leaning hard. shoulders. symbiosis. sincere. but the pain is nontransferable, dear. the care and support only highlight the simultaneous intimacy and distance of the laboring process—a structural and physiological distance combined with an intimate affect.[37] like a defect or taint inscribed in the very fact of existence.[38] the fuck need. the escape need to get out of oneself . . . to break that most radical and unalterably binding of chains, the fact that the "i" is oneself.[39] because shame's whole intensity, everything it contains that stings us, consists precisely in our inability not to identify with this being . . . and make others forget our basic nudity.[40] the impossibility of hiding or transcending one's own insurgent physicality. convulsions. excretions. soil—the least human part of the body, in the sense that no other element of this body is as undifferentiated from the corresponding element in other animals.[41] and amid the precipitous, renegade filthiness:

34. Lingis, "To Die with Others," 109–10.
35. Ahmed, "No."
36. Deleuze and Guattari, *A Thousand Plateaus*, 232–309.
37. Stevenson, "The Psychic Life of Biopolitics," 602.
38. Rolland, "Getting Out of Being by a New Path," 10.
39. Levinas, *On Escape*, 55.
40. Ibid., 63–64.
41. Bataille, "The Big Toe," 20.

"don't worry." the nurses worry. this is not normally how things go—the part where she keeps saying no. still, they go, "her special day," "whatever she needs," "she's doing great," "it's not straight lines, no standard time."

a season.

and then. obstetrician enters. assumes command. "you're in good hands."

physician and staff ready for completion. the point of intensity of a dramatization. a kind of rupture—in anguish . . . at the limit of tears.[42] exploding bones.

touchdown.

and then. ecstasy. breathe. sigh. game over.

"this is so. i want my baby. let me hold it. i want to hold my baby."

and then. diagnosis: retained placenta. stuck. low blood pressure. life-threatening. crisis.

treatment: emergency removal. more chemicals to induce wrenching squeezing dislodging the stubborn afterbirth.

"you're in good hands." jerks.

and then. diagnosis: cord won't budge. translation: manual removal.

"no! fuck no! what? are you fucking serious? with your fucking arm?"

why, if the female attending has thinner arms, is the male resident in latex gloves?

hands-on learning experience.

do not let how-to manuals breathing classes gift registries teddy bears balloons fool you. this is some elaine scarry shit—shrieks, screams, shattering language.[43]

nurses know say something something anesthesia fentanyl midazolam diazepam ketamine something something fucking tylenol something! something!

she's adamant. no. a short word; a snap, perhaps. no as negative speech; a complaint. no what you say when you do not want to proceed; when you do not agree to something. no as an address; delivered to a person or made against a system or given in a situation. no what you announce by what you do or do not do with your body; as gesture, as withdrawal.[44]

42. Bataille, *Inner Experience*, 18.
43. Scarry, *The Body in Pain*.
44. Ahmed, "No."

low pressure dark blood drop unconscious. pulpy fuchsia profusions dyeing. womb coming down, the world turned over.[45] go out, come back in.

and then. nurses know you poor thing.

buckets. fresh blankets.

sleep.

before the horrific hemorrhaging, there was a rush of beta-endorphins and oxytocin, just as the manuals describe, hormones also widely secreted during sexual activity and orgasm.

"this is so. i want my baby. let me hold it. i want to hold my baby."

she had already loved the baby for months. she now sees its face, swollen and scrunched. cradles its slimy, amniotic, purple body, and lays it on her chest dripping with sweat. this is what manuals call skin-to-skin. the warm, fleshy contact and embrace facilitate breastfeeding, and the rushing hormones relieve stress and let the milk down.

"i love you. i am your mom. i can't wait to get to know you. i will love you forever."

this boundless, infinite love does not know what it seeks. the not-knowing is the essential.

the baby, cooing, pees, and, with no postural axis, wobbles and flails, coltish, splayed, rubbing its head across swollen breasts, its mouth open for latching, suckling, keen on connecting with a key physical feature, an areola. and as transcendent as the moment was for me, i feel ashamed of my own impulsive, object-oriented glance. the first thing i did when the baby emerged was look for a key physical feature. i saw penis. and i breathed a sigh of relief.

45. Goo Goo Dolls, "Black Balloon."

13 Broken Flowers

<u>Life Sciences</u>

She finished her book. The essential component of the tenure dossier. And now. More free time. Time for trying. Even though I was still using drugs and alcohol, we wanted another one. This is what science refers to as "replacement-level fertility." Manny needed someone to pick on and tickle. I needed additional reasons to get sober.

Such genre of sex can be laborious, not much fun—a regimentation. Try and try again. Popular websites offer magical-thinking recommendations, such as the myth about lying flat for a half hour after sex.

Trying is might-as-well-experimental-focusing-doing. All for the purpose of a literal finishing. Are you, we, finished?

Sleep.

Science suggests that the evolutionary reason why males release oxytocin and prolactin during sex—chemicals that cause sleepiness—is to enhance pair-bonding with the female mate. Nurdling, snuggling, snoozing reins males in and contributes to prairielands domesticity. Male reproductive fitness is increased as they ensure sperm retention with females remaining in that horizontal position and participate in relation-ship commitment.[1]

And who says romantics are hopeless?

Like everything under the sun, the functionalism of straightaway snores and nucleated nesting got going among early hominids on the African savanna hundreds of thousands, maybe millions of years ago.

Doesn't the mumbo-jumbo nonsense of says-so science provide the worse half with an alibi to nod off neglectfully? Was the savanna so parched and platonic? Wasn't there sex open to the night, biochemical resistances of an instinctual falling away? Wasn't there *Homo erectus ergaster* hooking up? ("Sipping and sucking in the darkness of the hive. Touching and taking, rubbing and writhing. That liquid world of intimate intensities.")[2] Caresses unaware of what they seek.[3] Directionless desires escaping the functional logic of finished.

Expecting

Trying must be in the summer for a timed-right birth at the end of the fol-lowing year's spring semester to ensure the longest possible parental leave. The planned parenthood of the professoriate.

August.

She happily told me about tender breasts, fatigue, and nausea—symp-toms interpreted as signs. This was good—good to be waking up throwing up. Uncomfortable indications.

With Manny at preschool, the sweethearts headed to Schnucks, where they went straight to the apples, then left at the flowers to the pharmacy. They bought two kits and headed home, an upbeat, expectant anxious.

They surged upstairs.

Pink is positive.

A delicate rose.

1. Kruger and Hughes, "Tendencies to Fall Asleep First after Sex Are Associated with Greater Partner Desires for Bonding and Affection."
2. Raffles, *Insectopedia*, 262.
3. Levinas, *Time and the Other*, 89.

She peed again.

Pink is positive.

They picked up Manny. He vaguely understood something about something something something. "Take good care of." "Good role model." "Learn to share." "Same school." "The playground on the weekends."

And then. Now. Expecting. Alonging. How far alonging? A light at the end of the tunnel.

And then. The first visit. The look, see, listen. The nurse glides the wand to browse a dark figuration surrounded by circular grayscale smears and snowdrifts. Tidal whooshing. Around smudging. And then she prints a few Polaroids for their fridge. This is the life.

Natural Causes

Everyone comes to see, in one way or another, the heartache of the process of giving life.

"Our life *gives life* to others," Alphonso Lingis writes. "The possibility of giving life, giving one's own life to another, is an essential feature of our existence. [. . .] A parent would kill or die for his or her child."[4]

In the commingling of matter in the fallopian tube, another matter can come into existence. There is great societal debate about the name for this itness. It is, no matter what, already death, dying, as it will, unavoidably, at some point, perish, peter out.

Think of the normative long view of "a life."[5] Setting forth. Whooshes. Alonging. See the light. Jammies. Erectus. Reading writing arithmetic. Backpacks. That weight. Meet mingle mate. Finished. Snores. This is the life. Kedron and me and Manny. And after the ultrasound, there's Henry, too.

Afterlives

Manny was there in Texas when Grandma died at ninety-five. She was spirited until the last breath. Going in and out of Hungarian, touching base with her immigrant mother who died in Connecticut half a century

4. Lingis, "To Die with Others," 109, 113.
5. Berlant, "Intimacy," 1.

earlier, half-conscious, Grandma kept telling the same spent joke, making sure no one forgot her vivacity in the face of her impairments and deteriorations—that lewd, bawdy, blue streak.

"What do sex and Campbell's Soup have in common? Mmm, mmm, good."

"Grandma!"

Over Manny's head. Everyone hollered, lovingly massaging her arms, applying a damp cloth to her forehead and shoulders.

She died, amid the consoling presence of family, from natural causes related to organ failure. As the respiration slowed, we clasped her hands.

She made the best Christmas cookies, an Old World recipe.

She loved when spring training came around, talked about her Mets.

She sent Manny ten bucks every month to play pool at Fitz's on the Loop, his favorite restaurant.

When I was Manny's age, she took me to Burger King in Norwalk for kids' meals.

It was good that she went. She could barely get around. She had pain throughout her body. She had skin cancers and was all the time being biopsied. She was in the doctor's office on a regular basis.

"[T]here is [. . .] love in wanting someone to die," Lingis writes. "When someone we love who has been suffering dies, we feel a sense of relief. [. . .] Death appears as a deliverance from dying—from the suffering of dying."[6]

Death can also appear as a snatching. A child dies—utter "why." We cry and wail and scream and throw things at walls and punch walls and go on benders and bottle it up because death is not a biological phenomenon.

"We want time for her to flourish, knowing that her life is a radiance shed on others, on us," Lingis continues. "We can desperately want someone to live because we have not yet shown our love for her enough, not yet loved her enough."[7]

Fridge magnets. Framed pictures. A mantel culture haunted by "all the things that we failed to say."[8] An unfinished archival existence. Death as "impossibly painful immortality."[9] The preemptive loss of all alonging.

6. Lingis, "To Die with Others," 111.
7. Ibid.
8. Lingis, *Irrevocable*, 169.
9. Schine, "Elegy to the Void."

Joan Didion writes of the "unending absence that follows, the void [. . .] the relentless succession of moments."[10] Reflecting on the death of her daughter, Didion submits that "the fear is not for what is lost," but rather "for what is still to be lost."[11]

Point A, Point B

I think about you every day.

We never saw you. The ultrasound worked. You kinda didn't. Latched too soon. Stuck. Jammed. A pearl. Pearl jam. That's okay. That's how I am.

Maybe you were flustered or frazzled. Maybe you didn't know what to do. Or there was an accident or a wrong turn. Or it was hard. Not straightforward. Or what lay ahead was scary. Believe me, it is.

The nurses and doctors didn't say "B." They switched, as they do.[12] In dehumanizing, disowning, and delegating references to abnormality and tissue, you became scientific, advanced, and medical for the sake of absolving a Catholic hospital.

Good doctor—white coat caduceus name badge title—swivels, leans forward. Fetal tissue surgery-related trauma fallopian tube future infertility hemorrhage who knows general anesthesia laparoscopic tiny incision lower abdomen. Do you have any questions?

Her hospital gown had moments earlier been the medium of access to lubricate abdomen and image angel. Now it indicated another patienthood, a different look, see, listen—the "unwilled susceptibility" of an emergency operation.[13]

The first being Manny's umbilical cord, the retained placenta, this was the second time she faced her own mortality in the process of giving life.

The doctor's office radiates happy baby birth. Bright splashes. Soothing murals and spirituals. Hanging crosses. Bible verses.

Institutions, theologians, and clinicians who want to get away with what they otherwise hold to be murder refer to a small percentage of pregnancies with the word "ectopic," from the Greek "ek-topos," meaning out

---

10. Didion, *The Year of Magical Thinking*, 189.
11. Didion, *Blue Nights*, 188.
12. Saunders, "Lesley's Story," 13.
13. Butler, *Giving an Account of Oneself*, 91.

of place. They have drawn a line, nominally and procedurally exteriorizing the fallopian tube, to condone an act religiously and morally prohibited for other embryos, an act befalling a clumpy you. This hospital doesn't excise embryonic tissue except in this circumstance—a medical logic and predication of salvation and intervention resting on a denial of earlier and elsewhere ascriptions of sacredness, a partition to make this not "A."[14] Because, look, see, listen. "A" and "B" can't go together. For it to not be "A," you couldn't be "B," even though an ectopic, an errantly implanted fertilized egg, is biologically like photogenic humanities for cubicle tack boards and water coolers being imaged in other consultation rooms down the hall. Because that which might be called "A" is here only permissible given a cataclysmic diagnosis and an unwanted gurney, the transmutation of ontology, the disavowal of legitimacy, the "social forms that have made certain kinds of losses ungrievable," to quote Judith Butler.[15] They take it back and make believe and nothing started and nothing's ending.

("I pace around the parking lot. Then I walk down to buy her flowers. [. . .] Now she's feeling more alone, than she ever has before. And she broke down and I broke down.")[16]

I don't know what.

We never talk about it, you.

We never talk about it.

I don't know what it's like . . . to be close to death and need to be rescued at the expense of a love in formation. Torn from desire and choice and forced into alienating terminologies and directed to social work with talk of unfortunately.

Scholars and other writers describe "the realness problem of pregnancy loss," where "the social construction of [. . .] 'baby'" is annulled, "as if nothing of any significance took place," in the words of Linda Layne, who discusses how "[t]he cultural denial of pregnancy loss challenges the validity of the cultural and biological work already undertaken in constructing that child and belittles the importance of the loss."[17] Patients experience embarrassment, fault, and culpability, feeling blameworthy for

14. Dickens, Faundes, and Cook, "Ectopic Pregnancy and Emergency Care."
15. Butler, *The Psychic Life of Power*, 185.
16. Ben Folds Five, "Brick."
17. Layne, *Motherhood Lost*, 17.

investing in horizons and attachments.[18] Everybody was iPhone-expecting to look, see, listen. Grain glimpses. Amazon wish lists. A nursery awaiting whimsical wallpaper or blue or pink accent walls. There were projections, picked-outs, publicizing and personalizing speculations, and it's a sudden imperceptibility, a collapsed universe, the death of God. To have blindly loved a pregnancy that is an "aporetic juncture," a "dead end," and it's an evacuation of undecidability, loss experienced as a kind of stupidity.[19]

Name[20]

Every other is absolutely other.[21]

"There cannot be a replacement for the non-substitutable," so goes Emmanuel Levinas's theory of existence, "nor a substitute for the irreplaceable."[22]

Anthropologists study naming rituals. Some cultures wait weeks after birth. Maybe they know better.

Maybe because we already had a boy. Maybe because we liked the name. Maybe because we wanted a flower. We were 100/0. Down there with the tattoos for Manny and Kedron, right down there on my ankle alongside עמנואל and Ked , the logo for the shoes, a one-of-a-kind, young-love tattoo, I couldn't wait to get one for you: a tattoo of a rose.

It is not, "would have been." It is, "was." Your name was Rose, a tender, delicate flower, the prettiest of flowers, and the most Catholic name, outdone only by Mary.

"Second-rate, mediocre" is how one woman sorrowfully describes her ectopic embryo in a poem.[23]

Stuck moving. A pearl. A jam. That's okay. That's how I am.

18. Hey et al., *Hidden Loss.*
19. Ronell, *Stupidity,* 70.
20. Goo Goo Dolls, "Name."
21. Derrida, *The Gift of Death,* 78.
22. Desmond, "Philosophies of Religion," 168.
23. Hey, "Valerie's Poem," 8.

August and Everything After[24]

You were named after a whiskery great aunt who divorced after a month of marriage during the Great Depression and then went celibate, carrying rosary beads throughout the twentieth century and forgetting everything except the names of a whole generation of Italian American ballplayers.

I rubbed her chilly, exposed back. "[W]e stroke the truss of the shoulders," Lingis writes. "Unable to restore a loss, we offer the support of our body to the weight of the grief. [. . . We] lay our hand [. . .] in a touch of consolation."[25]

I don't remember if we ever heard like a heartbeat or anything or saw a visualization or if the ultrasound technician was just like, "Let me get the doctor."

We never talk about it. There's too much. It's too hard.

"Leaving flowers on your grave, show that I still care. Black roses and 'Hail Mary's' can't bring back what's taken from me. I reach to the sky and call out your name. And if I could trade, I would.[26] Faeries, come take me out of this dull world, for I would ride with you upon the wind, run on top of the disheveled tide, and dance upon the mountains like a flame.[27] Excuse me if I break my own heart tonight.[28] To escape their solitude and sadness, Mexicans not only use the party, but also the vehicle of alcohol. Party nights can also be nights of mourning.[29] Thanks to the fiesta the Mexican opens out . . . without them we would explode. They free us from the thwarted impulses, the inflammable desires that we carry with us. Our fiestas are explosions. There is nothing so joyous as fiesta night, but there is also nothing so sorrowful. Fiesta night is also a night of mourning.[30] This is a cultural syndrome. Social suffering. It's a case study for medical anthropology . . ."

"Bullshit fuck you've been drinking since grad school. A man thinks, that by mouthing hard words, he proves that he understands hard

---

24. Counting Crows, *August and Everything After*.
25. Lingis, *Irrevocable*, 3, 13.
26. The Offspring, "Gone Away."
27. Yeats, "The Land of Heart's Desire," 71–72.
28. Whiskeytown, "Excuse Me While I Break My Own Heart Tonight."
29. Palafox, "Cantinas and Drinkers in Mexico," 177.
30. Paz, *The Labyrinth of Solitude*, 52–53.

things.[31] You're treading. It's exhausting. The billows and the waves pass over you. The waters compass about you, even to the soul: the depth closes you round about, the weeds are wrapped about your head.[32] . . . Grow old with me! The best is yet to be."[33]

In the early spring, I ran out to grab a twelve-pack at Schnucks and made that stop in the parking lot of Manny's preschool. Got turned around. Turned around.

That summer we tried again.

Pink is positive.

August and everything after.

Manny and I tickle Henry.

"Beep, beep," he blurts out. Day care for "Back up, stop it."

He slides blocks back and forth on the living room floor. Drops clinking coins into a glass jar and plucks them out and does it again and again. Repeatedly opens and closes the fridge door and rejoices: "Did it!" Builds Duplo towers (the big block LEGOs for toddlers) and then topples them, a recovery playground.

"Oh no. Happen."

We gesture to help resurrect it.

"Beep, beep."

Moat making.

"Mo-chee."

"Cheese? Okay, hold on."

"No no, mo-chee."

"Cheese or no cheese?"

"Mo-chee."

"Okay, hold on."

"No no, mo-chee."

"Do you see the trees? Yeah, out the window. That's great, Henry. Good job."

"No no, mo-chee."

"Oh! Marching! The ants go marching one by one, hurrah, hurrah."

31. Melville, *White-Jacket*, 263.
32. Jonah 2:3, 2:5.
33. Browning, "Rabbi Ben Ezra," 781.

"Just like your brother, Henry. Nippling on your first two fingers, the other hand wrapped around your noggin, fidgeting with your earlobe, wudging."

(Cue "Beautiful Boy [Darling Boy]" by John Lennon and Yoko Ono.)[34]

And then. A friend of Manny's moved to a farther-out suburb, not returning to his school. Manny's first-grade teacher was reassigned to second grade. He hoped for her again but was placed in a different classroom. Henry transitioned up to another room and got a plastic potty. And everything is going fine.[35]

"There was an empty Coke can on the bookshelf. I know it's a little thing. I don't want to make a big deal. But it's the kind of thing that would be meaningful. I don't want to have to clean up after you."

("She lies and says she's in love with him, can't find a better man. She dreams in color, she dreams in red, can't find a better man.")[36]

<u>Rose</u>

I am the oldest, and then my brother, a little more than a year younger, and then my sister, nearly a decade younger. My parents took care of Aunt Rose. An Old World deal. She was my mom's aunt on her dad's side. Pete's sister.

Aunt Rose, always wearing the same hand-knit cardigans and sweaters for geriatric insulation, had unkempt gray hair, profuse nostril hair, facial hair, ear hair, benign lesions and moles on her face, and a battery of questions about the Yankees of baseball's golden age, like a game of pepper.

How's Phil Rizzuto doing this year? Billy Martin? Joe DiMaggio? Yogi Berra? Frank Crosetti?

Even us buffs were baffled. *Who's Crosetti?*

She would sacrilegiously switch to the Brooklyn Dodgers, asking about Roy Campanella, Ralph Branca, Sal Maglie, Cookie Lavagetto, Carl Furillo. Cognitively declined, she conjured a subway series of Italian

34. Lennon and Ono, "Beautiful Boy (Darling Boy)."
35. Soderbergh, *And Everything Is Going Fine.*
36. Pearl Jam, "Better Man."

Americans, Americanized immigrant labor, men who fought in the war, men who smoked (and, in DiMaggio's case, advertised) cigarettes.

Sitting next to Aunt Rose involved caretaking for dementia. At dinner, every night, my brother and I jockeyed for positions at the other side of the table, mortified by the disgusting idea of whiskers falling into our mashed potatoes and gravy. The old maid chomped and smacked. Her dentures a mandible of loud and hard jowl chews. Cool and grossed-out teenagers protesting, "grody" and "gnarly"; we tussled for faraway. Despite the neurodegeneration, Aunt Rose knew the game. Snarled at us. Scolded us: "ungrateful." "Boys," she said. "You boys." "My boys." "Here boys." "There boys."

She'd lapse into exhortations for rapture, pleading for death: "Oh dear, Jesus, Mary."

"Fine," we snickered. "Our father, who aren't in heaven."

She was like Tony Soprano's mom—senile and streaky mean, mischievous, wanting to die, and, furthermore, someone whom everyone wanted to die.

My sister was more gracious, agreeably sitting next to Aunt Rose. And Aunt Rose, in her nineties, stuck with an abridged vocabulary, nicknamed her "my doll." Not "doll." But "my doll."

"I'm not your doll."

There's a story about Aunt Rose chaperoning my mom's sister, taking the train to see the Beatles for their famous first performance at Shea Stadium in Queens. But I can't picture Aunt Rose in the City or at a rock concert or in the sixties.

"Where's my coffee?"

"You just drank it."

"Where are my cookies and crackers?"

"You dunked them in your coffee for a half hour."

"We never have pork chops."

"They're on your plate every week."

Look, see, listen; she forgot. Every other is absolutely other. Living lifetimes and lapses in minutes and meals.

She was attentively regarded, never neglected, a sick and persnickety great-aunt treated with the respect accorded elders. Every morning she had "coffee and." She had an inventory of hard candy and crocheting supplies on hand. They did the laundry and the dishes and in the last years, the showering and sheggy wiping. On weekends, they plopped her on the couch for *The Lawrence Welk Show* on PBS, lovingly and patiently maintaining this rose, thorny, prickly, and stuck in insane repetitions about Depression-era batting averages and the babying of a doll.

14 Stagecoach

A couple of years after we relocated from the East Coast to St. Louis, some of our friends from Guatemala—a husband and wife and their two-year-old daughter—came to visit. Kedron was pregnant, so it was Manny's-age years ago. We did not yet know the sex, gender, hard sciences, soft sciences—that "'it-ness' of the classified object world."[1]

Kedron and I had been living in Guatemala during summers for a decade, at first as expatriate backpackers and Spanish language learners, then as anthropology graduate students. We spent the bulk of our time living in Tecpán, a mostly Maya town in the central highlands. Tecpán is known for nontraditional export agricultural production that complements the subsistence cornfields known as milpa. I cowrote an anthropology book about this interesting agrarian world as a graduate student.[2] Tecpán is also known for its thriving clothing industry, which involves the production of knockoffs. The logos and styles of global brands are lifted for manufactured clothing sold cheaply throughout the highlands. Kedron spent several summers in Guatemala learning Kaqchikel, one of the many Mayan

1. Mody, *Cultural Identity in Kindergarten*, 150.
2. Fischer and Benson, *Broccoli and Desire*.

languages. She then lived for more than a year in Tecpán and went on to write a book about the regional apparel industry, the country's clothing and fashion styles, and the intensifying enforcement of anti-counterfeiting laws. Multinational apparel companies use intellectual property laws to target poor people in places like Guatemala for stitching ponies, pumas, and crocodiles on their shirts and sweaters.[3]

Kedron and I have developed very close ties with a few families in Tecpán. We regard them, and they regard us, as kin. We are co-parents in one family. We can be called upon at any moment to fulfill a range of obligations. It is a serious and meaningful spiritual, moral, economical, and social relationship and commitment. Kedron and I do things to support families that have, with such generosity, supported our anthropological work. These involvements are embedded in compromisos and refrains, return trips to Tecpán, regular communication, and bonds of trust that transcend one keyword.

Introduction

A student in the campus chapter of a global health organization took my "Introduction" class. Idealistic, energetic, and aspirational, she wants to make a difference in the world. She is white and comes from affluence. She is like many of my students—premed, majoring in anthropology (my fault), and concerned with the trendy theme of culture and global health. A dominant paradigm is "cultural competence," the idea that health outcomes are improved if clinicians and program managers understand and address cultural issues of patient populations.[4]

Anthropologists have been critical of this paradigm for presuming that a static thing called "culture" causes or solves health conditions. This view homogenizes groups, assumes that patients are overdetermined by culture, but clinicians are neutral and unmarked, and suggests that the main determinant of health is the culture and behavior of a target population.[5] Moreover, the emphasis on culture in global health and humanitarianism

3. Thomas, *Regulating Style.*
4. Betancourt et al., "Defining Cultural Competence."
5. Fassin, "Culturalism as Ideology"; Kleinman and Benson, "Anthropology in the Clinic"; Taylor, "The Story Catches You and You Fall Down."

32. Peter in Antigua, Guatemala, 2004. Photograph by Kedron Thomas.

is part of a dominant, sentimental worldview that problematically frames "condition[s] in terms of suffering rather than the geopolitical situation."[6]

My student asked me to give a lecture to the group on culture and health in Guatemala. They were preparing a summer trip there for volunteer medical work in an impoverished town. I am occasionally asked to do such lectures for student organizations that do southerly stints for good intentions and résumé checkboxes for medical school applications. In this case, I wanted to dispense with the notion that Guatemala is other and talk about how the United States might be understood otherwise instead.

I began with slides of myself hulking along the thin—too thin for my big body—sidewalks of the colonial town of Antigua, a prime tourist destination with cobblestone streets, a leisurely central park, and surrounding volcanoes named Pacaya, De Agua, Acatenango, and Fuego, this highland

6. Fassin, "Humanitarianism as a Politics of Life," 501.

town where I first fell in love with the country, where every day I passed a man with no legs begging for money on my way to Spanish class. The photographs were taken by Kedron. I have on shorts. An American thing to do. Guatemalans generally do not wear shorts. I am not sure why. Maybe modesty. In the photographs, I am also noticeably tall. My head hits overhanging shingled roofs. I stand above Catholic schoolgirls in the street beside me.

My time in Guatemala made me feel things, with such difficulty, that I had not felt before. I became more critically aware of corporeality, race, and gender, and experienced the power embodied in something as simple as following a sidewalk or having blond hair. People called me "canchito," a Guatemalan colloquialism, playful and perhaps pejorative, meaning "little blondie." People touched my hair, marveled at my light hair. And while street dogs bark at everyone, when they barked at me, people chuckled with schadenfreude, telling me that the dogs like carne blanca—white meat. Over time, I came to see myself in terms of that keyword.

"Gringo" refers to a white person, usually an American. It can be mundane and innocuous. It can also have disparaging and resistant meaning, referring to a figure of imperial power, someone who, as Gloria Anzaldúa writes, is "locked into the fiction of white superiority";[7] someone who feels "the prerogative," to quote Judith Butler, "to be the one who transgresses the sovereign boundaries of other states, but never to be in the position of having one's own boundaries transgressed";[8] a white man who travels to Latin America for sex;[9] someone who believes they "must know best";[10] someone who lounges on beaches and drinks margaritas and looks down on the global south.

International volunteer programs. Plane tickets, passports, preparedness, perhaps parents paying for it all, what Ron Krabill critiques as a "self-satisfied big emotional experience of an exotic adventure in helping others."[11] The university is a market for clamors and fervors of periphery involvement, for participation in "life-building on the bottom of

7. Anzaldúa, *Borderlands/La Frontera*, 29.
8. Butler, *Precarious Life*, 39.
9. Rivers-Moore, *Gringo Gulch*.
10. Stanley, *A Critical Auto/Ethnography of Learning Spanish*, 123.
11. Krabill, "American Sentimentalism and the Production of Global Citizens," 53.

contemporary class society," to quote Lauren Berlant.[12] While this travel-experience framework is advertised as relevant and transformative, it feeds into "the illusion that awareness and enthusiasm are sufficient for social change," which, Krabill writes, "seriously diminishes possibilities for alternatives," such as "a relentlessly self-reflexive engagement with the realities of global inequality, the politics of that inequality, and our varying individual and collective responsibilities within them."[13]

My presentation discussed anthropology as a different travel and engagement practice—less overdetermined, more open-ended, as in Renato Rosaldo's phrase "deep hanging out,"[14] involving, Stacy Leigh Pigg writes, "the questioning of received certainties through a responsiveness to multiple viewpoints and contested perspectives," an ethic arising from "sitting, being, noticing, and reflecting."[15]

I told the students that perhaps the point of travel is to feel awkward and uncomfortable, involving what Gayatri Chakravorty Spivak discusses as "unlearning one's learning."[16] Not primarily aiming to know otherness in someone else's shoes, but rather what it is to stand in one's own shoes.

Powerpoint

I shifted the presentation to Wikipedia. Screen grabs. As if to say, "You could have looked this up online if you were so interested." Alas, my role, it seems, is to certify and commoditize knowledge that is readily and freely available to anyone.

"This stuff happened," I said. "The 1954 Guatemalan coup d'état was a covert operation by the CIA that deposed the democratically elected Guatemalan president Jacobo Árbenz and installed the military dictatorship of Carlos Castillo Armas, the first in a series of US-backed authoritarian rulers in Guatemala. Árbenz instituted land reforms grant-

12. Berlant, "Nearly Utopian, Nearly Normal," 275.
13. Krabill, "American Sentimentalism and the Production of Global Citizens," 53.
14. Renato Rosaldo, quoted in Clifford, "Anthropology and/as Travel," 5.
15. Pigg, "On Sitting and Doing," 127.
16. Spivak, "An Interview," 24.

33. Lake Atitlán, Sololá, Guatemala, 1999. Photograph by Josef Koudelka (Magnum Photos).

ing property to landless peasants. The United Fruit Company, whose highly profitable business had been affected by the end to exploitative labor practices in Guatemala, engaged in an influential lobbying campaign to persuade the US to overthrow the Guatemalan government. Secretary of state John Foster Dulles and his brother CIA director Allen Dulles had close ties to the United Fruit Company. The CIA armed, funded, and trained a force of 480 men led by Carlos Castillo Armas. Castillo Armas quickly assumed dictatorial powers, banning opposition parties, imprisoning and torturing political opponents, and reversing the social reforms."[17]

I told the students about how the coup was the beginning of decades of US-backed counterinsurgency activities in Guatemala, culminating in the eighties with the genocidal killing of more than two hundred thousand

17. Wikipedia, "1954 Guatemalan Coup d'état."

people, mostly Mayas, specially targeted because of racism and a belief that rural people were affiliated with guerilla fighters.[18] The Gipper "materially and morally [. . .] supported" the genocide in the name of fighting communism and backing Guatemala's violent president.[19]

More screen grabs from Wikipedia.

"The Guatemalan syphilis experiments were United States-led human experiments conducted from 1946 to 1948. Doctors infected various impoverished groups with syphilis, gonorrhea, and chancroid, without the informed consent of the subjects. The populations involved consisted of child and adult commercial sex workers, prisoners, soldiers, orphans, leprosy patients, and mental health patients. The experiment resulted in at least 83 deaths. In 2010, President Obama formally apologized to Guatemala for the ethical violations that took place. Guatemala condemned the experiment as a crime against humanity. Multiple unsuccessful lawsuits have since been filed in the US."[20]

Student groups volunteer to build wells, measure infants, and shadow doctors in some sort of post- and/or neocolonial field of global health and humanitarianism, aspects of what Michel Foucault calls "biopower."[21] These undertakings, not without questionable and problematic political and moral valences, extend what Ann Stoler refers to as "imperial durabilities."[22]

One year in Tecpán, there was a pair of Peace Corps volunteers conducting women's initiatives—workshops to teach Maya people about hygiene, maternal and child health, and nutrition. These volunteers, working in an institutional vestige of the Cold War, were in their early twenties, advising Maya women, some of them midwives (well beyond the young Americans in age), how to raise children and make families. Guatemalans roll their eyes like they roll their Rs.

My goal in the presentation was to raise doubts about an illusory competence crash course on Guatemala, a how-to manual for interacting with Maya people, a knowledge of disaster without "the larger disasters behind

18. Navarro, "Guatemalan Army Waged 'Genocide.'"
19. Grandin, "Guatemalan Slaughter Was Part of Reagan's Hard Line."
20. Wikipedia, "Guatemalan Syphilis Experiments."
21. Foucault, *The History of Sexuality*, 140.
22. Stoler, *Duress*.

it,"[23] an engagement with ailments apart from reckoning.[24] I wanted the students to realize why the word "health" should be situated alongside words like "history," "power," "structure," "inequality," and "injustice," and not simply "culture."[25]

Gringolandia

To claim to be "without borders" (as in Doctors, and, more recently, Engineers, Chemists, Teachers, etc.) is such a gringo thing to say. Emilio, Alma, and Ixq'anil are not without borders. Kedron wrote a letter to the State Department vouching for them and attesting that they would return home after their stay with us. They were issued temporary visas.

The State Department issues special travel warnings for Americans headed to Guatemala, making vague reference to the high levels of violent crime there. Absent an explanation, the violence seems random, endemic mayhem lacking a historical relationship to the very agency once headed by Dulles. Guatemala seems to exist in an ahistorical "outer zone,"[26] where naturalized violences impact and implicate emboldened and vulnerable gringos as potential victims rather than perpetrators or participants.

A few clicks.

The Wikipedia page on "Crime in Guatemala" clearly outlines historical and geopolitical causes of violence in Guatemala. A quick Google search brings up numerous reports by scholars and activists that link exorbitant homicide levels, violent policing and security efforts, human rights abuses, and the "war on drugs" waged by the United States.[27]

Emilio has a small business, carrying on a tradition of apparel manufacturing that goes back generations in Tecpán. Several of his elders were killed during the genocide. Emilio's family belongs to an emerging middle class. They are not malnourished and living in extreme poverty like most Maya.

23. Cole, "The White-Savior Industrial Complex."
24. Nelson, *Reckoning.*
25. Farmer, "An Anthropology of Structural Violence"; Metzl and Hansen, "Structural Competency."
26. Lingis, "Anger," 200.
27. Main, "The U.S. Re-Militarization of Central America and Mexico."

34. From left: Matthew Broderick as Ferris Bueller, Mia Sara as Sloane Peterson, and Alan Ruck as Cameron Frye at the Sears Tower observation floor in *Ferris Bueller's Day Off* by John Hughes, 1986 (CBS/Getty Images).

Emilio, Alma, and Ixq'anil flew into O'Hare so we could see the big city. It was their first time in the States. "Welcome to gringolandia," they joked. We went to the Shedd Aquarium. Way overpriced, not worth it, everyone agreed. We loitered around the parks along Lake Michigan and ate hot dogs piled with diced white onion, sweet pickle relish, tomato slices, sport peppers, and celery salt. "Chicago style!" I raved. Emilio and Alma were like, "What's the big deal?" Tecpán evenings are strolls in the central plaza, snacking on shucos, a sandwich of ham, pepperoni, salami, a sliced hot dog, sausages, bacon, sauerkraut, guacamole, mustard, mayonnaise, ketchup, and salsas. We went to Gino's East. "Chicago style!" I raved. Emilio and Alma were like, "This isn't real pizza." We ascended the Sears Tower to the 103rd story, the Skydeck, and stood on the Ledge, a glass balcony jutting four feet out, where one can look straight down onto Wacker Drive.

"The city looks so peaceful from up here."

"Anything is peaceful from one thousand, three hundred and fifty-three feet."[28]

28. Hughes, *Ferris Bueller's Day Off.*

Field of Dreams[29]

The highway down Illinois to St. Louis was corn.

We went up the Arch, the Gateway to the West, where Thomas Jefferson, and something about Manifest Destiny, and hunting and trapping, and Indians, a canoe trip, look at all the land, so much work to do, fell in love, and happily ever after.[30] And then we hit the zoo, the Science Center, and a Cardinals game. This was before Michael Brown was shot to death, so our friends didn't once say "Ferguson" or "la policía."

Baseball is not entirely foreign to our friends. The sport was spread along the lines of the hemispheric vision of the Monroe Doctrine through American imperialism and is popular among US Latinxs and Latin Americans.[31] But, as Indigenous Maya people, Emilio and Alma are not entirely legible in terms of these dominant ethnicity and nationality categories.[32] And baseball doesn't do it for them like soccer. It is not kinesthetically dynamic, aesthetically graceful, and thrillingly exciting in the way that soccer is regarded as "o jogo bonito," as they say in Brazil—the beautiful game.

I get it. I was in Tecpán in the summer of 2002 with an alarm clock that went off at, like, 2:00 a.m. because of the time change with Japan so I could wake up with twentysomethings, young Maya men who work in apparel factories, and I was then twentysomething, and we watched Brazil win the World Cup, got drunk before sunrise, so, yeah, I get the soccer madness. And that morning made me a little less gringo. And a sport that bores me to bits was for the span of a few hours, during a dark, rum-soaked predawn, with pirated cable running to a staticky screen, enjoyable—a delirium.

The first reference to Manifest Destiny appeared in 1845 in a magazine arguing for the territorial expansion of the United States.[33] This was around the same time as the first organized baseball games, some played on a site in Hoboken called Elysian Fields,[34] a reference to the Greek

29. Robinson, *Field of Dreams*.
30. Clark, *Paul Bunyan*.
31. Regalado, *Viva Baseball!*
32. LeBaron, "When Latinos Are Not Latinos."
33. Pratt, "The Origin of 'Manifest Destiny.'"
34. Butterfield, "Cooperstown? Hoboken? Try New York City."

mythological Elysium, which, according to Homer, is a paradise at the limits of the earth.[35]

In its very spatial and temporal order, baseball dramatizes the outward expansion of territory and time. Centered on a node called "home," the ballfield widens into a space called the "outfield."[36] The ultimate goal is to hit a home run that "sails clear of the park [. . .] beyond the boundaries of the game itself," without borders.[37] And unlike other sports, governed by a clock, baseball has the "open-endedness" of "inning time."[38] A game can theoretically go on forever, evoking the "mythic innocence" and pastoral connotations that are related to the settler colonialism and imagining of a boundless frontier that occurred alongside the sport's historical formation.[39]

Our friends, likely not drawn into these nostalgias, marveled at the enormity of Busch Stadium and got decked out in Cardinals gear—red hats and tees. They bought one of those big number one foam hands. We busily snapped photos of each other. Ate pretzels and cotton candy. Ate hot dogs. Mustard only, I insisted.

None of us really cared about balls and strikes. Amid the lethargy of the old ballgame, we were sustained in refreshments and "atmospheric attunements."[40] The organ periodically returned to a short fanfare, a six-note sequence, da da da DUT da DUD, with fans then shouting, "Charge!" We were caught up in this familiarizing tune, a classic feature of the ballpark's "melodic landscape."[41]

"Charge?"

"Yeah, it kinda means ¡vámanos!, except it's militaristic."[42]

The rousing electricity of the wave slunk smoothly around the crowd, fans undulating, awaiting tidal advances, refrains in which, to quote

35. Anderson, "Calypso and Elysium."
36. Shore, *Culture in Mind*, 81.
37. Ibid., 88.
38. Ibid., 77.
39. Ibid., 79; Fortier, "Stealing Home."
40. Stewart, "Atmospheric Attunements."
41. Deleuze and Guattari, *A Thousand Plateaus*, 318.
42. Anderson, "Give Him Credit for the Charge."

Kathleen Stewart, "[p]ublic feelings world up as lived circuits of action and reaction."[43]

We had a blast, indulging in ridiculousness, resisting any impulse to translate baseball for the sake of cultural competence or assimilation, enjoying commensality and collective sensory stimulations, the "[s]ynthetic experiences" that are "generative repetitions of care and potentiality."[44] The improbability and amusement of being together in gringolandia, taking in a sport of absurd, arbitrary, and sedimented law and design—something like a border. We delighted in a somewhat nonnormative and liminal occasion at the ballpark constituted around confianza and familiarity, like my spirited madrugada in Tecpán a decade prior.

Civilization

There we were, hosting original Americans, people genetically, archaeologically, and culturally related to ancestors who crossed the Beringia land bridge without borders over ten thousand years ago, whose civilization supposedly disappeared a thousand years ago, whose family members were arrested, tortured, disappeared, terrorized, raped, burned alive, and otherwise massacred by US-backed military forces over the last century,[45] who were likely the only Indigenous people at the ballpark, who were granted impermanent, "nonimmigrant" visas (already verging on "illegal") and traveling with contraband (apparel embroidered with counterfeit logos), who hollered "Charge!" and made waves while occupying purchased seats on land purchased by Jefferson in the Louisiana Purchase (a big home run for America), a country named after Amerigo Vespucci, whose descendants in Chicago have gotten way off track with their pizza, a country where there are sports teams named Braves, Chiefs, and Rangers (named after the Texas Rangers, the irregular, armed groups formed in the 1830s to wipe out Mexicans and Native Americans), and Aztecs, and, up in Portland, Trail Blazers, a team originally named the Pioneers, except

43. Stewart, "Worlding Refrains," 339.
44. Ibid., 353.
45. Schirmer, *The Guatemalan Military Project*.

that name was already in use by Lewis & Clark College, which is a Missouri River ride from St. Louis to the Pacific Northwest.

And when Donald Trump imposed his travel ban, Cardinals outfielder Dexter Fowler, a Black man whose wife is Iranian American, issued a heartfelt statement to the media underlining the resulting obstacles of visiting family in Iran, and Cardinals online fan pages erupted with racism, one post telling him to "go back where he came from."[46] Perhaps meaning his previous spot on the Chicago Cubs roster? Or his birthplace of Atlanta? But Missouri itself was purchased by Jefferson to emplace African descendants there.

Kedron and I live in a trenchantly segregated metropolitan area defined by possessive investments in upholding geographical and social boundaries and inequalities, where policing is a hyperbolic, racialized system of revenue generation from minor offenses and the everyday.[47] Part of the angry interiority from which I write aims at the historical configuration of Guatemala as a china shop where authorized, bullish students and professionals without borders peruse and pick up pieces of wreckage wrought by incursions and policies long and still advanced by their own elected officials. Humanitarian aspirations hatched at a university that is a physical fortress, where the legal offenses of the students themselves—substance use, underage drinking, sexual crimes, online piracy—are not muscularly policed. Where grandiose "global" initiatives and international partnerships are built very near the "local" spot where Michael Brown was killed.

I was honored that my student asked me to lecture. I was also frustrated by the presumptions about cultural difference and college making a difference. When Jefferson famously praised the importance of an educated public for the success of economy and democracy, he left out the part about fundamentally exploitative relationships between educated and subordinated groups.[48] My presentation was motivated by an inner temper related to travels, dwellings, and relations. Emilio and Alma have repeatedly welcomed Kedron and me into their concrete block home on the outskirts of Tecpán, sharing meals and conversations, establishing

46. Ortiz, "Fowler Won't Lash Out, or Back Down, from Comments on Travel Ban."

47. Lipsitz, "The Possessive Investment in Whiteness"; US Department of Justice, Civil Rights Division, *The Ferguson Report*.

48. Conant, *Thomas Jefferson and the Development of American Public Education*.

foundations of confianza across many divides. Even though they're not living in the deepest poverty, given Guatemala's patchwork and largely private education system, the idea that Ixq'anil might go to college, let alone become a doctor, is a stretch, except for the fact that a couple of gringo anthropologists are in her corner.

Jean-Luc Nancy characterizes anger as the "political sentiment par excellence" because it deals with "the inadmissible, the intolerable," the far reaches of social change.[49] The orienting framework of global health is expertise, not anger. These are clinical vacuum responsibilities for a distanced outer zone, where maladies are timeless and bounded. But as I explained in my presentation to the student group, the conditions are, in fact, coeval and connective. Globalizing gringos wear apparel assembled in maquiladoras. Free-trade agreements allow gringos to purchase coffee, tea, fruits, and vegetables cheaply produced in contexts of poverty and exploitation in Guatemala. The scaling purview of global health (all that resonates in and hangs on the oft-repeated word "Hopkins") conceals these kinds of (post/neo)colonial histories and relations, which also include the dependence of wealthy research universities and medical centers on proximate impoverished and policed laboring classes in places like Ferguson.

"A local refugee clinic this semester," my student tells me, "a summer in Guatemala, then North St. Louis next summer, a gap year, then Hopkins."

Interventions "at home," "in the community," and "in country" are entwined, interchangeable stylings of "the them, the there." These are substitutable target populations limned in absolving technical jargon: "resource-poor," "resource-constrained," "underdeveloped," "underserved," "disadvantaged," and "challenged." Not-angry idioms formulate the effects of historical and relational extractive activities as happenstance, further ennobling postures of paternalism, compassion, and culturalism as decontextualizing forces of "anti-politics."[50] Whereas the experts are positioned as neutral and rational, the people they study and engage with are a "socially complex population," defined by an array of factors, variables,

49. Nancy, "La Comparution/The Compearance," 375.
50. Ferguson, The Anti-Politics Machine.

and determinants.⁵¹ Advanced sounding. Technical. Congenial discourse. A courteous way of insinuating that so-and-so have a bad deal. Not an inkling of anger; it's polite.

Shithole Biopolitics

Isn't this code-speak to avoid saying royally (I mean, also, democratically) fucked?

Global south. Penetrated. Plundered. Bottom. Controllable. Submissive. Behind. Subpar. Substandard. Pants sagging low. Down there. Down and out. At the bottom. Bottom feeder. Under-privileged, -employed, -educated, -achieving, -appreciative, -neath, -class, malaria nets, a spell. Cannot spell. Culture-bound. Bound by cultural barriers.

The so-called receptive role. "[A]n opportunity for medical students and other health professionals to see first-hand the challenges faced by patients navigating a complex health care system," in the words of one program report. To "reinforce core-values of service in medicine [. . .] and practice skills necessary for cross-cultural interactions."⁵²

Cultural difference and social complexity. Competence and awareness. Tops and bottoms. Assumptions. Assimilations. Accoutrements. Tailored interventions. Vibrant pictures of diversity and inclusion in the brochures and hallways of medical schools and academia. White coats. Traditional huipiles. A planet of hierarchical and disparate stages and spheres. Bill and Bill (Clinton and Gates) may be distinguished from Trump in graciously not using the word "shithole." But global health continues to operate on an outer zone imagined as a "[f]ilthy," "disgusting" space, to cite Dipesh Chakrabarty's analysis of the language and culture of British colonialism.⁵³ A zone imagined as a "strange phantasmagoria" of "chaos," "dirt and disorder," and "dirt and disease," with "unsanitary conditions" and "defecat[ion] everywhere."⁵⁴ A zone symbolically distilled in the figure of the stereotypical "bazaar," "a place where one comes across

51. Weissman et al., "Global Health at Home," 942.
52. Ibid., 943, 945.
53. Chakrabarty, *Habitations of Modernity*, 67.
54. Ibid., 67–68.

strangers,"[55] a metaphor, like shithole, to envision and disparage "a place that is designated as *outside*,"[56] where "[a]mbiguity and risk [...] are inherent to the excitement,"[57] where modernist visions and governmentalities of growth and improvement drive projects to make spaces of "urban beauty, public health, and efficient policing" and intersect with "vigorously productive and efficient capitalism."[58]

Kedron and I have conscientiously decided not to invest in tobacco and other characteristically unethical industries. We put our retirement savings in the "Social Choice" mutual fund available through our university's 401(k) plan. This fund exclusively picks companies said to have solid environmental, social, and ethical performance. Among the top holdings in our portfolio are Microsoft, Coca-Cola, Pepsi, and a few pharmaceutical companies. These are the ethical standard-bearers. Big Shots. Big Screens. Big Gulp. Extra Large Fries. And, um, what else is on the list? Hasbro.[59] Seriously. But I'm not gonna put my money under the mattress. And who knows about the future of Social Security?

Global health consternates in classrooms, competence workshops, and pizza parties over the persistence and prevalence of health problems affecting "the them, the there," while the ethical society's future and everyone's retirement depend on global flows of sweetened beverages, junk food, propertied software, and corporatized medicine and health care. To quote Spivak, "[w]hy not develop a certain degree of rage against the history that has written such an abject script?"[60]

Global health resounds with euphonious choruses. "Hopkins, Hopkins." A university sued for $1 billion for leading the Guatemalan syphilis experiments.[61] "Gates, Gates." A foundation that emphasizes profit-oriented business strategies in health care and has participated in notable exploitations and degradations, investing in Big Oil while funding health programs in regions experiencing fossil fuel pollution and related health

55. Ibid., 72.
56. Ibid., 69.
57. Ibid., 74.
58. Ibid., 77.
59. Ethisphere, "The 2022 World's Most Ethical Companies."
60. Spivak, "Questions of Multi-culturalism," 62.
61. Dance, "Hopkins Faces $1 Billion Lawsuit over Role in Government Study That Gave Subjects STDs."

problems,[62] backing intellectual property laws to maintain protections for Microsoft Office and pharmaceuticals—the same body of laws that criminalize Maya apparel makers in Guatemala.[63]

Global health is counterproductive in failing to "reason out the need for the need."[64] It is profitable across a continuously recolonized bottom imagined in terms of inferiority. It is constitutionally incapable of confronting capitalism and industrialism as drivers and vectors of ill health and environmental ruin. Enthused efforts to clean and cultivate a chimerical planet of stereotyped "shitholes" are necessarily "mum's the word" about how shit happens. I once used the word "problems" in a global health curriculum meeting, referring to, oh, I don't know, problems. A colleague corrected me, asserting that the appropriate word is "challenges." It reminded me of how the state of Texas substituted the phrase "free-enterprise system" in public textbooks for the word "capitalism," claiming that the latter term has a "negative connotation."[65]

And yet are Maya people healthier in the era of sweatshops and soda pop than an erstwhile period of widespread subsistence agriculture? Do the towering office buildings—such as Torre Citibank, of the affluent Zona Viva in downtown Guatemala City—represent such great heights,[66] a better civilization than the stone pyramids at El Mirador, Tikal, and Chichén Itzá—pyramids built for the skies and gods?

The World

A tricky thing in these student presentations and in teaching the anthropology of global health is getting into critique without devolving into revolutionary flailing, impractical theorizing, structural-violence hovering, or hopes-and-dreams shattering.

I want the students in my "Introduction" class to learn ethnographic and ethical orientations that positively influence their lives. But I fear that my vocation, for all the fulfillment of being an educator, is a market for

---

62. Piller, Sanders, and Dixon, "Dark Cloud over Good Works of Gates Foundation."
63. Aneja, "The Gates Foundation and the Anatomy of Philanthrocapitalism."
64. Cole, "The White-Savior Industrial Complex."
65. McKinley Jr., "Texas Conservatives Win Curriculum Change."
66. The Postal Service, "Such Great Heights."

spice, selling social and cultural otherness knowledge and skills for credentials within a class system.[67] I am confused and despondent as an anthropologist as I attempt to negotiate complicities, comfort levels, and conversations and keep a commitment to critique without canceling my course or continuing to run in circles looking for a corner.

When I departed graduate school to work in St. Louis—I'll never forget—Arthur imparted two final words of advice and mentorship. I looked up to him, as anthropologist and person. His advice has challenged and sustained me in many ways. He emphasized the value of critical and ongoing self-reflection. Arthur's other parting message was an encouragement to try to make some positive difference in the world—however small.

National Pastime

We were in the upper deck, decked out, out in the sun, out in the heat, three Maya and two partly unlearned, kindred gringos. Hot dogs, the rollicking organ, and the motional wave. Our friends held up the big number one hand in the middle of an all-gringo crowd that a few years later would chant "Let's go, Darren!" for police officer Darren Wilson, to heckle Black Lives Matter protesters outside the ballpark.[68]

Emilio and Alma saved up to pay most of the cost of their three international plane tickets. And we toured St. Louis, hitting up Ben & Jerry's every night on the Loop. I felt a little embarrassed and contrite.

"I wish you could see New York and the Grand Canyon and Disney World and Hollywood and Yellowstone and all the monuments in Washington, DC. You really should see Washington."

They would fly into Dulles or Reagan. Why are the two airports in our nation's capital named after gringos who fucked up a hapless country?

67. Bourdieu and Passeron, *Reproduction in Education, Society and Culture.*
68. Goldstein, "St. Louis Cardinals Fans Taunt Black Protestors Urging Justice for Michael Brown."

15 The Red Balloon

<u>little red</u>

torn and frayed.[1] poor. thing. folksy. threadbare. not purchased at a store.

you get a hankering sometimes in guate. this one summer, it was mangos. ningunos en aquellos días. no sé. i lay around thinking of permutations: salsas, chutneys, sweets, lollipops, cheesecake, smoothies, ice cream. mango everything.

and then. there was the summer when kedron and i adventurously scavenged textile markets for a week around the lake. sololá el mejor. at the end of a vendor's table, un rojo solitario. reminded me of prince's anthem "little red corvette."[2] as well as that delightful french movie *the red balloon,* about a boy who follows a balloon around paris as it whips and whirls with the wind.[3] movies about boyhood. my favs. my forever fav: *murmur of the heart.*[4] oh, my heart! *my own private idaho.*[5] oh, mike!

1. The Rolling Stones, "Torn and Frayed."
2. Prince, "Little Red Corvette."
3. Lamorisse, *The Red Balloon.*
4. Malle, *Murmur of the Heart.*
5. Van Sant, *My Own Private Idaho.*

sweet and lorn. entirely torn. of woman born.[6] my kinda guy. my kinda movies.

i fell in need with el rojo. rescue scarf. dishevels revels. colorful, embroidered design of jagged lines. raggedy, deteriorating seams and hemlines. i had to make it mine.

and then the other day on campus, la seño me preguntó, "what's with the red scarf? i've always wanted to ask."

and now i remember a joke that a friend of ours, a kaqchikel guy from tecpán, likes to tell.

i was doing something or other in the capital and caught a late bus back, one of the express red ones at that hectic stop across from tikal futura. the bus was jam-packed.

el ayudante me dijó, "¡córrase canchito!"

"okay, okay!" (now a little less gringo. interpellation. becoming. otherwise. blah blah.)

and there he was, my friend. in the middle of the smoosh. i squoze my way back to sit with him, frustrating the other passengers. (now a little more gringo. unfinished. blah blah.) he and i perked up in seeing each other and exchanged trivials, like, "how's the schlep? how's your day?"

the pan-american highway.

an hour and a half later we stepped down and out and then up and around to tecpán's parque central and along a road past milpas and that weekend i think we did eat italian, yeah, we made lasagna, went to the domingo mercado for the ingredients because i cook good italian (de mis abuelos on my mom's side), but we never could get the water to a rolling boil at that altitude, entonces la lasagna era muy al dente.

(¡córrase canchito!)

okay, okay. the joke. this friend is a goofy guy. he always says, "la seño quiere lasagna para la cena." that's the joke.

anyways, back to campus. the other day, i was in this committee meeting with la seño, a senior faculty member in another department. and she was like, "what's with the red scarf? i've always wanted to ask."

"it's from guatemala. i go there a lot. i love it there."

6. Rich, *Of Woman Born.*

a few weeks later, en route to another one of those meetings, i was wearing the tattered scarf, but this time, right before entering the conference room, i got frightened. attire. the institutional magnifier. there i was with little red, and i didn't wanna gawd forbid—to be read as some sorta id, moi, instead of the empty signifier, the operationally arid, fitted self-presentation they hired.[7] shame. yeah, it's a shame. the sense surround. at the coat rack in the hall i swung around, stealthily tucked the scarf into my winter jacket, and then to the meeting darted down.

and get this: the building—smack dab in the heart of this fortified academic garrison, busy hallway of open office doors—was robbed. my jacket fucking stolen during the meeting.

el mundo esfumó.

mi mente immediately went to mis llaves. i was now locked out of my car, and the car was stranded in the parking lot, and the kids were at school, and . . . it was an ordeal for a week.

and i forgot about you-know-what. until a few days later, work dinner with an outside speaker. as the restaurant door opened with another party, cold air rushed about our table, where everyone had moments earlier agreed: defaix chablis les lys and some sorta napa valley—and triple cream. the candidate. the search committee. and right then the chilling realization hit me.

"oh no, little red!"

sig. smidge. smitten. my pet, my baby. melancholy. the most special thing to me. de sololá. fifteen years worn. friend forlorn. and now four years sober, i asked the waiter over. drinking diet coke, i needed it harder. a cup of coffee.

and then. the weekend.

and then. monday morning. the building admin phoned.

"they found your jacket in a garbage bin in the basement."

"the keys?"

"not there."

"and, um, a red scarf?"

"yes, it's in the pocket."

poor. thing.

7. Goffman, *The Presentation of Self in Everyday Life.*

<u>sure thing</u>

there was the summer when i palled around with the students in an intensive kaqchikel language program in panajachel. gringo friends did classes during the weekdays. i read in bars and cafés. one of the teachers, a kaqchikel guy, thirtysomething (i was like twenty-four), he drank with all of us at night. he and i became friends. one sunday we were squatting on the steps of, i dunno, a hostel or something, and he asked me if he could divulge something.

i said, "sure thing."

"soy gay," he said.

i was a brash graduate student not wasting time in the language course for my press in academic books. he wore traje and was culturally and spiritually related to that lake atitlán turf. he dug my scarf. he liked to eat and drink as much as me. we talked philosophy. who knows? maybe something from my own experience was important to this unlikely camaraderie.

we embraced and, like, i just asked about his family, and, like, a context.

"no sé," he said, "no say no way."

no sé. he and i were friends. maybe we related in lost religion. maybe we basically bonded. there was admissibility there, like no pasa nada. i actually said something like that to him, like "whatever." and it was special to me—that share and at once complete care and no worries, no cares. laying bare and together being there.

a few years later, i gave a toast at my brother's wedding. i didn't talk about marriage or memories. i talked about how my brother is a brother to randoms and strangers, and how, as a sociomoral thing, jesus questioned who his brothers were, suggesting a community "beyond kinship," a "community of those who have nothing in common."[8]

my friend, an intellectual, a language instructor, we kept company for a short while, talking guatemala, and then the set dissipated or changed or the street reappeared as a clearing, and the safe density of a cloistered stair was a gone-there, and i don't exactly remember, but i think we

8. Lingis, *The Community of Those Who Have Nothing in Common*, 157.

shuffled away, and it was a sweet, fleeting commensurable between a man coded up and down and all around and, of course, inside as traditional, and a rather traditional guy reading foucault for self-satisfied spacing and every night drinking rum and planning to hop to san pedro for some fun.

the corner

when we say so-and-so is "in my corner," as in a supportive person, that's a boxing term. there's a one-min break between each three-min round. the boxers go to their respective corners of the ring for downtime. sitting on small stools, they huff and puff, wanting it to end or wanting to go at it again. they each have a "cornerman," a trainer and assistant who squirts water into the boxer's mouth, applies jellies and medicines to the wounds on their face, discusses tactics and techniques for what is coming at them in the next round, offers encouragement, sustaining words, maybe makes them angry, maybe calms them down. they are there for the boxer. the boxer is in their hands.

pepper

o connecticut! my connecticut! the four seasons. the limited access merritt parkway overpass friezes, each one architecturally distinctive. the reliable leaves and unhurried streams. the high school. the boys club. the reservoir. the charter oaks and glades overgrown. the bucolic back roads.

debris crunches underneath sneaks. i last the length of a few boxing rounds and then need a break—time out. you crack up. we plop down—a couple of stumps or a tree trunk. now what?

an idea. in baseball, before a game, coaches and players smack hits to other players at close range and they catch and speedily return the balls. standard pregame warm-ups to facilitate hand-eye coordination. it's called "pepper" for its tempo, like a dash of pepper.

okay, here we go. round one. quick. quick.

ice cream flavor

place in the city

extra spending money, spencer's or sam goody

movie

tv show

book

better lemonheads, the candy or the band

better band, nirvana or pearl jam

famous person to have dinner with

okay. break. me, cornerman: "i want to talk to you, i want to shampoo you, i want to renew you again and again. applause, applause, life is our cause."[9]

now, again, round two. quick. quick.

type of tea

way to eat cheese—no, i know, "macaroni and" . . . all right then, in general italian

food if not strawberry shake, kraft shells easy to make, or lasagna in the oven

straight man or top banana

on the roster, hanukkah or santa

thanksgiving cranberry jello mold, less or more

best song by the doors

most enviable in the city can't-afford-it store

in-the-city building been-up-there highest floor

a good memory

okay, okay. that was fun. now whaddya want to do? how about . . . truth or . . . a dare. go ahead, look up there! surface to air. ponder rows and columns of sequenced squares. a table. preposterous idea. the big bang, you know. bond, compound. like when people have chemistry. things coming together. a joyous science.[10] an etiology of love and lament and laughter.

9. Mitchell, "All I Want."
10. Nietzsche, *The Gay Science*.

strawberry fields forever.[11] and i'm gonna get "82" tattooed on me. my letters, laden. condensation. i mean, come on. i have music and i have heart.
i know how it feels, being a part. and how this here, on this makeshift tree
bench, it would never finally resolve or sum if not for the inescapable,
gravity and revolves, back to earth and the inevitable sun.

you know, they say it started from a void; everything is elemental. but
it doesn't feel accidental. it feels like a board of ladders and chutes. from
where i sit, at 82, i see across the universe to 92.

Pb

my friend went through a tragic, awful thing in high school. the lunch
table, video games, drew us together. now he works on wall street. lives
somewhere "upper." we text infrequently. he buttons about bodegas. harps
on me to get on the horn. but twenty years we haven't spoken. there's too
much. scared to catch up. scared to give an account of myself all grown up.

the date. fate. his "moms" (he spoke new york) had tickets. i wasn't
flunking calc, but very near. technically in the clear. that night in the
bronx, doc gooden pitched a once-in-a-lifetime witness, an occur. a no-
hitter, blanking, um, i forget who. but i got a tattoo. 5-14-96. random tix.
saber. being there.

this past october, the yanks were in the playoffs (again). late in one
game, a text notification. an exclamation point. "my man gary sanchez!"
the catcher hit a home run. haven't seen each other in decades. but the
skies are an ocean of ships. the air transmits. blast soaring far beyond the
playing pitch. the city. st. louis. worlds simultaneous.

sometimes it's an effort-life of working through, wanting something to
be true or untrue. we're torn and frayed—undone and forever remade. no
without or before. not anymore. a tenured colleague manipulated and
took advantage of me when i didn't have tenure, when i had so much to
lose, my career and my health, she was engaging in harassment and abuse.
she had power and say-so, and she pursued me and treated me in ways
that threatened me so, emotionally damaged me, inappropriateness
terrible to know, part of what propelled me into that major medical

11. The Beatles, "Strawberry Fields Forever."

breakdown and sent me into the hospital those years ago. and then she didn't let it go. she harassed me and wrote nasty notes. and i'm traumatized and shouting out.

we're torn and frayed—undone and forever remade. i know exactly what it's like to be couch-locked. absolute unfreedom. one hundred percent. i get it. i feel it. i'm able to say these things—to say palabras. i have a seat at the table.

guatemala. the highlands. el frío. the factor of the bundle. wool blankets. seven, nine, eleven, thirteen at a time. maybe fifteen. saber. no one cares. and the stare. frigid pila. attunements to water and air. exposures and ratchets to a world. maybe a real world.

so much time doing nothing. hanging around with strangers for days. days like seasons without reasons. street people. vendors. kids playing soccer in that, you know, that scrubby cancha in the roadside ruins that you pass on the hike to el cerro de la cruz in antigua.

public buses otherwiseness. puttering municipal parks. loafing the lake. santa catarina. santa cruz. the one without electricity. the one with yoga studios. the one with tree forts. maybe that's all the same one. saber. palopos. pana. san pedro. a postgrad phase for psychedelic coast colonizing. that bubblegum beachhead. gringo beats ready for a phish concert growing milpa and buds in between. that fog funk of expat life inhaled as bush was bombing "the them, the there." an old tz'utujil woman went up and down the streets selling kind cookies.

but it ain't me.[12] i didn't fit in. just looking for a spin—a scene and dopamine. and there, opportunity, an airy alternative along a drag of artifice and whim, gringos washing clothes and themselves en el lago, antiwar backpacker-troopers hopped up on molly lurching back to bunk beds in hostels en la madrugada as maya men and women and their kids hauled stick bundles or bundles of wool blankets or baskets of aguacates or mangos from the public transit boats up that steep climb into a real world.

an expat haunt overlooking the dock. open all night. one of the best nights of my life. yo estaba clavado en un bar como maná.[13] epic smoking on futons with a random assortment of foreigners against a hostel-culture

12. Dylan, "It Ain't Me Babe."
13. Maná, "Clavado en Un Bar."

soundscape of oasis, manu chao, radiohead, and coldplay. a friendly few from denmark and me riding high ranting about bush. i didn't realize denmark was participating in the world party.[14] "yes," they stressed, noting the presence of a danish submarine in the persian gulf. i reminded them that iraq has limited access to the gulf and lacked a navy. "entonces, the submarine?" i sarcastically thanked these proud northern people for their country's vigilant cosmo nonengagement in placid underwaters. we played protest and pretense and drank and smoked on a volcano's edge and a ledge above the lake and in a place said to be postwar. guatemala.

when the sun rose, i took a water taxi back to pana. then a bus to tecpán, where i lived in a house on the outskirts. every morning it was just me and the muchacha from an aldea. and lazy me, i hadn't learned any kaqchikel. didn't take language courses amid the vanity bonfires and wanderlusts. uneasy about glottal stops—to tell the truth, i feared inability. she was mostly monolingual. we used gestures and expressions. palabras sin palabras. she made scrambled eggs with those, you know, those dried, salted river shrimps. not my thing. but i ate them. she laughed out loud at the hard swallow on my face. she is one of the most gracious people i have known. when i go on return visits, we sit in that kitchen and have spiced tea and panes and inhabit queer silence at an apparent end of the earth.

hanging out with teenage tecpaneco apparel factory workers. way too into reggaeton, these sueteros. not my thing. (now a little less gringo. interpellation. becoming. otherwise. blah blah.) we drifted streets carefree. an escapist new wave movie. before the buzz-by era of the tuk-tuk. saunters without startles or sidesteps. shucos, atoles, cigarettes. euphoric and romantic in and about losing myself and becoming something else. losing my religion.[15]

visiting family and friends in guate, there's a ritual called, simply, palabras. it's exchanging words with another person or a group with great humility, formality, and generosity. it's an oral performance. grammatology.[16] vulnerability in language as the organic source of society.[17] being present to each other in colloquy. requisite confrontation with intimacy. laden and

14. World Party, *Private Revolution.*
15. R.E.M., "Losing My Religion."
16. Derrida, *Of Grammatology.*
17. Rousseau, *Essay on the Origins of Languages.*

leaden words. palabras, parables, plumbing (Pb). confianza kinship without guarantees.[18] maybe like the surprise and susceptibility of an anthropology.

when saying palabras, doña loops in refrains extemporaneously. multiple languages at the same time. "matyox chawe," she expresses gratitude in kaqchikel. delivers repetitious sequences for anticipation and familiarity. like jazz. hooks. grappling hooks. she gets into people. winds and works personalizing, grateful, mournful improvisations across and around the dining table. everybody hanging on words. gold crowns smile. doña peppers, crescendos, falls off for a wink, perdures, like a boxer trundling from the corner. decants and presents. pouring out plenty. spending, expending, wasting. burning. sacrificial chemistry.[19] it's a virtuosic performance of impression strings like the ad-lib pockets and grooves of a jam band concert. indexing presence and hereness in edifying individual addresses.[20] undulating waves of words. iterative and cumulative expressions, properly garrulous.

doña, don, the daughters, sons-in-law, children prod me to consume chile. a game of pepper. a dare. a heaping spoonful of chiltepe with a staling tortilla. an inside joke. "pedro," they call me. "san pedro," they go. the man who's been coming to tecpán for years, "a real tecpaneco," they kid. let's see si el rey can stomach the hot stuff. endearing sarcasm across divides. asymmetrical bonds gestured and transmitted in the timbre and emoting of palabras and the subtle gist of jokes.

18. Hall, "The Problem of Ideology—Marxism without Guarantees."
19. Bataille, *The Accursed Share.*
20. Benveniste, *Problems in General Linguistics,* 217–22.

16 Planet of the Apes

Text

Beto died. I thought you would want to know.

A short text message about a migrant worker.

It had been a couple of years since hearing from the tobacco grower who sent me this text. This was not the grower from chapter 2, but another one of my main interlocutors. The last time I had heard from him was when I visited North Carolina after sending growers my book. We had met in a small wooden office building in the middle of his farm operation. "The book was not well received in the community," he said.

He had harsh words for me. "You don't create jobs," he said. "You don't make anything. Anthropology isn't worth shit."

I did not have an answer then. I did not respond. Things felt too acrimonious for discussion, and I had not yet come to grips with the regret I was carrying.

Anthropos Today

I am a card-carrying member of a sometimes—a lot of times—bad-faith discipline of Normans and malers, seniors and juniors, mores and lesses, base and superstructure, what many experience as a hierarchical, competitive, and exploitative profession of people who more or less on whole loudly support egalitarianism and equity more or less on whole.

Maybe anthropology isn't worth shit. Maybe the theoretical sophistication, political positioning, and good intentions are ways to obscure, absolve, and validate possessive investments in lifestyle and class among the fieldworkers. Methods for making moola. For an enterprising, appropriative arboreality, hierarchies built atop and around hierarchies.

The mechanics of anthropology aren't that different: extract who, what, where. Construct—culture. A value "inscribed in the balance books, recorded in the economy of capital."[1] Teach do. It's iffy. The significant difference, real or imagined, is that this moral science extraction and investment works in various ways to confront and challenge colonialism and capitalist globalization, the world-historical systems of extractivism and enterprise that anthropologists more or less on whole more or less expound and oppose more or less.

Hotel Lobby

The more a path is used, the more a path is used.[2]

Enter the field. Works and lives.[3] Take notes. Write it down. Write it up. Control-P.

Advance and accrue in analyzing and engaging the belows and betweens of class society. Mix business and pleasure in studying "the them, the there." Clamber, climb, sprint, for "here come the carrots and sticks," an "American way of death."[4] It's a game of craps—the hard six, the hard eight.[5] It's throwing a curriculum vitae out for a time and a date. It's casting a line.

(Cue "A Day in the Life" by the Beatles.)[6]

The elevators open onto thousands of people who are saving the planet and standing in line at Starbucks. Muzak in the lobby is easy listening.

1. Massumi, *A User's Guide to Capitalism and Schizophrenia*, 49.
2. Ahmed, *What's the Use?*, 40.
3. Geertz, *Works and Lives*.
4. Mitford, *The American Way of Death Revisited*, 230.
5. Anderson, *Hard Eight*.
6. The Beatles, "A Day in the Life."

Catch up with classmates, colleagues, friends, frenemies. Oh no, the nemesis! Navel gaze (name tags). Run into or run away (faces). Eat on the fly.

Check out a late-breaking session. Listen to aestheticized stories about suffering. Call everything emergent.

It feels and smells like a funeral or a funeral casino or casino capitalism.[7] Markets smell. Some markets "communicate calm" and are "an atmosphere of cordial and safe exchange," Fernando Coronil observes. Other markets are "homogenizing and impersonal." Others are "defined by the high-energy movements of [. . .] shifting risks" or the "smell" of "fear," and "no effort can dispel a sense of disorder and lack, the stink of abjection."[8]

Sit on the floor like more or less everyone, mostly the lesses. Sit Indian style for anthropology. Sit beside and between large planters with decorative plants that are either real or fake. Sit in stirs of frantic laptopping. The hotel, the whole conference, is commotion, a meet/meat market of fashionable intellectual zonings and circuited alarmings. Flail with everyone else as frogs fall. Enmesh with the worlding sense about caring more and doing more and anthropology's crucial role in stopping the rain.[9] Plan a session for next year's conference on the Anthropocene, new ethnographies of contemporary exodus, and the politics of exhaustion.[10] Check out big-name panels. Gawk at oh my gawd gods in the lobby. Some recognizables go without name badges. For some it's look-see. For some it's look-at-me. But more or less everyone is wearing a scarf (oh, little red!), an element of style for matching, mingling, modish marathoning. For this is like any other real world. It's a day in the life and tonight's the night.[11]

Go down the escalators. Make a pitch to a publisher in the expo. Fifteen minutes—hi, hello. Browse handsome, erudite books—books for sunken library stacks, one semester's worth of use in a class, and/or burial in a desk's mounting amass. Stickers for award winners. Complementary glasses of wine. Precious titles and covers. There is something in the air.

7. Klima, *The Funeral Casino*.

8. Coronil, "Smelling Like a Market," 119.

9. Creedence Clearwater Revival, "Who'll Stop the Rain."

10. Welander and De Vries, "Refugees, Displacement, and the European 'Politics of Exhaustion.'"

11. Young, *Tonight's the Night*.

Some transferring spirit trance, a swarming market smell, a scent path of intersecting modes of being and having.[12] Commercializing, mellow spherics and tonics cloud and dissimulate the loopiness of a structuring difference and repetition.[13] The books are all about who, what, where. A collection of other others. The beats and veins and refrains more or less the same. The dismal truth, more or less, that the problems are distributional, signifying, and materiality dynamics having to do with highers and lowers.

Meander to the suite. Escalators and elevators, levels and plains leading to Salons 1, 2, and 3, the Palladian Room, the Empire Room, and the Regency Ballroom. There are pungencies, precarities, and passionate attachments in a small society working within and against systems. A small society of kings and queens upstairs, a tree museum down below,[14] and a middling belly core of Joes and schmoes and a grab-and-go.

The long medium short medium long short list sets up a setup of musical chairs.

There's a glass of water and a snack bar.

It's who, what, where. A half hour—hi, hello.

Be sure to remember the number one rule about being and having—having to be. Have high-quality leather or microfiber.[15] Have key contributions. Have guile about a research agenda for the next three to five years. Love two or three courses, lowers and uppers. Discuss strengths. No signs of interruption, disarticulation, or lack.[16] A being-for-itself is in the hot seat. Be in touch.

It's a rodeo, an unpopular remnant from centuries ago with little audience, a few big shots from Brazil, venerations of multispecies adventure, and betters and worses placed according to opaque judgments about timing, technique, aesthetics, degree of difficulty, and performance. It's out of the gates and on the clock. Hang tight. There's no slack. There are risks and injuries and glories. It's wild out there.

(Cue "Hold On" by John Lennon.)[17]

---

12. Marcel, *Being and Having.*
13. Deleuze, *Difference and Repetition.*
14. Mitchell, "Big Yellow Taxi."
15. Kelsky, "On to the Conference Interview!"
16. Ibid.
17. Lennon, "Hold On."

Take the elevator downstairs. There are literal and metaphorical revolving doors. Circle jerks holding court or holding on. Hit the hotel bar. Refer to people as quote unquote a name. When someone drops a name, nonchalantly play along in building a referential chain. This is the calling, method acting. There is nothing outside the text.[18] Having ethnography and citationality is being anthropological. Being in touch, having the touch, scanning surfaces, navigating a world, playing a field—having and doing ethnography on and within anthropology is essential for membering within it and being remembered. Getting a bite at the hotel bar is part of the process of getting a bite.

Musical Chairs

Who is oppressed and how much and who else and who opposes oppression and how much and how do oppressions and oppositions fit together or fall apart and I know you are but what am I? The words "precarity," "activism," "patriarchy," "decolonization," "diversity and inclusion," "open access," "the canon," "Ivy League," and "Chicago" are substituted into the mad lib. And no one agrees more! Seats at the table and seats near the table and back seats wanting better seats and a bigger, wider table.

The calliope starts to play. The festivities are structured around incentivizing optimism and hope about inclusivity and equity.[19] Support for the revolt. But there is limited seating on the anthropology boat. In fact, everybody is chasing down a cushier pad as they sit in solidarity with the crowds in the general admission section. Rock stars and rising stars and worker bees and wannabes all want the same thing: a little T & A (tenure in a city).[20]

Enough Already

Just a few years after bombs over Baghdad[21]—the Connecticut colonial, the snacks and military picture books, the television connected to cable—

18. Derrida, Of Grammatology, 159.
19. Berlant, Cruel Optimism; Mondesire, "A Black Exit Interview from Anthropology."
20. The Rolling Stones, "Little T & A."
21. Outkast, "B.O.B."

veteran anthropologist Nancy Scheper-Hughes described an anthropology that passes muster. Following decades of deconstruction, she proposed a stopgap to end an "obsessive, self-reflexive hermeneutics in which the self, not the other, becomes the subject of anthropological inquiry. [W]eary of [...] postmodernist critiques," she wrote, "I am inclined toward a compromise that calls for the practice of a 'good enough' ethnography."[22] Notwithstanding the relativism, empirical indeterminacy, and problematic colonial dynamics of anthropology, Scheper-Hughes claimed that methodological rigor and modest reflexivity were sufficient grounds for anthropologists to be able to make expert political and moral claims. She wrote passionately about anthropology's ethical imperative for "giving voice" and "speak[ing] truth to power."[23] She named this "militant anthropology."[24] Critique-driven research and representation for illuminating, analyzing, and combating injustice and suffering.

This grand framework significantly influenced my tobacco studies. I did militant anthropology. Because there are injustices and people suffering. Because there is tenure in a city. And there is fear of gods and idol worship. And the repurposed trees are stories about forests. Forests of symbols.[25] Forest people.[26] Every book is "another country heard from."[27] It's a felling and processing mill operation for making cloud forests and arboreal hierarchies and "really, really ridiculously good-looking" campuses.[28] It's jumping around a ditch, avoiding underneaths, losing sight of the trees for questions of how forests think.[29] The books are pulp fiction.[30] Soylent green.[31] It was who, what, where in North Carolina, the appropriative assembly of a tree fort for good-enough anthropology. It was a portrait of a still life in the pursuit of a lifetime.

Is reforestation possible on Amazon?

22. Scheper-Hughes, *Death without Weeping*, 28.
23. Ibid.
24. Scheper-Hughes, "The Primacy of the Ethical."
25. Turner, *The Forest of Symbols*.
26. Turnbull, *The Forest People*.
27. Geertz, *The Interpretation of Cultures*, 23.
28. Stiller, *Zoolander*.
29. Kohn, *How Forests Think*.
30. Tarantino, *Pulp Fiction*.
31. Fleischer, *Soylent Green*.

"Anthropology isn't worth shit," the tobacco grower told me.

Scheper-Hughes burned bridges. So did I. We wrote books about the ugliness of other people's works and lives. Scrutinized their stuff and critiqued their lifeworlds in the service of megaphonic militant anthropology.

Guilt about my work in North Carolina and uneasiness with the sanctimonious claims of much anthropology led to permissive letter writing and writing about myself. Driving around St. Louis wearing out a Pearl Jam album—wanting to be honest about hypocritical and self-serving exploitations enmeshing my discipline and institution. The denial that anthropology operates in textual and graphical modes that approximate voyeurism, pornography, consuming, and hoarding.[32] The public secrets about the circumspection, performativity, theatricality, duplicity, espionage, and conspiracy inherent in fieldwork.[33] I thought about some sorta grunge anthropology. Embracing negative affect and downbeat realism. Writing about the badness and dilemma that have characterized my work and work-life. Giving a sense of the anthropologist as complicit, self-seeking, entrepreneurial. Accepting the reality that the philosophies and institutions and income-generating activity that sustain my life—anthropology and higher education—are perhaps not concretely remaking the world as they promise.

It is not surprising that such ambivalences are normally obscured in the discipline given controlling discourses that frame reflexivity and autobiography as "associated with pleasure, with frilliness," as being "too precious, a bit too full of itself, or self-indulgent (always a no-no in anthropology)," Ruth Behar explains. These literary modes are deemed a "distraction from the reality at hand that needs to be analyzed rigorously and unselfishly."[34] The point is to "not spotlight the ethnographer carrying out the work," as Behar puts it.[35] Consequently, one effect of ethnographic writing is the construction of an ontological rift: the construction of the author as an academic expert who enters into a context and subject matter but ultimately comes to stand above and apart from them through

32. Pine, "Last Chance Incorporated"; Stewart, *A Space on the Side of the Road.*
33. Castañeda, "The Invisible Theatre of Ethnography"; Pels, "Professions of Duplicity."
34. Behar, "Ethnography in a Time of Blurred Genres," 153.
35. Ibid.

analysis and interpretation.[36] This process makes the author seem like a fundamentally different class of person than the people being studied. Enlightened. Omniscient. Evolved. The anthropologist's work must conform to genre specifications and scientific paradigms to be deemed legitimate and authoritative. The anthropologist must perform cultural ideals of autonomy, cohesion, privacy, and sanity to have a chance at succeeding in the discipline, which covers over the intimate, personal, and patchwork nature of research—and life in general.[37] These dynamics of separation, objectification, othering, and selving underpin an enshrined, colonial model of extractive knowledge production.[38] According to Behar, the genre conventions of anthropology are also an essential strategy for maintaining the discipline's commodity value, "maintaining the sobriety and respectability of anthropology within the university system."[39] It is about standing out as a science with culture knowledge products, holding onto "our academic departments; our scientific grants; the jobs that eventually allow us to settle down."[40]

Recording

"Anthropology isn't worth shit."

A grunge thing to say. This farmer who met me at his office—and a couple of years later sent me the text message—was holding back feelings of anger and disdain that were probably too deep-seated, too heated to let loose in the moment, at the whim of an impromptu visit. I don't recall many specific sentences from that half-hour meeting. But I have a lasting

36. Fabian, *Time and the Other;* Foucault, "What Is an Author?"; Haraway, *Primate Visions;* Haraway, "Situated Knowledges."

37. Durban, "Anthropology and Ableism"; Günel, Varma, and Watanabe, "A Manifesto for Patchwork Ethnography."

38. Allen and Jobson, "The Decolonizing Generation"; Behar and Gordon, *Women Writing Culture;* Clifford, *The Predicament of Culture;* Clifford and Marcus, *Writing Culture;* Gupta and Ferguson, *Anthropological Locations;* Gupta and Ferguson, *Culture, Power, Place;* Harrison, *Decolonizing Anthropology;* Marcus and Fischer, *Anthropology as Cultural Critique;* McClaurin, *Black Feminist Anthropology;* Rosaldo, *Culture and Truth.*

39. Behar, "Ethnography in a Time of Blurred Genres," 154.

40. Ibid.

imprint—he was betrayed by someone he trusted. He hurled swears across farm equipment catalogues and stacks of paper.

"We told you everything about us. You never told us anything about yourself," he objected.

After a while, he and I exited the office. He was leery of me. "Hang on— were you recording that?" He pointed to the lanyard dangling out of my pocket.

I pulled out my car keys, attached to the nylon cord.

A decade prior, we were palling around country roads in his pickup truck, with him speaking frankly to me as someone integrated into the farm world. Now he thought I was a spy.

Goodbye

We were in Austin at my parents' house visiting for the holidays, family gathered around the TV, kind of watching, mostly chitchatting.

My phone sounded on the other side of the room. Kedron, over there, checked the notification for me.

"It's North Carolina," she said.

My heart skipped a beat. Maybe holiday greetings. Maybe something situational or tragic had transpired. Maybe it was that long-awaited reconnection with the man from chapter 2.

She handed me the phone.

Beto died. I thought you would want to know.

I looked at the name of the sender. My heart sank—because of the news. And because it was not from chapter 2, the man who drives the F-150, the man who refuses to speak to me.

Beto was robust, brokeback brawn and bulk. He was fucked up a lot, a mess of physical health, an alcoholic and type 2 diabetic. He was a hard-working, up-early-for-cotton-tobacco-soybeans-whatever-in-spite-of-the-heat-and-hangovers migrant who had crossed the border a handful of times since the nineties. He was accumulating cash, remitting some to Guadalajara, and gleaning a collection of pirated DVDs at weekend flea markets throughout that sandy loam section of Carolina del Norte—action flicks, rodeo competitions, and porn.

35. Beto supervises a farm labor crew in eastern North Carolina, 2005. Photograph by Kedron Thomas.

The labor camp down the road was where the other migrant workers resided. Beto, an informal crew leader, speaking substantial English and charged with coordinating the crew's daily schedule and transporting workers from field to field, had a nearby mobile home, however shoddy and dilapidated, allotted as a perk. Every day at midday, Beto hosted the crew for lunches of stews, tortillas, pickled vegetables, and discount beer.

Across a decade of regular visits, I saw Beto get fatter and settle down. While his acquisition of properties in Guadalajara through remittances expanded, he was no longer there, perhaps never going back. Not physically there for years, for fear of Border Patrol and law enforcement and maybe not being able to return to the United States, and perhaps also because of the deepening of roots in North Carolina, with reliable sources of work and income during the wintertime and developing relationships with local white women—poor women who regularly hung around the labor camps, sometimes as sex workers.

When I returned some years later, I wanted to see Beto during the lunch break and give him a copy of my book. But I had to go through Beto's employer, the grower who had harsh words for me about anthropology and whose suspicion was piqued by the lanyard dangling out of my pocket. He initially balked at the idea of granting me access to the trailer, which he owns and which is located beside his farm office. But despite his contempt for my discipline, and for me, he graciously granted me permission.

Beto's face had grown swollen and pale, his characteristically buoyant, affable personality diminished. He was chugging beer and shoveling food. The squalor of the trailer wasn't new to me. But Beto nonetheless seemed embarrassed about cans on the floor and on a simple folding table in the kitchen. Maybe he was humbly receiving an old friend in tidying up or making motions. It was almost one o'clock. Time to head back to the fields. I gave him a copy of *Tobacco Capitalism* and confessed that I wasn't sure when I would return. Flipping through the pages, he thanked me. He saw pictures of migrants he had previously known who had moved on to other areas. No one knows where or what or whether or whatever.

"Todo bien, Pedro."

I didn't know that at that very moment he was rapidly descending, on the verge of dying. I said adios and left the trailer and drove west to

Raleigh and farther west back to Kedron's family's farm. I never saw Beto again.

The Machine

Beto died. I thought you would want to know.

I sent a short reply, asking for details.

Beto was reportedly on dialysis at a clinic in the region but didn't always show up. Migrants commonly avoid health care for fear of deportation and the inevitable impediments of financial resources, transportation, and social stigma.[41] And access to a transplant is impossible for an undocumented immigrant. Organs are illegal to purchase. The transplant system requires citizenship. Beto flew back to Guadalajara with a plan to procure a kidney there. He was then going to cross the border once again without documentation after surgery. He died at some point during this process in his hometown.

Kinship

Someone told Jesus, "Your mother and brothers are standing outside, wanting to speak to you." He replied, "Who is my mother, and who are my brothers?"[42] On another occasion, Jesus was more forceful, instructing, "If anyone comes to me and does not hate father and mother, wife and children, brothers and sisters—yes, even their own life—such a person cannot be my disciple."[43]

This is a conception of ethics as heretical and paradoxical.[44] When Jesus went to eat at a prominent religious leader's house, there was a man "suffering from abnormal swelling of his body." Jesus broke the law, healed him on the Sabbath,[45] a radical approach to morality and politics, an affinity for what Donna Haraway might call "oddkin."[46]

---

41. Quesada, Hart, and Bourgois, "Structural Vulnerability and Health."
42. Matthew 12:47–48.
43. Luke 14:26.
44. Žižek, *The Puppet and the Dwarf.*
45. Luke 14:2–4.
46. Haraway, *Staying with the Trouble.*

The movie *My Own Private Idaho* is effusive and florid to a fault.[47] There's a sequence of images—salmon swimming upstream interspersed with Mike nuzzling up to his mother. River Phoenix. Such a symbolic name!

The main plotline entwines a biblical contrast involving two ideal types. Wrestling with the affluence and power of his polite-society father, Keanu Reeves joins a group of queer sex workers on the streets of Portland, finding something communal and gratifying there. For his part, Phoenix lacks knowledge of his origins and his family's whereabouts and belongs to the road in a more significant way.

Amid the desolations of the Gipper years, released right around the time of the craze for those WWJD ("What would Jesus do?") bracelets, the grunge film poses this very question—an ethics of legalism and conformity or heterodox theology and practice. The mutuality of a community of strangers and orphans in shelled-out slums. Or the American dream of a radiant marriage, the inheritance of riches, and the mayor's mansion.

Two funerals proceed simultaneously at the end of the film. One is for Portland's mayor, the patriarch, the lineage event with Reeves, now reformed, and formally attired, in the front row beside his new wife. The other funeral is for Bob, the dingily dressed, thieving father figure who had, throughout the movie, been the leader of the lost boys. The priest presiding over the upright citizen funeral reads a medley of passages, including, "For where your treasure is, there shall your heart be also,"[48] and "For whatsoever a man soweth, that shall he also reap,"[49] passages that refer specifically to the morality and economy of kinship and keeping.

Meanwhile, at the cemetery's edge, a coterie of misfits and punks in colorful garb chant "Bob," riotously moshing, banging and clanging folding metal chairs, plodding up and down on a wood casket. Phoenix leaps and twirls, his arms outstretched above his head, pointing irreverently toward society. A close-up of his face catches him in rapture.

---

47. Van Sant, *My Own Private Idaho.*
48. Matthew 6:21.
49. Galatians 6:7.

36. River Phoenix as Mike Waters in *My Own Private Idaho* by Gus Van Sant, 1991 (Moviestore Collection/Alamy Stock Photo).

Jesus leapt up, his arms outstretched, above his head, in the Sermon on the Mount, and he proclaimed, "No one can serve two masters. Either you will hate the one and love the other, or you will be devoted to the one and despise the other. You cannot serve both God and money."[50]

Aversions to Christianity led me into the pagan discipline. Wonder and confusion about these passages still impassion me. I wake up flummoxed, sweating in agons, in debates with men about social issues and what I perceive as hypocrisies, and the question, WWJD? A tobacco grower. A conservative relative. The pastor of the church of my upbringing. My true father.

Ten minutes—hi, hello, fuck you—shitstorm, storming out.

"I know, I know, it's a legal product and an individual choice. That's basically my position," a grower told me in an interview in 2005, during my fieldwork. "If you smoke, sip liquor, it's up to you. But it still nags at me. I can't quit tobacco because I've got a family, and at my age."[51]

I quoted these statements in *Tobacco Capitalism* as part of that book's analysis of what I was thinking about as fraught moral life in a harmful industry. I did not mention that the office in which I was typing away—the computer, the books and shelves, the whole timber of the place—is sustained by a university's financial ties to fossil fuels, agribusiness, and defense contractors.

"Being a Christian," the grower went on in the interview, "I want to be a righteous person in whatever way. But I grow tobacco. Does that make me un-Christian? Would Jesus grow tobacco? Would he vilify me for growing tobacco?"[52]

After two decades of thinking about the contradictions of good Christians who, say, grow tobacco, or support harsh policies, or are involved in any number of problematic dependencies and complicities, and after asking, time and again, WWJD?, I am running in circles and looking in mirrors and studying the politics of exhaustion. I have thought about simplicities and complexities, hypocrisies and ideologies, contextual factors and kinships, corporate influences and religious nuances,

50. Matthew 6:24.
51. Benson, *Tobacco Capitalism*, 141.
52. Ibid., 140–41.

moral worlds and practical imperatives. And it just seems like a stuck moving jam. Good enough?

Revelation

After I had railed in my book against tobacco agribusiness and that agrarian world, analyzing hypocrisy and harm, the grower who texted me did me a good one.

Emmanuel Levinas elliptically defines "[t]he entire life of a nation" as "the formal sum of individuals standing *for themselves*" and "living and struggling for their land, their place."[53] People go about their business, following laws, pursuing self-interests. But Levinas also criticizes this theory of society, writing of another "way of understanding the meaning of the human." He writes of "the *for-the-other* [. . .] in which, in the adventure of possible holiness, the human interrupts the pure obstinacy of being and its wars."[54]

The grower reached out to someone toward whom he rightly holds resentment, and he did something he didn't need to do. A man whose livelihood I publicly problematized and whose professed Christianity I have difficulty appreciating. A two-sentence elegy honored the odd kinship between a begrudged, muckraking anthropologist and a migrant worker. That "send" entered through a wound. It entered a painful inner space of loss and regret related to my ethnography. A satellite connection is all there is between the sender and me. I had hurt him badly—to the point of rejection. I never really acknowledged another potential for him, did I? A well of goodness. The capacity and willingness to transgress us for the sake of us, for the sake of kindness. A good-enough ethnography fuming about surrounding social problems excluded this chance. He was forest, the pure obstinacy of being.

Good Faith

I vote. I support abolishing plastic drinking straws (and all the other issues). We invest in the "Social Choice" mutual fund for ethical savings.

---

53. Levinas, "The Other, Utopia, and Justice," 231.
54. Ibid.

There are accumulating college funds for the kiddos. TurboTax has it all in order. Oil changes and emissions up to date. We go organic and fair trade. I am personable in the checkout line and considerately hold doors open for others. We own fuel-efficient cars. We dependably pay the mortgage, credit cards, and home maintenance.

"Yet what I have to do is not determined by what I can do," Alphonso Lingis writes. Paul Gauguin fled to the Marquesas, abandoning his family for artistic inspiration.[55] What an adventure!

I didn't know that Beto needed a kidney. Giving resources to Beto would have involved subtracting from savings accounts, environmentalist cars, sustainable grocery shopping, anthropology conferences, erstwhile drug abuse, holiday trips to Austin, and cell phones to receive bad news.

Some things are undoable, such as running off to become an artist or fleeing the family to foster a suffering subject.[56] The immediacy and gravity of practicalities "prevails over what is undoable."[57] Stakes and pulls and responsibilities, keeping it all going—the little life—confounds sacrifice.

FADE IN:

<u>DREAM SEQUENCE</u> – EXT./INT. CAR – DAY

PETER idles at a red light on the way home from work. He rolls down the window to talk to the BEGGAR he sees on this corner every day on the short commute. The BEGGAR has no footwear and wears a holey raglan sweater. His dark hair, matted. He struggles, in short hobbles, strides, and skips, to canvas the cars, hampered, ill-health. One hand holds up loose-fitting light-wash jeans. His other RATTLES a RED SOLO CUP affixed to the back of a placard that says nothing more than "Thank you for your help. God bless."

---

55. Lingis, "Theoretical Paradox and Practical Dilemma," 26.
56. Robbins, "Beyond the Suffering Subject."
57. Lingis, "Theoretical Paradox and Practical Dilemma," 27.

BEGGAR

No worries. Leave it up to distributional dynamics.
The solution culture. Go ahead, keep driving,
everybody. It's all good. The donations and
government dole do make their way down here.

PETER

(relieved)
Honestly, I would if I could. But giving what I
have to the famished would give both them and
myself and my children but one meal before we all
starved. It cannot be imperative to do so.[58]

END DREAM SEQUENCE.

FADE OUT.

Ethics as Usual

Society is the solution because it is also the problem. The structuring of practicalities and habitations. An ordinary ethics of privatism.[59] Everything in its right place.[60]

I'm extremely fucking busy. The kids are driving me crazy. I'm working on us-actuality. I'm working on anthropology. I teach, I do (performatives, utterances), I work, I play. Am I good enough, am I okay? How many lives will this book save? How much will it increase my pay? NPR every day— and we donate in other ways. Oddkin remittance outlays—money from our rich-kid-tuition-dollar salaries, forwarded on to friends and family in Guate.

The disabled custodian in my building has severe back problems. There's cash for him in an envelope.

58. Ibid.
59. Lambek, *Ordinary Ethics*.
60. Radiohead, "Everything In Its Right Place."

Or there are emails of tenured outrage and demands from a militant anthropologist sent to the university's higher administration, giving voice and standing with.

Or there's a proposition for redistributing resources across all employees. But this is a university of pay scales and prestige. And I would love to know if the progressive profs who live in the exclusive school districts or shell out for private schools will be okay with "negative raises" and other changes needed to afford campus workers a larger piece of the pie—so their kids can go to the exclusive schools, too.

Or there's a formal, individual resignation in protest of the unfair labor practices.

The university hires a real anthropologist.

Or there's a switcheroo to help the custodian and Beto, too. Going all in. Checking a new box on the investment form, a different button. Moving my monthly contributions to the hardcore, venture capital, aggressive, fuck-Africa-and-fuck-everything-else fund. Higher returns on death diamonds. Straight into my friend's upper abdomen. But all the custodians have back problems. And I do, too. And there's saving for a rainy day. And what about our compromisos in Guate? What about the man with no legs?

Okay. Load the jump program.[61] More peacekeeping profits. Mass detention pensions. Banana plantations. All-hours maquiladoras. Toxic production water. Shock systems. Condos at sea. Refugee camp rental fees. Shifting jet streams. Oedipus industrial complex. Infant labor. Fingertip zaps. E-waste. The ditch.

I'm not sure where this line of thinking would end. I'm afraid and unwilling to start down that path or deviate at all from the one I'm on. The more a path is used the more a path is used.[62]

---

61. The Wachowskis, *The Matrix*.
62. Ahmed, *What's the Use?*, 40.

FADE IN:

EXT./INT. CAR – AFTERNOON

PETER gets off work and heads to the preschool to fetch HENRY. Stops at the red light. Puts the Prius in park. The BEGGAR loiters on the corner. Empty packs of cigarettes. Crumpled bags of chips. Crushed plastic water bottles. Crinkled cups.

DISSOLVE TO:

<u>DREAM SEQUENCE</u> – EXT./INT. CAR

PETER fiddles with the car stereo. Turns it down. Looks around.

> PETER (V.O.)
>> (whispers to himself)
>> Suppose God most especially pitches his tent
>> among the homeless.[63]

PETER rolls down the front door window and tilts his head toward the BEGGAR.

> PETER
>> Hi, hello. Come on in. Yeah, there's a seat. Right
>> here. Next to me, in the front. Don't worry. I'm a
>> mess, too. You can take a shower at my house if
>> you want to. There's a bedroom and all the time in
>> the world and a shelf in the fridge that's all yours.

Another intersection. PETER pulls through, becoming overzealous, as his personality is wont to do.

> PETER (CONT'D)
>> Let's be serious. A gift is truly a gift only to the
>> extent that there is an element of impetuousness,

---

63. Caputo, *The Weakness of God*, 33.

recklessness in it. Giving is a passionate act that
puts the giver at risk.[64]

(switching gears)

Are there others where you come from? Because
there is more room. Upstairs. The basement. We
don't even really use the sitting room. There are
mattresses and blankets and electric bills and
plumbing and water heaters and, Jesus Christ, how
many are you? We need another refrigerator and
prepared dinners and I've defaulted on my mortgage
and I'm sacrificing my kids and destroying my
marriage and all I've got left is tenure in a city.

END DREAM SEQUENCE.

DISSOLVE TO:

EXT./INT. CAR (BACK TO SCENE)

Light turns green. PETER picks up HENRY. Then pizzas. Then home for
dinner, baths, bedtime. Tomorrow is teaching. And pasta. The next day,
tacos. Then bistro night. On Friday, the Loop for burgers, fries, and capchuk. A thirty- to fifty-year agenda.

FADE OUT.

True Story

I received the university's email alert about the death of that man. I then
googled the news item and read about it online.

*October 12, 2018. Body Discovered near Washington University's
North Campus Building. Investigators found the body of a 20–30-year-
old white male with a puncture wound. He was pronounced dead at the
scene. The identity of the victim is not known at this time.*[65]

64. Lingis, *Dangerous Emotions*, 174–75.
65. Millitzer, "Body Discovered near Washington University's North Campus Building."

This was like a personal nonrelationship. I passed him every day for years. We have a guest bedroom.

The Regret

Beto died. I thought you would want to know.

The signal crossed a space between forested remotes, contrasting and intersecting complicities in the life and death of a stranger. A criminalized, nicknamed, more or less homeless man, a migrant whose labors fed into beneficial mattering for our own enterprises, the grower's farm and my scholarship.

I placed the phone on the coffee table in front of me and dedicated a few minutes of quiet to Beto. Candles of holiday spice scents burned there in my parents' house on a mantel cluttered with little-life portraits.

Weekly meetings at the synagogue. Weekly therapy sessions in a banal office park. Monthly psychiatric consultations. Conversations with Kedron. Family time. The catharsis of writing this book.

And things just fade, as we keep moving.[66]

Albina Press

The letter that is chapter 2 in this book was published in an academic journal in 2018 and mailed to the addressee.

I also mailed a copy to Mom. She read and reread it. Cried. Gained insights into stuff I've been struggling with for years and she didn't know a lot about. Said she was going to give it to you.

Weeks went by, and I didn't hear anything.

Kedron and I were teaching a summer course in Portland. One morning, I was sitting at the Albina Press coffee shop, writing more of this book. I called Mom. She told me that she printed the article in big font, like you like—easier to read. She wanted to put me on speakerphone, with you standing there. But I wanted to talk to you directly.

"I want to get to know you," you said. "I want to have a relationship with you. We might not be as different as you think. I don't know, maybe some

66. Nietzsche, "On the Uses and Disadvantages of History for Life."

stuff that I did . . . what you have gone through. We'll walk on the beach when you come to Florida."

I teared up. Mom got back on the phone.

"That was the best conversation I've ever had," I told her.

Harvest Moon

She smashed a cell phone one morning in graduate school. I had also shattered one against our apartment's plaster wall. We said goodbye so many times, always last goodbyes. A relationship of broken flowers.[67]

Manny quips "smoochie, smoochie" as we leave him with the babysitter. Date night. Humboldt Fog.

"Do you still think of me favorably? I hope that you do. Please say you remember how good it was. Even if it's so hard, please remember the way that we were in our own little world back when we were young. How good it was. Even if it's so hard, please recall the time that we said that we'd never regret."[68]

FADE IN:

DREAM SEQUENCE – INT. ST. LOUIS – PETER AND KEDRON'S HOUSE – KITCHEN – DAY

MUSIC CUE: "Harvest Moon" by Neil Young.[69]

Flower garden in backyard visible through broad picture window. PETER and KEDRON stand close, hand in hand, like children, like when they waltzed at their wedding. They take short back-and-forth strides as MUSIC plays on a portable pill speaker on the counter.

END MUSIC CUE

END DREAM SEQUENCE.

FADE OUT.

67. Jarmusch, *Broken Flowers.*
68. The Courteeners, "How Good It Was."
69. Young, "Harvest Moon."

Bridge

The impetus for this book is a consciousness that I have gained about anthropology, stemming from my experience as a twentysomething graduate student doing research that involved methods of extraction that were essential for me to succeed professionally. These problematic methods are the foundation of a discipline premised upon the idea of capturing the perspectives of "subjects" in "good enough" ways. Going somewhere called the "field." Doing something called "work." Getting something called "data." Making something called an "argument." For me, it was a means of getting a good job and attaining elite orbits of material and symbolic capital. And together with the rest of the discipline, I have used language of progressive ethical and political commitments to recast what is essentially a commercial enterprise as part of a world-redeeming mission. My book is a highly critical study of capitalism called *Tobacco Capitalism*. I earn royalties, and it got me tenure.

No matter how much things fade, I'm never forgetting that resounding silence in North Carolina.

Living the Dream

We'll see what happens in Florida. Your Social Security years. I'm happy for you guys. It will be modest and chill. You and Mom have worked hard for so long. Gave your kids a good life. Taught us to respect people and hold the door open. Took care of elders. It's great that you're finally on Medicare, even though you've always opposed state-run health care. And you deserve to have a place on the beach to relax and rest and eat well and enjoy life. You deserve a place that, in a few short years, will be underwater.

Say, do you remember that one time you encouraged me to do a presentation on how global warming is a hoax in my middle school science class? (Cue "Ironic" by Alanis Morissette.)[70]

Come on in, Dad. The water's fine. A wooden ship. You and me. Strangers to each other despite the biologicals and baseball games.

70. Morissette, "Ironic."

Nineties guy. Sixtysomething. Stuck moving. Who knows? We're in for a long one. Remember what you told me on the phone when I was in Portland? You said that you want to get to know me.

Have you ever seen *Lifeboat?*[71] It defined the genre we're in. Stuck-togetherness. You know—saloons, cellblocks, snow-ins, shipwrecks, panic rooms, and the 3:10 to Yuma.[72] So many setups! *Planes, Trains and Automobiles* is a total crack-up.[73] And even *When Harry Met Sally . . . .*[74] There's even some of this in the Han Solo and Chewbacca galley.[75] I call Han! These stories where people are forced into confinement or a predicament and need to figure it out.

Just you and me. I brought along a desert island trunk. The low I love.[76] On purpose, some stuff I knew you wouldn't like. You're stuck with me, Dad. Let's stretch.

Here's a mixtape that I made for our trip. I call it "wooden ships." I made it for you. Soundtrack for the three-hour tour.

1. "wooden ships"—crosby, stills & nash
2. "all i want"—joni mitchell
3. "ode to my family"—the cranberries
4. "where do the children play?"—cat stevens
5. "don't dream it's over"—crowded house
6. "no rain"—blind melon
7. "over the hills and far away"—led zeppelin
8. "le vent nous portera"—noir désir
9. "sinnerman"—nina simone
10. "i follow rivers"—lykke li
11. "sober"—childish gambino
12. "unknown legend"—neil young
13. "high and dry"—radiohead

71. Hitchcock, *Lifeboat*.
72. Daves, *3:10 to Yuma*.
73. Hughes, *Planes, Trains and Automobiles*.
74. Reiner, *When Harry Met Sally . . . .*
75. Lucas, *Star Wars: Episode IV—A New Hope*.
76. Dumm, *A Politics of the Ordinary*, 8.

14. "society"—eddie vedder

15. "ironic"—alanis morissette

16. "last goodbye"—jeff buckley[77]

    The first track. That one is for you, a classic from our road trips. Remember? We wore that cassette out, man. You and me sitting in the front of the camper. Rand McNally. KOA campgrounds. National parks. Ken Burns. All of that is why I'm a professor.

    Go on. Press play. And turn it up.

    Just you and me, Dad. We're in for a long one. This boat is loaded with baggage. You're not gonna like everything I have to say. Same for me. Nobody said it was easy. No one ever said it would be this hard.[78] I'm grateful for everything you've given me as a father. I have so much love and respect for you. There is room for both of us in this dinghy. Whaddya want to talk about?

77. See the bibliography for references for the songs in this playlist.
78. Coldplay, "The Scientist."

Credits

AUTHOR'S PUBLICATIONS

A modified version of chapter 2 was previously published as "Tobacco Capitalism, an Afterword: Open Letters and Open Wounds in Anthropology." *Journal for the Anthropology of North America* 21, no. 1 (2018): 21–34.

A modified section of chapter 12 was previously published as "Natural Beauty." *Journal for the Anthropology of North America* 22, no. 2 (2019): 90–92.

Nicholas Samaras's text on page 45 is from "Wind Telephone" in *Prairie Schooner* (Spring 2018). © 2018 University of Nebraska Press. Reproduced by permission of University of Nebraska Press.

Jean-Paul Sartre's text on page 76 is from *No Exit and Three Other Plays*, translated by Stuart Gilbert. © 1946 Stuart Gilbert. Renewed © 1974, 1975 Maris Agnes Mathilde Gilbert. Used by permission of Alfred A. Knopf, an imprint of the Knopf Doubleday Publishing Group, a division of Penguin Random House LLC. All rights reserved.

John B. Thompson's text on page 168 is from the editor's introduction to *Language and Symbolic Power,* by Pierre Bourdieu, edited and introduced by John B. Thompson, translated by Gino Raymond and Matthew Adamson. Published by Harvard University Press. © 1991 Polity Press. Used by permission. All rights reserved.

Justin Thomas Trudeau's text on page 45 is from "Stooging the Body, Stooging the Text: Jack Kerouac's *Visions of Cody*" in *Text and Performance Quarterly* (October 2007). © 2007 Taylor & Francis. Reproduced by arrangement with Taylor & Francis Group.

Tom Wolfe's text on page 83 is from *The Right Stuff.* © 1977 Tom Wolfe. All rights reserved. Reprinted by permission of Macmillan/Farrar, Straus and Giroux and Janklow & Nesbit Associates.

COMEDY

Joke written and recorded by Steven Wright on page 70 is from "Water" on *I Have a Pony*, published by Pyramids and Ponies Music. © 1985 Warner Bros. Records, Inc. Used by permission of Steven Wright.

MOVIES AND TELEVISION

Excerpts from *Leaving Las Vegas* on pages 110 and 160 are reproduced courtesy of MGM Media Licensing and Studio Canal S.A.S. © 1995 Initial Productions, S.A. All rights reserved.

Excerpts from *The Matrix* on pages 97 and 292 are granted courtesy of Warner Bros. Entertainment, Inc. © 1999 Warner Bros. All rights reserved.

Excerpt from *On the Waterfront* on page 51 is reproduced courtesy of Columbia Pictures. © 1954, 1982 Columbia Pictures Industries, Inc. All rights reserved.

Excerpt from *South Park* on page 172 is used with permission by Comedy Central. © 2022 Viacom International, Inc. All rights reserved.

Excerpt from *When Harry Met Sally . . .* on page 96 is granted courtesy of Warner Bros. Entertainment, Inc. © 1989 Castle Rock Entertainment. All rights reserved.

SONGS

Lyrics recorded by Ryan Adams & the Cardinals on page 126 are from "The End." Words and music by Ryan Adams and Michael Panes. © 2005 Songs of Universal, Inc., Barland Music, and Psilu Music. All rights for Barland Music administered by Songs of Universal, Inc. All rights for Psilu Music administered by BMG Rights Management (US) LLC. All rights reserved. Used by permission. Reprinted by permission of Hal Leonard LLC.

Lyrics recorded by Ben Folds Five on page 239 are from "Brick." Words and music by Ben Folds and Darren Jessee. © 1996 Sony Music Publishing (US) LLC and Hair Sucker Songs. All rights administered by Sony Music Publishing (US) LLC. International copyright secured. All rights reserved. Reprinted by permission of Hal Leonard LLC.

Lyrics recorded by Coldplay on pages 192 and 299 are from "The Scientist." Words and music by Guy Berryman, Jon Buckland, Will Champion, and Chris Martin. © 2002 by Universal Music Publishing MGB Ltd. All rights in the United States administered by Universal Music—MGB Songs. International copyright secured. All rights reserved. Reprinted by permission of Hal Leonard LLC.

Lyrics recorded by Counting Crows on page 2 are from "Round Here." Words and music by Adam Duritz, David Bryson, Charles Gillingham, Matthew Malley, Steve Bowman, Christopher Roldan, David Janusko, and Dan Jewett. © 1993 Songs of Universal, Inc., Jones Falls Music, and PW Ballads. All rights for Jones Falls Music and PW Ballads administered by Songs of Universal, Inc. All rights reserved. Used by permission. Reprinted by permission of Hal Leonard LLC.

Lyrics recorded by the Courteeners on page 296 are from "How Good It Was." Words and music by Liam Fray. © 2014 Universal Music Publishing Ltd. All

Bibliography

Abu-Lughod, Lila. *Veiled Sentiments: Honor and Poetry in a Bedouin Society*. 30th anniversary edition. Berkeley: University of California Press, 2016 [1986].

Adams, Ryan. "New York, New York." Track 1 on *Gold*. Lost Highway Records, 2001.

Adams, Ryan, & the Cardinals. "The End." Track 2 on *Jacksonville City Nights*. Lost Highway Records, 2005.

Adams, Vincanne, Nancy J. Burke, and Ian Whitmarsh. "Slow Research: Thoughts for a Movement in Global Health." *Medical Anthropology* 33, no. 3 (2014): 179–97.

Ahmed, Sara. "No." *Feministkilljoys* (online), June 30, 2017.

———. *On Being Included: Racism and Diversity in Institutional Life*. Durham, NC: Duke University Press, 2012.

———. *The Promise of Happiness*. Durham, NC: Duke University Press, 2010.

———. *What's the Use? On the Uses of Use*. Durham, NC: Duke University Press, 2019.

Alcott, Louisa May. *Little Women, or, Meg, Jo, Beth and Amy*. Boston: Little, Brown and Company, 1968 [1868].

Allen, Catherine J. *The Hold Life Has: Coca and Cultural Identity in an Andean Community*. 2nd ed. Washington, DC: Smithsonian Books, 2002 [1988].

Allen, Jafari Sinclaire, and Ryan Cecil Jobson. "The Decolonizing Generation: (Race and) Theory in Anthropology since the Eighties." *Current Anthropology* 57, no. 2 (2016): 129–48.

Almodóvar, Pedro, dir. *All about My Mother*. Sony Pictures Classics, 1999.

American Psychiatric Association. *Highlights of Changes from DSM-IV-TR to DSM-5*. Washington, DC: American Psychiatric Association, 2013.

Anderson, Bruce. "Give Him Credit for the Charge." *Sports Illustrated,* November 12, 1990.

Anderson, Paul Thomas, dir. *Hard Eight*. Samuel Goldwyn Company, 1996.

———, dir. *Magnolia*. New Line Cinema, 1999.

Anderson, Warwick. "The Trespass Speaks: White Masculinity and Colonial Breakdown." *American Historical Review* 102, no. 5 (1997): 1343–70.

Anderson, Wes, dir. *Rushmore*. Buena Vista Pictures, 1998.

Anderson, William S. 1958. "Calypso and Elysium." *Classical Journal* 54, no. 1 (1958): 2–11.

Andrews, Michael. "Mad World," featuring vocals by Gary Jules. Track 17 on *Donnie Darko: Music from the Original Motion Picture Score*. Enjoy Records and Everloving Records, 2001.

Aneja, Urvashi. "The Gates Foundation and the Anatomy of Philanthrocapitalism." *The Wire* (online), March 23, 2016.

Anzaldúa, Gloria. *Borderlands/La Frontera: The New Mestiza*. San Francisco: Aunt Lute Books, 1987.

Appadurai, Arjun. *Modernity at Large: Cultural Dimensions of Globalization*. Minneapolis: University of Minnesota Press, 1996.

Arcade Fire. "Neighborhood #1 (Tunnels)." Track 1 on *Funeral*. Merge Records, 2004.

Armstrong, Louis, and His Orchestra. "When the Saints Go Marching In." Track 1 on *Louis Armstrong Classics: New Orleans to New York*. Decca Records, 1950 [1938].

Attfield, Judy. "Design as a Practice of Modernity: A Case for the Study of the Coffee Table in the Mid-century Domestic Interior." *Journal of Material Culture* 2, no. 3 (1997): 267–89.

Bailey, Michael, Mary Kirkbride, and Manal Omar. *Rising to the Humanitarian Challenge in Iraq*. Oxford: Oxfam International, 2007.

Bakhtin, M. M. "Forms of Time and of the Chronotope in the Novel: Notes toward a Historical Poetics." In *The Dialogical Imagination: Four Essays,* edited by Michael Holquist, translated by Caryl Emerson and Michael Holquist, 84–258. Austin: University of Texas Press, 1981 [1975].

Ball, Alan. *American Beauty: The Shooting Script*. New York: Newmarket Press, 1999.

The Band. "The Weight." Track 5 on *Music from Big Pink*. Capitol Records, 1968.

Barboza, David. "U.S. Group Accuses Chinese Toy Factories of Labor Abuses." *New York Times*, August 22, 2007.

Barker, Clive, dir. *Hellraiser*. Entertainment Film Distributors, 1987.

Barry, Ann Marie Seward. *Visual Intelligence: Perception, Image, and Manipulation in Visual Communication*. Albany: State University of New York Press, 1997.

Barth, Fredrik, ed. *Ethnic Groups and Boundaries: The Social Organisation of Culture Difference*. Long Grove, IL: Waveland Press, 1998 [1969].

Barthes, Roland. *Mythologies*. Translated by Annette Lavers. New York: Hill & Wang, 1972 [1957].

Bataille, Georges. *The Accursed Share: An Essay on General Economy*. Vol. 1, *Consumption*. Translated by Robert Hurley. New York: Zone Books, 1991 [1949].

———. "The Big Toe." In *Visions of Excess: Selected Writings, 1927–1939*, edited by Allan Stoekl, translated by Allan Stoekl, with Carl R. Lovitt and Donald M. Leslie Jr., 20–23. Minneapolis: University of Minnesota Press, 1985 [1929].

———. *Inner Experience*. Translated by Stuart Kendall. Albany: State University of New York Press, 2014 [1954].

Baudrillard, Jean. *America*. Translated by Chris Turner. London: Verso, 1988 [1986].

———. *The Gulf War Did Not Take Place*. Translated by Paul Patton. Bloomington: Indiana University Press, 1995 [1991].

Baumbach, Noah, dir. *Kicking and Screaming*. Trimark Pictures, 1995.

The Beatles. "Carry That Weight." Track 15 on *Abbey Road*. Apple Records, 1969.

———. "A Day in the Life." Track 13 on *Sgt. Pepper's Lonely Hearts Club Band*. Capitol Records, 1967.

———. "Don't Let Me Down." Track 9 on *Hey Jude*. Apple Records, 1970 [1969].

———. "The Long and Winding Road." Track 10 on *Let It Be*. Apple Records, 1970.

———. "Strawberry Fields Forever." Track 8 on *Magical Mystery Tour*. Capitol Records, 1967.

Behar, Ruth. "Ethnography in a Time of Blurred Genres." *Anthropology and Humanism* 32, no. 2 (2007): 145–55.

———. "Introduction: Out of Exile." In *Women Writing Culture*, edited by Ruth Behar and Deborah A. Gordon, 1–29. Berkeley: University of California Press, 1995.

———. *The Vulnerable Observer: Anthropology That Breaks Your Heart*. Boston: Beacon Press, 1996.

Behar, Ruth, and Deborah A. Gordon, eds. *Women Writing Culture*. Berkeley: University of California Press, 1995.

Belton, Robert J. *Alfred Hitchcock's* Vertigo *and the Hermeneutic Spiral*. Cham, Switzerland: Palgrave Macmillan, 2017.

Ben Folds Five. "Brick." Track 3 on *Whatever and Ever Amen*. Epic Records, 1995.

Benjamin, Walter. "Little History of Photography." In *Selected Writings*. Vol. 2, part 2, *1931–1934*, edited by Michael W. Jennings, Howard Eiland, and Gary Smith, translated by Edmund Jephcott and Kingsley Shorter, 507–28. Cambridge, MA: Harvard University Press, 2004 [1931].

———. "The Task of the Translator." In *Selected Writings*. Vol. 1, *1913–1926*, edited by Marcus Bullock and Michael W. Jennings, translated by Harry Zohn, 253–63. Cambridge, MA: Harvard University Press, 2004 [1921].

Benson, Peter. *Tobacco Capitalism: Growers, Migrant Workers, and the Changing Face of a Global Industry*. Princeton, NJ: Princeton University Press, 2012.

Bento, Berenice. "Necrobiopower: Who Can Inhabit the Nation-State?" *Cadernos Pagu* 53 (2018): e185305.

Benveniste, Émile. *Problems in General Linguistics*. Translated by Mary Elizabeth Meek. Coral Gables, FL: University of Miami Press, 1971 [1966].

Berger, Phil. "Tyson-Spinks Bout Pits Rage against Strategy." *New York Times*, June 26, 1988.

Bergman, Ingmar, dir. *Shame*. Svensk Filmindustri, 1968.

———, dir. *Wild Strawberries*. Svensk Filmindustri, 1957.

Berlant, Lauren. *Cruel Optimism*. Durham, NC: Duke University Press, 2011.

———. *The Female Complaint: The Unfinished Business of Sentimentality in America*. Durham, NC: Duke University Press, 2008.

———. "Genre Flailing." *Capacious: Journal for Emerging Affect Inquiry* 1, no. 2 (2018): 156–62.

———. "Intimacy: A Special Issue." In *Intimacy*, edited by Lauren Berlant, 1–8. Chicago: University of Chicago Press, 2000.

———. "Nearly Utopian, Nearly Normal: Post-Fordist Affect in *La Promesse* and *Rosetta*." *Public Culture* 19, no. 2 (2007): 273–301.

———. "Slow Death (Sovereignty, Obesity, Lateral Agency)." *Critical Inquiry* 33, no. 4 (2007): 754–80.

Bernstein, Robin. *Racial Innocence: Performing American Childhood from Slavery to Civil Rights*. New York: New York University Press, 2011.

Berra, Yogi. *When You Come to a Fork in the Road, Take It! Inspiration and Wisdom from One of Baseball's Greatest Heroes*, with David Kaplan. New York: Hyperion, 2002.

Betancourt, Joseph R., Alexander R. Green, J. Emilio Carrillo, and Owusu Ananeh-Firempong II. "Defining Cultural Competence: A Practical Framework for Addressing Racial/Ethnic Disparities in Health and Health Care." *Public Health Reports* 118, no. 4 (2003): 293–302.

Better Than Ezra. "Desperately Wanting." Track 8 on *Friction, Baby*. Elektra Records, 1996.

Beyoncé. "All Night." Track 11 on *Lemonade*. Columbia Records and Parkwood Entertainment, 2016.

Bhabha, Homi K. *The Location of Culture*. London: Routledge, 1994.

Biehl, João. "Ethnography in the Way of Theory." *Cultural Anthropology* 28, no. 4 (2013): 573–97.

Biehl, João, and Peter Locke, eds. *Unfinished: The Anthropology of Becoming*. Durham, NC: Duke University Press, 2017.

Blake, William. "A Cradle Song." In *The Complete Poetry & Prose of William Blake*, edited by David V. Erdman, 468–69. Berkeley: University of California Press, 2008 [1794].

Blind Melon. "No Rain." Track 7 on *Blind Melon*. Capitol Records, 1992.

Blink-182. "What's My Age Again?" Track 5 on *Enema of the State*. MCA Records, 1998.

Bluth, Don, dir. *The Land before Time*. Universal Pictures, 1988.

Bourdieu, Pierre, and Jean-Claude Passeron. *Reproduction in Education, Society and Culture*. 2nd ed. Translated by Richard Nice. London: Sage, 1990 [1977].

Bourguignon, François J. Foreword to *Economic Growth, Poverty, and Household Welfare in Vietnam*, edited by Paul Glewwe, Nisha Agrawal, and David Dollar, vii–viii. Washington, DC: World Bank, 2004.

Bowden, Mark. "The True Story of 'The Marine on the Tank' and One of the Most Emblematic Images of Vietnam." *Vanity Fair*, May 20, 2017.

———. "Why Are We Obsessed with Superhero Movies?" *New York Times*, July 6, 2018.

Bowie, David. "Young Americans." Track 1 on *Young Americans*. RCA Records, 1975.

Boyz II Men. *Cooleyhighharmony*. Motown Records, 1991.

Braxton, Toni. "Un-Break My Heart." Track 4 on *Secrets*. Arista Records and LaFace Records, 1996.

Brettell, Carolyn B., ed. *When They Read What We Write: The Politics of Ethnography*. Westport, CT: Greenwood Publishing Group, 1993.

Brooks, James L., dir. *As Good as It Gets*. TriStar Pictures, 1997.

Brown, Frederick Z. "Rapprochement between Vietnam and the United States." *Contemporary Southeast Asia: A Journal of International and Strategic Affairs* 32, no. 3 (2010): 317–42.

Browning, Elizabeth Barrett. "Nature's Remorses." In *Last Poems*, 97–100. London: Chapman and Hall, 1862.

Browning, Robert. "Rabbi Ben Ezra." In *The Poems*. Vol. 1, edited by John Pettigrew, supplemented and completed by Thomas J. Collins, 781–87. New Haven, CT: Yale University Press, 1981 [1864].

Buckley, Jeff. "Last Goodbye." Track 3 on *Grace*. Columbia Records, 1994.

Buck-Morss, Susan. *The Origin of Negative Dialectics: Theodor W. Adorno, Walter Benjamin, and the Frankfurt Institute*. New York: Free Press, 1977.

Burnett, Courtney. "Avant Gardener." Track 3 on *The Double EP: A Sea of Split Peas*. House Anxiety, 2013.

Burns, Ken, dir. *The Civil War*. PBS, 1991.

Burns, Ken, and Lynn Novick, dirs. *Baseball*. PBS, 1994-2010.

———. "Vietnam's Unhealed Wounds." *New York Times*, May 29, 2017.

Bush, George W. "Campaign Speech, Bentonville, Arkansas, November 6, 2000." In *Oxford Essential Quotations*. 6th ed., edited by Susan Ratcliffe. Oxford: Oxford University Press, 2018.

———. "Remarks by the President from the USS *Abraham Lincoln*." San Diego, California, May 1, 2003.

Butler, Judith. *Frames of War: When Is Life Grievable?* London: Verso, 2009.

———. *Giving an Account of Oneself*. New York: Fordham University Press, 2005.

———. *Precarious Life: The Powers of Mourning and Violence*. London: Verso, 2004.

———. *The Psychic Life of Power: Theories in Subjection*. Stanford, CA: Stanford University Press, 1997.

Butterfield, Fox. "Cooperstown? Hoboken? Try New York City." *New York Times*, October 4, 1990.

The Byrds. *Sweetheart of the Rodeo*. Columbia Records, 1968.

———. "Turn! Turn! Turn! (To Everything There Is a Season)." Track 1 on *Turn! Turn! Turn!* Columbia Records, 1965.

Capra, Frank, dir. *It's a Wonderful Life*. RKO Radio Studios, 1946.

Caputo, John. *The Weakness of God: A Theology of the Event*. Bloomington: Indiana University Press, 2006.

Carmichael, Hoagy. "Stardust." Track 16 on *Stardust, and Much More*. Bluebird Records, 1989 [1933].

The Carters. "LoveHappy." Track 9 on *Everything Is Love*. Parkwood Entertainment, Sony Music Entertainment, and Roc Nation, 2018.

Castañeda, Quetzil E. "The Invisible Theatre of Ethnography: Performative Principles of Fieldwork." *Anthropological Quarterly* 79, no. 1 (2006): 75-104.

Celermajer, Danielle. "Apology and the Possibility of Ethical Politics." *Journal for Cultural and Religious Theory* 9, no. 1 (2008): 14-34.

Chakrabarty, Dipesh. *Habitations of Modernity: Essays in the Wake of Subaltern Studies*. Chicago: University of Chicago Press, 2002.

———. "Reviews: History and Historicality." *Postcolonial Studies* 7, no. 1 (2004): 125-30.

Chapman, Tracy. "Fast Car." Track 2 on *Tracy Chapman*. Elektra Records, 1988.

Chaucer, Geoffrey. *The Canterbury Tales: Complete.* Edited by Larry D. Benson. Boston: Houghton Mifflin, 2000 [1387–1400].

Childish Gambino. "Sober." Track 1 on *Kauai.* Glassnote Records, 2014.

Chmiel, Matt. "A Man Walks into a Boxing Ring." *The Awl* (online), June 18, 2014.

Clark, Les, dir. *Paul Bunyan.* Walt Disney Productions, 1958.

Clifford, James. "Anthropology and/as Travel," *Etnofoor* 9, no. 2 (1996): 5–15.

———. *The Predicament of Culture: Twentieth-Century Ethnography, Literature, and Art.* Cambridge, MA: Harvard University Press, 1988.

Clifford, James, and George E. Marcus, eds. *Writing Culture: The Poetics and Politics of Ethnography.* 25th anniversary edition. Berkeley: University of California Press, 2010 [1986].

CNN. "Franks Holds Press Briefing." CNN (online), March 2, 2003.

———. "The World's 50 Best Foods." CNN (online), April 13, 2021.

Cohen, Esther. *The Modulated Scream: Pain in Late Medieval Culture.* Chicago: University of Chicago Press, 2010.

Coldplay. *Parachutes.* Capitol Records and Nettwerk Records, 2000.

———. "The Scientist." Track 4 on *A Rush of Blood to the Head.* Capitol Records, 2002.

Cole, Nat King. "Stardust." Track 1 on *Love Is the Thing.* Capitol Records, 1957.

Cole, Teju. "The White-Savior Industrial Complex." *Atlantic* (online), March 21, 2012.

Columbus, Chris, dir. *Home Alone.* 20th Century Fox, 1990.

Conant, James Bryant. *Thomas Jefferson and the Development of American Public Education.* Berkeley: University of California Press, 1962.

Conniff, Richard. "Is Connecticut Really New England?" *Yankee Magazine,* June 13, 2016.

Conover, Ted. "Cattle Calls." *Harper's Magazine,* October 2015.

Conrad, Joseph. *Heart of Darkness and Other Tales.* Edited by Cedric Watts. Oxford: Oxford University Press, 2002 [1899].

Coppola, Francis Ford, dir. *Apocalypse Now.* United Artists, 1979.

Cordero, Abac. "ABS-CBN, GMA, TV5 Join Hands to Air Pacquiao Fight: Networks Unite for Historic Broadcast." *Philippine Star,* March 27, 2015.

Coronil, Fernando. "Smelling Like a Market." *American Historical Review* 106, no. 1 (2001): 119–29.

Costello, Elvis. *My Aim Is True.* Stiff Records, 1977.

Costs of War Project. "2015 Costs of War Executive Summary." Watson Institute for International and Public Affairs. Providence, RI: Brown University, 2015.

Counting Crows. *August and Everything After.* Geffen Records, 1993.

———. "Mr. Jones." Track 3 on *August and Everything After.* Geffen Records, 1993.

———. "Round Here." Track 1 on *August and Everything After*. Geffen Records, 1993.

The Courteeners. "How Good It Was." Track 2 on *Concrete Love*. [PIAS] Cooperative, 2014.

The Cranberries. "Linger." Track 7 on *Everybody Else Is Doing It, So Why Can't We?* Island Records, 1993.

———. "Ode to My Family." Track 1 on *No Need to Argue*. Island Records, 1994.

Crapanzano, Vincent. *Tuhami: Portrait of a Moroccan*. Chicago: University of Chicago Press, 1980.

Creedence Clearwater Revival. "Who'll Stop the Rain." Track 9 on *Cosmo's Factory*. Fantasy Records, 1970.

Crist, Judith. "Basic Bergman Truth." *New York*, January 13, 1969.

Critchley, Simon. *On Humour*. London: Routledge, 2002.

Crosby, Stills & Nash. "Wooden Ships." Track 6 on *Crosby, Stills & Nash*. Atlantic Records, 1969.

Crosby, Stills, Nash & Young. "Our House." Track 7 on *Déjà Vu*. Atlantic Records, 1970.

Crowded House. "Don't Dream It's Over." Track 4 on *Crowded House*. Capitol Records, 1986.

The Crystals. "Then He Kissed Me." Track 15 on *The Best of the Crystals*. Phil Spector Records, 1992 [1963].

Dance, Scott. "Hopkins Faces $1 Billion Lawsuit over Role in Government Study That Gave Subjects STDs." *Baltimore Sun*, April 1, 2015.

Das, Veena. *Critical Events: An Anthropological Perspective on Modern India*. Oxford: Oxford University Press, 1995.

Dave, Naisargi N. "Witness: Humans, Animals, and the Politics of Becoming." *Cultural Anthropology* 29, no. 3 (2014): 433–56.

The Dave Brubeck Quartet. *Jazz Goes to College*. Columbia Records, 1954.

Daves, Delmer, dir. *3:10 to Yuma*. Columbia Pictures, 1957.

Debord, Guy. *The Society of the Spectacle*. Translated by Donald Nicholson-Smith. New York: Zone Books, 1995 [1967].

Deep Blue Something. *Home*. Interscope Records, 1995.

Deleuze, Gilles. "Control and Becoming." In *Negotiations, 1972–1990*, interview by Antonio Negri, translated by Martin Joughin, 169–76. New York: Columbia University Press, 1995 [1990].

———. *Difference and Repetition*. Translated by Paul Patton. New York: Columbia University Press, 1994 [1968].

———. *Nietzsche and Philosophy*. Translated by Hugh Tomlinson. New York: Columbia University Press, 1983 [1962].

Deleuze, Gilles, and Félix Guattari. *Anti-Oedipus: Capitalism and Schizophrenia*. Translated by Brian Massumi. Minneapolis: University of Minnesota Press, 1983 [1972].

———. *A Thousand Plateaus: Capitalism and Schizophrenia*. Translated by Brian Massumi. Minneapolis: University of Minnesota Press, 1987 [1980].

DeLillo, Don. *Falling Man*. New York: Scribner, 2007.

———. *Underworld*. New York: Scribner, 1997.

Derrida, Jacques. *The Gift of Death*. Translated by David Wills. Chicago: University of Chicago Press, 1995 [1992].

———. *Of Grammatology*. Translated by Gayatri Chakravorty Spivak. Baltimore: Johns Hopkins University Press, 1976 [1967].

———. *On the Name*. Edited by Thomas Dutoit. Translated by David Wood, John P. Leavey Jr., and Ian McLeod. Stanford, CA: Stanford University Press, 1995 [1993].

———. *The Work of Mourning*. Translated by Pascale-Anne Brault and Michael Naas. Chicago: University of Chicago Press, 2001 [1981–98].

Desmond, William. "Philosophies of Religion: Marcel, Jaspers, Levinas." In *Continental Philosophy in the 20th Century*. Vol. 8 of the *Routledge History of Philosophy*, edited by Richard Kearney, 131–74. London: Routledge, 1994.

de Waal, Frans B. M. "Bonobo Sex and Society." *Scientific American* 272, no. 3 (1995): 82–88.

Dickens, B. M., A. Faundes, and R. J. Cook. "Ectopic Pregnancy and Emergency Care: Ethical and Legal Issues." *International Journal of Gynecology & Obstetrics* 82, no. 1 (2003): 121–26.

Dickinson, Greg. "The *Pleasantville* Effect: Nostalgia and the Visual Framing of (White) Suburbia." *Western Journal of Communication* 70, no. 3 (2006): 212–33.

Didion, Joan. *Blue Nights*. New York: Vintage, 2011.

———. *Slouching towards Bethlehem*. New York: Farrar, Straus and Giroux, 1968.

———. *The White Album*. New York: Farrar, Straus and Giroux, 1979.

———. *The Year of Magical Thinking*. New York: Vintage, 2005.

Dimock, Wai-Chee. *Through Other Continents: American Literature across Deep Time*. Princeton, NJ: Princeton University Press, 2006.

Diprose, Rosalyn. *Corporeal Generosity: On Giving with Nietzsche, Merleau-Ponty, and Levinas*. Albany: State University of New York Press, 2002.

Dire Straits. "Money for Nothing." Track 2 on *Brothers in Arms*. Warner Bros. Records, 1985.

DJ Jazzy Jeff & the Fresh Prince. "I Think I Can Beat Mike Tyson." Track 2 on *And in This Corner . . . .* Jive Records, 1989.

Dog's Eye View. "Everything Falls Apart." Track 2 on *Happy Nowhere*. Columbia Records, 1995.

Drake. "Passionfruit." Track 3 on *More Life: A Playlist by October Firm*. Cash Money Records, Republic Records, and Young Money Entertainment, 2017.

Drake, Nick. *Five Leaves Left*. Island Records, 1969.

Dumm, Thomas L. *A Politics of the Ordinary*. New York: New York University Press, 1999.

Dumont, Jean-Paul. *The Headman and I: Ambiguity and Ambivalence in the Fieldwork Experience*. Austin: University of Texas Press, 1978.

Durban, Erin L. "Anthropology and Ableism." *American Anthropologist* 124, no. 1 (2022): 8–20.

Durkheim, Émile. *Moral Education: A Study in the Theory and Application of the Sociology of Education*. Translated by Everett K. Wilson and Herman Schnurer. New York: Free Press, 1961 [1925].

———. *Suicide: A Study in Sociology*. Translated by John A. Spaulding and George Simpson. New York: Free Press, 1951 [1897].

Dwyer, Kevin. *Moroccan Dialogues: Anthropology in Question*. Baltimore: Johns Hopkins University Press, 1982.

Dylan, Bob. "A Hard Rain's A-Gonna Fall." Track 6 on *The Freewheelin' Bob Dylan*. Columbia Records, 1963.

———. "It Ain't Me Babe." Track 11 on *Another Side of Bob Dylan*. Columbia Records, 1964.

———. "The Man in Me." Track 10 on *New Morning*. Columbia Records, 1970.

Egendorf, Arthur. "Vietnam Veteran Rap Groups and Themes of Postwar Life." *Journal of Social Issues* 31, no. 4 (1975): 111–24.

Eliot, T. S. "The Love Song of J. Alfred Prufrock." In *The Poems of T. S. Eliot*. Vol. 1, *Collected and Uncollected Poems*, edited by Christopher Ricks and Jim McCue, 5–9. New York: Farrar, Straus and Giroux, 2015 [1915].

Ellsberg, Daniel. *The Doomsday Machine: Confessions of a Nuclear War Planner*. New York: Bloomsbury, 2017.

Elsaesser, Thomas, and Malte Hagener. *Film Theory: An Introduction through the Senses*. 2nd ed. London: Routledge, 2015 [2010].

Eminem. "The Real Slim Shady." Track 8 on *The Marshall Mathers LP*. Aftermath Entertainment and Interscope Records, 2000.

———. "White America." Track 2 on *The Eminem Show*. Aftermath Entertainment, Interscope Records, and Shady Records, 2002.

Etheridge, Melissa. "I'm the Only One." Track 1 on *Yes I Am*. Island Records. 1993.

Ethisphere. "The 2022 World's Most Ethical Companies." *Ethisphere Magazine*, Spring 2022.

Fabian, Johannes. *Time and the Other: How Anthropology Makes Its Object*. New York: Columbia University Press, 1983.

Fallows, James. "Shut Out: The U.S. Embargo on Vietnam Does Not Prevent Other Countries from Doing Business There, but It Does Prevent the Country from Rebuilding Itself." *Atlantic*, March 1991.

Farmer, Paul. "An Anthropology of Structural Violence." *Current Anthropology* 45, no. 3 (2004): 305–25.

Fassin, Didier. "Culturalism as Ideology." In *Cultural Perspectives on Reproductive Health,* edited by Carla Makhlouf Obermeyer, 300–317. Oxford: Oxford University Press, 2001.

———. "Humanitarianism as a Politics of Life." *Public Culture* 19, no. 3 (2007): 499–520.

———. "The Public Afterlife of Ethnography." *American Ethnologist* 42, no. 4 (2015): 592–609.

———. "Why Ethnography Matters: On Anthropology and Its Publics." *Cultural Anthropology* 28, no. 4 (2013): 621–46.

Ferguson, James. *The Anti-Politics Machine: "Development," Depoliticization, and Bureaucratic Power in Lesotho.* Minneapolis: University of Minnesota Press, 1990.

Fernandez, James W. "Silences of the Field." In *Silence: The Currency of Power,* edited by Maria-Luisa Achino-Loeb, 158–73. New York: Berghahn Books, 2006.

Figgis, Mike, dir. *Leaving Las Vegas.* United Artists, 1995.

Filoni, David, dir. *Star Wars: The Clone Wars.* Warner Bros., 2008.

Fischer, Edward F., and Peter Benson. *Broccoli and Desire: Global Connections and Maya Struggles in Postwar Guatemala.* Stanford, CA: Stanford University Press, 2006.

Fischer, Michael M. J. *Anthropology in the Meantime: Experimental Ethnography, Theory, and Method for the Twenty-First Century.* Durham, NC: Duke University Press, 2018.

———. *Emergent Forms of Life and the Anthropological Voice.* Durham, NC: Duke University Press, 2003.

Fitzgerald, F. Scott. "Benediction." In *Flappers and Philosophers,* 141–56. New York: Scribner, 1959 [1920].

———. *The Great Gatsby.* Edited by James L. W. West III. New York: Scribner, 2018 [1925].

Fitzgerald, Scott. "Local Family Says Unidentified Soldier Is Their Flesh and Blood." *Southern Illinoisan,* June 24, 2012.

Fleischer, Richard, dir. *Soylent Green.* Metro-Goldwyn-Mayer Studios, 1973.

Ford, John, dir. *Stagecoach.* United Artists, 1939.

Fortenberry, J. D. "Puberty and Adolescent Sexuality." *Hormones and Behavior* 64, no. 2 (2013): 280–87.

Fortier, Craig. "Stealing Home: Decolonizing Baseball's Origin Stories and Their Relations to Settler Colonialism." *Settler Colonial Studies* 6, no. 1 (2016): 1–22.

Foucault, Michel. *The Archaeology of Knowledge.* Translated by A. M. Sheridan Smith. New York: Pantheon, 1972 [1969].

———. *The Birth of the Clinic: An Archaeology of Medical Perception.* Translated by A. M. Sheridan Smith. New York: Vintage, 1973 [1963].

———. *Discipline and Punish: The Birth of the Prison.* Translated by A. M. Sheridan Smith. New York: Vintage, 1977 [1975].

———. *Fearless Speech.* Edited by Joseph Pearson. Los Angeles: Semiotext(e), 2001 [1983].

———. "Friendship as a Way of Life." In *Ethics: Subjectivity and Truth.* Vol. 1 of *The Essential Works of Foucault, 1954–1984,* edited by Paul Rabinow, interview by René Coccatty, Jean Danet, and Jean Le Bitoux, translated by John Johnston, 135–40. New York: New Press, 1997 [1981].

———. *The History of Sexuality.* Vol. 1, *An Introduction.* Translated by Robert Hurley. New York: Pantheon, 1978 [1976].

———. *Les mots et les choses: Une archéologie des sciences humaines.* Paris: Éditions Gallimard, 1966.

———. "Nietzsche, Genealogy, History." In *Aesthetics, Method, and Epistemology.* Vol. 2 of *The Essential Works of Foucault, 1954–1984,* edited by James D. Faubion, translated by Donald F. Bouchard and Sherry Simon, 369–91. New York: New Press, 1998 [1971].

———. "On the Genealogy of Ethics: An Overview of Work in Progress." In *Ethics: Subjectivity and Truth.* Vol. 1 of *The Essential Works of Foucault, 1954–1984,* edited by Paul Rabinow, interview by Hubert L. Dreyfus and Paul Rabinow, 253–80. New York: New Press, 1997 [1983].

———. *The Order of Things: An Archaeology of the Human Sciences.* Translated by A. M. Sheridan Smith. New York: Vintage, 1970 [1966].

———. "Sex, Power, and the Politics of Identity." In *Ethics: Subjectivity and Truth.* Vol. 1 of *The Essential Works of Foucault, 1954–1984,* edited by Paul Rabinow, interview by Bob Gallagher and Alexander Wilson, 163–73. New York: New Press, 1997 [1982].

———. "Structuralism and Post-Structuralism." In *Aesthetics, Method, and Epistemology.* Vol. 2 of *The Essential Works of Foucault, 1954–1984,* edited by James D. Faubion, interview by Gérard Raulet, translated by Jeremy Harding, 433–58. New York: New Press, 1998 [1983].

———. "Truth, Power, Self: An Interview with Michel Foucault, October 25, 1982." In *Technologies of the Self: A Seminar with Michel Foucault,* edited by Luther H. Martin, Huck Gutman, and Patrick H. Hutton, interview by Rux Martin, 9–15. Amherst: University of Massachusetts Press, 1988 [1982].

———. "What Is an Author?" In *Aesthetics, Method, and Epistemology.* Vol. 2 of *The Essential Works of Foucault, 1954–1984,* edited by James D. Faubion, translated by Josué V. Harari, 205–22. New York: New Press, 1998 [1969].

———. *Wrong-Doing, Truth-Telling: The Function of Avowal in Justice.* Edited by Fabienne Brion and Bernard E. Harcourt. Translated by Stephen W. Sawyer. Chicago: University of Chicago Press, 2014 [1981].

Freud, Sigmund. *Beyond the Pleasure Principle.* In vol. 18 (1920–1922) of *The Standard Edition of the Complete Psychological Works of Sigmund Freud,* translated by James Strachey, in collaboration with Anna Freud, assisted by Alix Strachey and Alan Tyson, 1–64. London: Hogarth Press, 1955 [1920].

———. "Mourning and Melancholia." In *On Murder, Mourning, and Melancholia,* edited by Adam Phillips, translated by Shaun Whiteside, 201–18. New York: Penguin, 2005 [1917].

Gabaccia, Donna R. *We Are What We Eat: Ethnic Food and the Making of Americans.* Cambridge, MA: Harvard University Press, 1998.

Gado, Frank. *The Passion of Ingmar Bergman.* Durham, NC: Duke University Press, 1986.

Gaston, Bill. *The Good Body.* Toronto: House of Anansi, 2000.

Geertz, Clifford. *The Interpretation of Cultures: Selected Essays.* New York: Basic Books, 1973.

———. *Works and Lives: The Anthropologist as Author.* Stanford, CA: Stanford University Press, 1989.

George Baker Selection. "Little Green Bag." Track 1 on *Little Green Bag.* Colossus Records, 1970.

Gildea, William. "Color of Money Is Gold for Tyson-Spinks." *Washington Post,* June 16, 1988.

Gin Blossoms. "Found Out about You." Track 8 on *New Miserable Experience.* A&M Records, 1992.

———. "Hey Jealousy." Track 2 on *New Miserable Experience.* A&M Records, 1992.

Ginsberg, Allen. "Howl." In *Collected Poems 1947–1997,* 134–41. New York: HarperCollins, 2006 [1956].

Ginsberg, Faye D. "The Case of Mistaken Identity: Problems in Representing Women on the Right." In *When They Read What We Write: The Politics of Ethnography,* edited by Carolyn B. Brettell, 163–76. Westport, CT: Greenwood Publishing Group, 1993.

Glass, Philip. *The Fog of War (A Film by Errol Morris): Music by Philip Glass.* Orange Mountain Music, 2003.

Glück, Louise. "A Summer Garden." In *Faithful and Virtuous Night,* 64–70. New York: Farrar, Straus and Giroux, 2014.

Godard, Jean-Luc, dir. *Band of Outsiders.* Columbia Films, 1964.

———, dir. *La Chinoise.* Athos Films, 1967.

Goffman, Erving. *The Presentation of Self in Everyday Life.* New York: Anchor Books, 1959.

Goldstein, Patrick. "Jimmy Swaggart Blasts Rock Porn." *Los Angeles Times,* August 3, 1986.

Goldstein, Sasha. "St. Louis Cardinals Fans Taunt Black Protestors Urging Justice for Michael Brown." *New York Daily News,* October 7, 2014.

Goodell, Gregory. *Independent Feature Film Production: A Complete Guide from Concept to Distribution.* Rev. ed. New York: St. Martin's Press, 1998 [1982].

Goo Goo Dolls. "Ain't That Unusual." Track 9 on *A Boy Named Goo.* Metal Blade Records and Warner Bros. Records, 1995.

———. "Black Balloon." Track 5 on *Dizzy Up the Girl.* Warner Bros. Records, 1998.

———. "Iris." Track 11 on *Dizzy Up the Girl.* Warner Bros. Records, 1998.

———. "Name." Track 6 on *A Boy Named Goo.* Metal Blade Records and Warner Bros. Records, 1995.

Gramsci, Antonio. *Prison Notebooks.* Vol. 3. Edited and translated by Joseph A. Buttigieg. New York: Columbia University Press, 2007 [1930–31].

Grandin, Greg. "Guatemalan Slaughter Was Part of Reagan's Hard Line." *New York Times,* May 21, 2013.

Grant, Beata. *Eminent Nuns: Women Chan Masters of Seventeenth-Century China.* Honolulu: University of Hawai'i Press, 2009.

Grateful Dead. "Sugar Magnolia." Track 3 on *American Beauty.* Warner Bros. Records, 1970.

Graves, Robert. *Good-Bye to All That: An Autobiography.* Rev. 2nd ed. New York: Anchor Books, 1998 [1929].

Gray, Rockwell. "Autobiography Now." *Kenyon Review* 4, no. 1 (1982): 31–55.

Greeley, Alexandra. "Phở: The Vietnamese Addiction." *Gastronomica* 2, no. 1 (2002): 80–83.

Greenberg, Harvey R. "My Own Private Idaho." *Film Quarterly* 46, no. 1 (1992): 23–25.

Grieco, Allen J. "Food and Social Classes in Medieval and Renaissance Italy." In *Food: A Culinary History from Antiquity to the Present,* edited by Jean-Louis Flandrin and Massimo Montanari (English ed. edited by Albert Sonnenfeld), translated by Clarissa Botsford, Arthur Goldhammer, Charles Lambert, Frances M. López-Morillas, and Sylvia Stevens, 302–12. New York: Columbia University Press, 1999 [1996].

Grier, Katherine C. *Culture and Comfort: Parlor Making and Middle-Class Identity, 1850–1930.* Rev. ed. Washington, DC: Smithsonian Books, 2010 [1988].

Guest, Haden. "Norman Mailer Collection." Harvard Film Archive (online), September 21–23, 2007.

Günel, Gökçe, Saiba Varma, and Chika Watanabe. "A Manifesto for Patchwork Ethnography." *Fieldsights* (online), June 9, 2020.

Gupta, Akhil, and James Ferguson, eds. *Anthropological Locations: Boundaries and Grounds of a Field Science.* Berkeley: University of California Press, 1997.

———, eds. *Culture, Power, Place: Explorations in Critical Anthropology.* Durham, NC: Duke University Press, 1997.

Gusterson, Hugh. "Studying Up Revisited." *PoLAR: Political and Legal Anthropology Review* 20, no. 1 (1997): 114–19.

Gutschow, Kim. "What Makes a Nun? Apprenticeship and Ritual Passage in Zanskar, India." *Journal of the International Association of Buddhist Studies* 24, no. 2 (2001): 187–215.

Habermas, Jürgen. *The Theory of Communicative Action*. Vol. 1, *Reason and the Rationalization of Society*. Translated by Thomas McCarthy. Boston: Beacon Press, 1984 [1981].

Halberstam, Jack. *The Queer Art of Failure*. Durham, NC: Duke University Press, 2011.

Hall, Stuart. "The Problem of Ideology—Marxism without Guarantees." *Journal of Communication Inquiry* 10, no. 2 (1986): 28–44.

Handelman, Susan A. *Fragments of Redemption: Jewish Thought and Literary Theory in Benjamin, Scholem, and Levinas*. Bloomington: Indiana University Press, 1991.

Haraway, Donna J. *Primate Visions: Gender, Race, and Nature in the World of Modern Science*. London: Routledge, 1989.

———. "Situated Knowledges: The Science Question in Feminism and the Privilege of Partial Perspective." *Feminist Studies* 14, no. 3 (1988): 575–99.

———. *Staying with the Trouble: Making Kin in the Chthulucene*. Durham, NC: Duke University Press, 2016.

Hardt, Michael, and Antonio Negri. *Multitude: War and Democracy in the Age of Empire*. New York: Penguin, 2004.

Hariman, Robert, and John Lucaites. "Public Identity and Collective Memory in U.S. Iconic Photography: The Image of 'Accidental Napalm.'" *Critical Studies in Media Communication* 20, no. 1 (2003): 35–66.

Harman, Graham. *Tool-Being: Heidegger and the Metaphysics of Objects*. Chicago: Open Court, 2002.

Harrison, Faye V., ed. *Decolonizing Anthropology: Moving Further toward an Anthropology for Liberation*. 3rd ed. Arlington, VA: American Anthropological Association, 2010 [1991].

Hasbro, Inc. *Playing with Purpose: 2016 Corporate Social Responsibility Report*. Hasbro (online), 2016.

Hausmann, Vincent. "Envisioning the (W)hole World 'Behind Things': Denying Otherness in *American Beauty*." *Camera Obscura* 19, no. 1 (2004): 112–49.

Hedling, Erik. "Shame: Ingmar Bergman's Vietnam War." *Nordicom Review* 29, no. 2 (2008): 245–59.

Henley, Don. "The Boys of Summer." Track 1 on *Building the Perfect Beast*. Geffen Records, 1984.

Herdt, Gilbert. *Guardians of the Flutes*. Vol. 1, *Idioms of Masculinity*. Chicago: University of Chicago Press, 1994 [1981].

Hey, Valerie. "Valerie's Poem." In *Hidden Loss: Miscarriage & Ectopic Pregnancy*. 2nd ed., edited by Valerie Hey, Catherine Itzin, Lesley Saunders, and Mary Anne Speakman, 8–9. London: Women's Press, 1996 [1989].

Hey, Valerie, Catherine Itzin, Lesley Saunders, and Mary Anne Speakman, eds. *Hidden Loss: Miscarriage & Ectopic Pregnancy*. 2nd ed. London: Women's Press, 1996 [1989].

Hitchcock, Alfred, dir. *Lifeboat*. 20th Century Fox, 1944.

———, dir. *Vertigo*. Paramount Pictures, 1958.

Holmes, Charles. "Kanye West, despite Himself, Is Bigger than Ever." *Rolling Stone*, October 25, 2019.

Horden, Peregrine, and Nicholas Purcell. "The Mediterranean and 'the New Thalassology.'" *American Historical Review* 111, no. 3 (2006): 722–40.

Horkheimer, Max, and Theodor W. Adorno. *Dialectic of Enlightenment: Philosophical Fragments*. Edited by Gunzelin Schmid Noerr. Translated by Edmund Jephcott. Stanford, CA: Stanford University Press, 2002 [1947].

Hornby, Nick. *About a Boy*. New York: Riverhead Books, 1998.

Horwitz, Richard P. "Just Stories of Ethnographic Authority." In *When They Read What We Write: The Politics of Ethnography*, edited by Caroline B. Brettell, 131–43. Westport, CT: Greenwood Publishing Group, 1994.

Howard, Ron, dir. *Cocoon*. 20th Century Fox, 1985.

Hughes, John, dir. *Ferris Bueller's Day Off*. Paramount Pictures, 1986.

———, dir. *Planes, Trains and Automobiles*. Paramount Pictures, 1987.

———, dir. *Sixteen Candles*. Universal Pictures, 1984.

Human Rights Watch. *Needless Deaths in the Gulf War: Civilian Casualties during the Air Campaign and Violations of the Laws of War*. New York: Human Rights Watch, 1991.

Hume, David. *A Treatise of Human Nature*. Vol. 1, *Texts*. The Clarendon Edition of the Works of David Hume. Edited by David Fate Norton and Mary J. Norton. Oxford: Oxford University Press, 2007 [1739].

Husserl, Edmund. *Logical Investigations*. Vol. 1. Edited by Dermot Moran. Translated by J. N. Findlay. London: Routledge, 2001 [1900–1901].

Imbruglia, Natalie. "Torn." Track 1 on *Left of the Middle*. RCA Records, 1997.

Irizarry, Lisa. "'Monopoly': How Board Game Got Its Boardwalk." *Seattle Times*, April 22, 2005.

Jackson, Peter, dir. *Lord of the Rings: The Fellowship of the Ring*. New Line Cinema, 2001.

The Jackson 5. "ABC." Track 3 on *ABC*. Motown Records, 1970.

James, Henry. *The Portrait of a Lady*. Edited by Philip Horne. New York: Penguin, 2011 [1881].

———. *The Wings of the Dove*. Edited by Millicent Bell. New York: Penguin, 2008 [1909].

Jamison, Kay Redfield. *An Unquiet Mind: A Memoir of Moods and Madness.* New York: Vintage, 1996.

Jarmusch, Jim, dir. *Broken Flowers.* Focus Features, 2005.

Jay-Z. "4:44." Track 5 on *4:44.* Roc Nation, 2017.

Jobson, Ryan Cecil. "The Case for Letting Anthropology Burn: Sociocultural Anthropology in 2019." *American Anthropologist* 122, no. 2 (2020): 259–71.

Judge, Mike, dir. *Office Space.* 20th Century Fox, 1999.

Kazan, Elia, dir. *On the Waterfront.* Columbia Pictures, 1954.

Kelly, Michael. "The American Way of War." *Atlantic,* June 2002.

Kelly, Richard, dir. *Donnie Darko.* Newmarket Films, 2001.

Kelsky, Karen. "On to the Conference Interview!" *The Professor Is In* (online), November 2, 2011.

Ker, David. "England in Old Times." *New York Times,* November 13, 1887.

Kerouac, Jack. *Visions of Cody.* New York: Penguin, 1993 [1972].

Kifner, John. "From Bombs to Burgers, Gulf War Involves Biggest Supply Effort Ever." *New York Times,* February 4, 1991.

The Killers. *Hot Fuss.* Island Records, 2004.

King, Carole. "It's Too Late." Track 3 on *Tapestry.* Ode Records, 1971.

King, Martin Luther, Jr. "I Have a Dream." In *A Testament of Hope: The Essential Writings and Speeches of Martin Luther King, Jr.,* edited by James Melvin Washington, 217–20. New York: HarperCollins, 1986 [1963].

Kleinman, Arthur. "'Everything That Really Matters': Social Suffering, Subjectivity, and the Remaking of Human Experience in a Disordering World." *Harvard Theological Review* 90, no. 3 (1997): 315–35.

———. "Experience and Its Moral Modes: Culture, Human Conditions, and Disorder." In *The Tanner Lectures on Human Values,* vol. 20, edited by G. B. Peterson, 357–420. Salt Lake City: University of Utah Press, 1999.

———. *The Illness Narratives: Suffering, Healing, and the Human Condition.* New York: Basic Books, 1988.

———. *What Really Matters: Living a Moral Life amidst Uncertainty and Danger.* Oxford: Oxford University Press, 2007.

Kleinman, Arthur, and Peter Benson. "Anthropology in the Clinic: The Problem of Cultural Competency and How to Fix It." *PLoS Medicine* 3, no. 10 (2006): e294.

Klima, Alan. *The Funeral Casino: Meditation, Massacre, and Exchange with the Dead in Thailand.* Princeton, NJ: Princeton University Press, 2009.

Klugh, Elgin L. "Delmos Jones and the End of Neutrality." In *The Second Generation of African American Pioneers in Anthropology,* edited by Ira E. Harrison, Deborah Johnson-Simon, and Erica Lorraine Williams, 52–67. Urbana: University of Illinois Press, 2018.

Kohn, Eduardo. *How Forests Think: Toward an Anthropology beyond the Human.* Berkeley: University of California Press, 2013.

Krabill, Ron. "American Sentimentalism and the Production of Global Citizens." *Contexts* 11, no. 4 (2012): 52–54.

Kravitz, Lenny. "It Ain't Over 'Til It's Over." Track 4 on *Mama Said.* Virgin Records, 1991.

Kruger, Daniel J., and Susan M. Hughes. "Tendencies to Fall Asleep First after Sex Are Associated with Greater Partner Desires for Bonding and Affection." *Journal of Social, Evolutionary, and Cultural Psychology* 5, no. 4 (2011): 239–47.

Kubrick, Stanley, dir. *Dr. Strangelove or: How I Learned to Stop Worrying and Love the Bomb.* Columbia Pictures, 1964.

———, dir. *The Shining.* Warner Bros., 1980.

Lacan, Jacques. *The Four Fundamental Concepts of Psychoanalysis: The Seminar of Jacques Lacan.* Book 11. Edited by Jacques-Alain Miller. Translated by Alan Sheridan. New York: W. W. Norton, 1981 [1973].

———. "The Function and Field of Language in Psychoanalysis." In *Écrits: The First Complete Edition in English,* translated by Bruce Fink in collaboration with Héloïse Fink and Russell Grigg, 197–268. New York: W. W. Norton, 2006 [1966].

———. *The Object Relation: The Seminar of Jacques Lacan.* Book 4. Edited by Jacques-Alain Miller. Translated by A. R. Price. Cambridge: Polity, 2020 [1956–57].

———. *The Other Side of Psychoanalysis: The Seminar of Jacques Lacan.* Book 17. Edited by Jacques-Alain Miller. Translated by Russell Grigg. New York: W. W. Norton, 2007 [1969–70].

———. "Seminar on 'The Purloined Letter.'" In *Écrits: The First Complete Edition in English,* translated by Bruce Fink in collaboration with Héloïse Fink and Russell Grigg, 7–48. New York: W. W. Norton, 2006 [1966].

Lambek, Michael, ed. *Ordinary Ethics: Anthropology, Language, and Action.* New York: Fordham University Press, 2010.

Lamont, Michèle. *The Dignity of Working Men: Morality and the Boundaries of Race, Class, and Immigration.* New York: Russell Sage Foundation, 2000.

Lamont, Roscoe. "Planet Notes." *Popular Astronomy* 29, no. 6 (1921): 340–48.

Lamorisse, Albert, dir. *The Red Balloon.* Lopert Pictures, 1956.

lang, k. d. "Constant Craving." Track 10 on *Ingénue.* Sire Records, 1992.

Lasseter, John, dir. *Toy Story.* Pixar Animation Studios, 1995.

Latour, Bruno. *Reassembling the Social: An Introduction to Actor-Network-Theory.* Oxford: Oxford University Press, 2005.

———. *We Have Never Been Modern.* Translated by Catherine Porter. Cambridge, MA: Harvard University Press, 1993 [1991].

Layne, Linda L. *Motherhood Lost: A Feminist Account of Pregnancy Loss in America*. London: Routledge, 2003.

Leavens, David A., and Kim A. Bard. "Tickling." *Current Biology* 26, no. 3 (2016): R91–R93.

LeBaron, Alan. "When Latinos Are Not Latinos: The Case of Guatemalan Maya in the United States, the Southeast and Georgia." *Latino Studies* 10, no. 1–2 (2012): 179–95.

Led Zeppelin. "Over the Hills and Far Away." Track 3 on *Houses of the Holy*. Atlantic Records, 1973.

Lee, Ang, dir. *The Ice Storm*. 20th Century Fox, 1997.

Lennon, John. "Hold On." Track 2 on *John Lennon/Plastic Ono Band*. Apple Records, 1970.

Lennon, John, and Yoko Ono. "Beautiful Boy (Darling Boy)." Track 7 on *Double Fantasy*. Geffen Records, 1980.

Levinas, Emmanuel. *Existence and Existents*. Translated by Alphonso Lingis. Pittsburgh, PA: Duquesne University Press, 2001 [1947].

———. *On Escape: De l'évasion*. Translated by Bettina Bergo. Stanford, CA: Stanford University Press, 2003 [1935].

———. "The Other, Utopia, and Justice." In *Entre Nous: Thinking-of-the-Other*, translated by Michael B. Smith and Barbara Harshav, 223–33. New York: Columbia University Press, 1998 [1991].

———. *Otherwise than Being, or Beyond Essence*. Translated by Alphonso Lingis. Pittsburgh, PA: Duquesne University Press, 1981 [1974].

———. "The Philosopher and Death." In *Alterity and Transcendence*, interview by Christian Chabanis, translated by Michael B. Smith, 153–68. New York: Columbia University Press, 1999 [1982].

———. *Time and the Other*. Translated by Richard A. Cohen. Pittsburgh, PA: Duquesne University Press, 1987 [1947].

———. *Totality and Infinity: An Essay on Exteriority*. Translated by Alphonso Lingis. Pittsburgh, PA: Duquesne University Press, 1969 [1961].

———. "The Trace of the Other." In *Deconstruction in Context: Literature and Philosophy*, edited by Mark C. Taylor, translated by Alphonso Lingis, 345–59. Chicago: University of Chicago Press, 1986 [1963].

Levi-Strauss, Claude. *Tristes Tropiques*. Translated by John Weightman and Doreen Weightman. New York: Penguin, 2012 [1955].

Limon, John. *Stand-Up Comedy in Theory, or, Abjection in America*. Durham, NC: Duke University Press, 2000.

Lingis, Alphonso. "Anger." In *On Jean-Luc Nancy: The Sense of Philosophy*, edited by Darren Sheppard, Simon Sparks, and Colin Thomas, 197–215. London: Routledge, 1997.

———. *The Community of Those Who Have Nothing in Common*. Bloomington: Indiana University Press, 1995.

———. *Dangerous Emotions*. Berkeley: University of California Press, 2000.

———. *The Imperative*. Bloomington: Indiana University Press, 1998.

———. *Irrevocable: A Philosophy of Mortality*. Chicago: University of Chicago Press, 2018.

———. "Theoretical Paradox and Practical Dilemma." *International Journal of Philosophical Studies* 12, no. 1 (2004): 21–28.

———. "To Die with Others." *Diacritics* 30, no. 3 (2000): 106–13.

Linklater, Richard, dir. *Slacker*. Orion Classics, 1990.

Linklater, Richard, and Kim Krizan. *Before Sunrise*. In *Before Sunrise and Before Sunset: Two Screenplays*, by Richard Linklater, 1–109. New York: Vintage, 2005 [1995].

Lipsitz, George. "The Possessive Investment in Whiteness: Racialized Social Democracy and the 'White' Problem in American Studies." *American Quarterly* 47, no. 3 (1995): 369–87.

Loggins, Kenny. "This Is It." Track 3 on *Keep the Fire*. Columbia Records, 1979.

Long, Steven, Derek Jacques, and Paula Kepos, eds. *International Directory of Company Histories*. Vol. 223, s.v. "Hasbro, Inc." Farmington Hills, MI: St. James Press, 1997.

Love, Heather. *Feeling Backward: Loss and the Politics of Queer History*. Cambridge, MA: Harvard University Press, 2007.

Lubitsch, Ernst, dir. *Design for Living*. Paramount Pictures, 1933.

Lucas, George, dir. *Star Wars: Episode IV—A New Hope*. 20th Century Fox, 1977.

Lykke Li. "I Follow Rivers." Track 2 on *Wounded Rhymes*. Atlantic Records, 2011.

Lynch, David, dir. *Mulholland Drive*. Universal Pictures, 2001.

Lyotard, Jean-François. *The Postmodern Condition: A Report on Knowledge*. Translated by Geoffrey Bennington and Brian Massumi. Minneapolis: University of Minnesota Press, 1984 [1979].

MacDowell, James. "Quirky: Buzzword or Sensibility?" In *American Independent Cinema: Indie, Indiewood and Beyond*, edited by Geoff King, Claire Molloy, and Yannis Tzioumakis, 53–64. London: Routledge, 2013.

Madness. "Our House." Track 7 on *The Rise & Fall*. Stiff Records, 1982.

Mailer, Norman, dir. *Maidstone*. Supreme Mix Productions, 1970.

———. *Why Are We in Vietnam?* New York: Picador, 1977.

Main, Alexander. "The U.S. Re-Militarization of Central America and Mexico." *NACLA Report on the Americas* 47, no. 2 (2014): 65–70.

Malinowski, Bronislaw. *Argonauts of the Western Pacific: An Account of Native Enterprise and Adventure in the Archipelagoes of Melanesian New Guinea*. London: Routledge, 2014 [1922].

Malle, Louis, dir. *Murmur of the Heart*. Orion Classics, 1971.

Maná. "Clavado en Un Bar." Track 6 on *Sueños Líquidos*. WEA Latina, 1997.

Mann, Aimee. *Magnolia: Music from the Motion Picture.* Reprise Records, 1999.

Marcel, Gabriel. *Being and Having: An Existentialist Diary.* Translated by Katharine Farrer. New York: Harper & Row, 1965 [1935].

Marche, Stephen. "*Dazed and Confused* Was the Definitive Movie about the '90s, Not the '70s." *Esquire,* March 6, 2013.

Marcus, George E. *Ethnography through Thick and Thin.* Princeton, NJ: Princeton University Press, 1998.

Marcus, George E., and Michael M. J. Fischer. *Anthropology as Cultural Critique: An Experimental Moment in the Human Sciences.* 2nd ed. Chicago: University of Chicago Press, 1999 [1986].

Martin, Emily. *Bipolar Expeditions: Mania and Depression in American Culture.* Princeton, NJ: Princeton University Press, 2009.

Martini, Edwin A. *Invisible Enemies: The American War on Vietnam, 1975–2000.* Amherst: University of Massachusetts Press, 2007.

Marty, Martin E. *Righteous Empire: The Protestant Experience in America.* New York: Dial Press, 1970.

Marx, Karl. *Capital: A Critique of Political Economy.* Vol. 1, *The Process of Capitalist Production.* Edited by Friedrich Engels. Translated by Samuel Moore and Edward Aveling. New York: International Publishers, 1967 [1867].

———. *A Contribution to the Critique of Political Economy.* Edited by Maurice Dobb. Translated by S. W. Ryazanskaya. New York: International Publishers, 1970 [1859].

Marx, Karl, and Friedrich Engels. *The Communist Manifesto.* Edited by Friedrich Engels. Translated by Samuel Moore in cooperation with Friedrich Engels. New York: International Publishers, 1948 [1848].

———. "Theses on Feuerbach." In *The Marx-Engels Reader,* 2nd ed., edited by Robert C. Tucker, 143–45. New York: W. W. Norton, 1978 [1845].

Massumi, Brian. *A User's Guide to Capitalism and Schizophrenia: Deviations from Deleuze and Guattari.* Cambridge, MA: MIT Press, 1992.

Mayer, John. *Battle Studies.* Columbia Records, 2009.

Mazzy Star. "Fade into You." Track 1 on *So Tonight That I Might See.* Capitol Records, 1993.

McClaurin, Irma, ed. *Black Feminist Anthropology: Theory, Politics, Praxis, and Poetics.* New Brunswick, NJ: Rutgers University Press, 2001.

McKinley, James C., Jr. "Texas Conservatives Win Curriculum Change." *New York Times,* March 12, 2010.

Mead, Margaret. *Coming of Age in Samoa.* New York: HarperCollins, 2001 [1928].

Mehlman, Jeffrey. "The 'Floating Signifier': From Lévi-Strauss to Lacan." *Yale French Studies* 48 (1972): 10–37.

Melville, Herman. *Moby-Dick, or, The Whale.* Vol. 6 of *The Northwestern-Newberry Edition of the Writings of Herman Melville.* Edited by Harrison Hayford, Hershel Parker, and G. Thomas Tanselle. Evanston, IL: Northwestern University Press, 2001 [1851].

———. *White-Jacket, or, The World in a Man-of-War.* Vol. 5 of *The Northwestern-Newberry Edition of the Writings of Herman Melville.* Edited by Harrison Hayford, Hershel Parker, and G. Thomas Tanselle. Evanston, IL: Northwestern University Press, 2000 [1850].

Memphis Minnie. "Soo Cow Soo." Track 11 on *Memphis Minnie & Kansas Joe Recordings in Chronological Order.* Vol. 3, *1931–1932.* Document Records, 1991 [1931].

Mendes, Sam, dir. *American Beauty.* DreamWorks Pictures, 1999.

———. Introduction to *American Beauty: The Shooting Script,* by Alan Ball, vii–viii. New York: Newmarket Press, 1999.

Metzl, Jonathan M., and Helena Hansen. "Structural Competency: Theorizing a New Medical Engagement with Stigma and Inequality." *Social Science & Medicine* 103 (2014): 126–33.

Miller, Christian. "With a Grin, Bush Answers Early Charges of Aloofness." *Los Angeles Times,* January 14, 2000.

Millitzer, Joe. "Body Discovered near Washington University's North Campus Building." FOX2Now (online), October 12, 2018.

Milne, David. *America's Rasputin: Walt Rostow and the Vietnam War.* New York: Hill & Wang, 2008.

———. "'Our Equivalent of Guerrilla Warfare': Walt Rostow and the Bombing of North Vietnam, 1961–1968." *Journal of Military History* 71, no. 1 (2007): 169–203.

Mingus, Charles. *The Clown.* Atlantic Records, 1957.

Mintz, Sidney. *Sweetness and Power: The Place of Sugar in Modern History.* New York: Penguin, 1985.

Mitchell, Joni. "All I Want." Track 1 on *Blue.* Reprise Records, 1971.

———. "Big Yellow Taxi." Track 10 on *Ladies of the Canyon.*" Reprise Records, 1970.

Mitford, Jessica. *The American Way of Death Revisited.* New York: Vintage, 2000 [1963].

Modest Mouse. "Float On." Track 3 on *Good News for People Who Love Bad News.* Epic Records, 2004.

Mody, Susan Laird. *Cultural Identity in Kindergarten: A Study of Asian Indian Children in New Jersey.* London: Routledge, 2005.

Mondesire, Zachary. "A Black Exit Interview from Anthropology." *American Anthropologist* 124, no. 3 (2022): 613–16.

Moreiras, Alberto. "Hybridity and Double Consciousness." *Cultural Studies* 13, no. 3 (1999): 373–407.

Morissette, Alanis. "Ironic." Track 10 on *Jagged Little Pill*. Maverick Records and Reprise Records, 1995.

———. "You Learn." Track 7 on *Jagged Little Pill*. Maverick Records and Reprise Records, 1995.

Morris, Errol, dir. *The Fog of War*. Sony Pictures Classics, 2003.

Moskowitz, Nona. "Engagement, Alienation, and Anthropology's New Moral Dilemmas." *Anthropology and Humanism* 40, no. 1 (2015): 35–57.

Munt, Sally R. "A Queer Undertaking: Anxiety and Reparation in the HBO Television Drama Series *Six Feet Under*." *Feminist Media Studies* 6, no. 3 (2006): 263–79.

Murray, Martin. *The Revolution Deferred: The Painful Birth of Post-Apartheid South Africa*. London: Verso, 1994.

My Morning Jacket. *Z*. ATO Records, 2005.

Nada Surf. "See These Bones." Track 1 on *Lucky*. Barsuk Records, 2008.

Nader, Laura. "Up the Anthropologist: Perspectives Gained from Studying Up." In *Reinventing Anthropology*, edited by Dell H. Hymes, 284–311. New York: Vintage, 1969.

Nancy, Jean-Luc. "*La Comparution*/The Compearance: From the Existence of 'Communism' to the Community of 'Existence.'" Translated by Tracy B. Strong. *Political Theory* 20, no. 3 (1992): 371–98.

Navarro, Mireya. "Guatemalan Army Waged 'Genocide,' New Report Finds." *New York Times*, February 26, 1999.

Neate, Rupert. "Trump and Atlantic City: The Lessons behind the Demise of His Casino Empire." *Guardian*, September 2, 2016.

Nelson, Diane M. *Reckoning: The Ends of War in Guatemala*. Durham, NC: Duke University Press, 2009.

Nelson, Maggie. *The Argonauts*. Minneapolis: Graywolf Press, 2015.

Neset, Arne. *Arcadian Waters and Wanton Seas: The Iconology of Waterscapes in Nineteenth-Century Transatlantic Culture*. New York: Peter Lang, 2009.

Newman, Randy. "Strange Things." Track 2 on *Toy Story: An Original Walt Disney Records Soundtrack*. Walt Disney Records, 1995.

The New Pornographers. "Challengers." Track 12 on *Challengers*. Matador Records, 2007.

Ngai, Sianne. *Ugly Feelings*. Cambridge, MA: Harvard University Press, 2005.

Nietzsche, Friedrich. *The Gay Science: With a Prelude in German Rhymes and an Appendix of Songs*. Edited by Bernard Williams. Translated by Josefine Naukhoff. Poems translated by Adrian Del Caro. Cambridge: Cambridge University Press, 2001 [1882].

———. *On the Genealogy of Morals and Ecce Homo*. Edited by Walter Kaufmann. Translated by Walter Kaufmann and R. J. Hollingdale. New York: Vintage, 1967 [1887].

———. "On the Uses and Disadvantages of History for Life." In *Untimely Meditations,* edited by Daniel Breazeale, translated by R. J. Hollingdale, 57–123. Cambridge: Cambridge University Press, 1997 [1876].

———. *Thus Spoke Zarathustra: A Book for All and None.* Edited by Adrian Del Caro and Robert B. Pippin. Translated by Adrian Del Caro. Cambridge: Cambridge University Press, 2006 [1883–85].

Nirvana. "Heart-Shaped Box." Track 3 on *In Utero.* DGC Records, 1993.

———. "Lithium." Track 5 on *Nevermind.* DGC Records, 1991.

———. *Nevermind.* DGC Records, 1991.

———. "Where Did You Sleep Last Night." Track 14 on *MTV Unplugged in New York.* DGC Records, 1994.

Noir Désir. "Le vent nous portera." Track 3 on *Des visages des figures.* Barclay, 2001.

Oasis. "Champagne Supernova." Track 12 on *(What's the Story) Morning Glory?* Creation Records, 1995.

The Offspring. "Gone Away." Track 7 on *Ixnay on the Hombre.* Columbia Records, 1997.

One Direction. "Story of My Life." Track 2 on *Midnight Memories.* Columbia Records, 2013.

O'Neill, Kevin Lewis. *Hunted: Predation and Pentecostalism in Guatemala.* Chicago: University of Chicago Press, 2019.

Ong, Aihwa. *Fungible Life: Experiment in the Asian City of Life.* Durham, NC: Duke University Press, 2016.

Ortiz, Jose De Jesus. "Fowler Won't Lash Out, or Back Down, from Comments on Travel Ban." *St. Louis Post-Dispatch,* February 21, 2017.

Ortner, Sherry B. "Dark Anthropology and Its Others: Theory since the Eighties." *Hau: Journal of Ethnographic Theory* 6, no. 1 (2016): 47–73.

Outkast. "B.O.B." Track 11 on *Stankonia.* Arista Records and LaFace Records, 2000.

———. "Ms. Jackson." Track 5 on *Stankonia.* Arista Records and LaFace Records, 2000.

Paine, Thomas. *Common Sense.* In *The Complete Writings of Thomas Paine.* Vol. 1, edited by Philip S. Foner, 3–72. New York: Citadel Press, 1945 [1776].

Palafox, Ricardo Avila. "Cantinas and Drinkers in Mexico." In *Drinking: Anthropological Approaches,* edited by Igor de Garine and Valerie de Garine, 169–80. New York: Berghahn Books, 2001.

Pandian, Anand. *A Possible Anthropology: Methods for Uneasy Times.* Durham, NC: Duke University Press, 2019.

Panksepp, Jaak. "Neuroevolutionary Sources of Laughter and Social Joy: Modeling Primal Human Laughter in Laboratory Rats." *Behavioural Brain Research* 182, no. 2 (2007): 231–44.

Parkes, Graham. Introduction to *Thus Spoke Zarathustra: A Book for Everyone and Nobody*, by Friedrich Nietzsche, translated by Graham Parkes, ix–xxxiv. Oxford: Oxford University Press, 2005 [1883–85].

Pasolini, Pier Paolo, dir. *Mamma Roma*. Arco Film, 1962.

Paz, Octavio. *The Labyrinth of Solitude and Other Writings*. Translated by Lysander Kemp, Yara Milos, and Rachel Philips Belash. New York: Grove Press, 1985 [1950].

Pearl Jam. "Better Man." Track 11 on *Vitalogy*. Epic Records, 1994.

———. "Corduroy." Track 8 on *Vitalogy*. Epic Records, 1994.

———. "Given to Fly." Track 4 on *Yield*. Epic Records, 1998.

Pels, Peter. "Professions of Duplexity: A Prehistory of Ethical Codes in Anthropology." *Current Anthropology* 40, no. 2 (1999): 101–36.

Petty, Tom. "Don't Fade on Me." Track 8 on *Wildflowers*. Warner Bros. Records, 1994.

———. "You Don't Know How It Feels." Track 2 on *Wildflowers*. Warner Bros. Records, 1994.

———. "You Wreck Me." Track 4 on *Wildflowers*. Warner Bros. Records, 1994.

Petty, Tom, and the Heartbreakers. "Don't Do Me Like That." Track 6 on *Damn the Torpedoes*. Backstreet Records and MCA Records, 1979.

———. "The Waiting." Track 1 on *Hard Promises*. Backstreet Records and MCA Records, 1983.

Phillips, Adam. *On Kissing, Tickling, and Being Bored: Psychoanalytic Essays on the Unexamined Life*. Cambridge, MA: Harvard University Press, 1993.

Phish. "Bouncing around the Room." Track 9 on *Lawn Boy*. Elektra Records, 1992.

———. "Possum." Track 10 on *Hampton Comes Alive*. Elektra Records, 1999.

Pierson, David P. "A Show about Nothing: *Seinfeld* and the Modern Comedy of Manners." *Journal of Popular Culture* 34, no. 1 (2000): 49–64.

Pigg, Stacy Leigh. "On Sitting and Doing: Ethnography as Action in Global Health." *Social Science & Medicine* 99 (2013): 127–34.

Piller, Charles, Edmund Sanders, and Robyn Dixon. "Dark Cloud over Good Works of Gates Foundation." *Los Angeles Times*, January 7, 2007.

Pine, Jason. *The Alchemy of Meth: A Decomposition*. Minneapolis: University of Minnesota Press, 2019.

———. "Last Chance Incorporated." *Cultural Anthropology* 31, no. 2 (2016): 297–318.

Portlandia. Season 2, episode 10, "Brunch Village." Directed by Jonathan Krisel. Aired March 9, 2012, on IFC.

Portugal. The Man. "Feel It Still." Track 4 on *Woodstock*. Atlantic Records, 2017.

The Postal Service. "Such Great Heights." Track 2 on *Give Up*. Sub Pop Records, 2003.

Povinelli, Elizabeth. "Geontologies of the Otherwise." *Fieldsights* (online), January 13, 2014.

Pratt, Julius W. "The Origin of 'Manifest Destiny.'" *American Historical Review* 32, no. 4 (1927): 795–98.

The Pretenders. "Brass in Pocket." Track 10 on *Pretenders*. Sire Records, 1979.

Priest, Dana. "Iraq New Terror Breeding Ground." *Washington Post*, January 14, 2005.

Prince. "Little Red Corvette." Track 2 on *1999*. Warner Bros. Records, 1982.

Puar, Jasbir, ed. "Precarity Talk: A Virtual Roundtable with Lauren Berlant, Judith Butler, Bojana Cvejić, Isabell Lorey, Jasbir Puar, and Ana Vujanović." *TDR/The Drama Review* 56, no. 4 (2012): 163–77.

Putnam, Pat. "'I'm Gonna Hurt This Guy': And Mike Tyson Did, Knocking Out Michael Spinks at 1:31 of Round Number 1." *Sports Illustrated*, July 4, 1988.

Puzo, Mario, and Francis Ford Coppola. *The Annotated Godfather: The Complete Screenplay*. Edited by Jenny M. Jones. New York: Black Dog and Leventhal Publishers, 2007 [1972].

Quesada, James, Laurie K. Hart, and Philippe Bourgois. "Structural Vulnerability and Health: Latino Migrant Laborers in the United States." *Medical Anthropology* 30, no. 4 (2011): 339–62.

Rabinow, Paul. *Reflections on Fieldwork in Morocco*. Berkeley: University of California Press, 1977.

Radford, Phil. "Hasbro Turns Over a New Leaf, Steps Up for Rainforests." *Huffington Post* (online), November 2, 2011.

Radiohead. "Everything in Its Right Place." Track 1 on *Kid A*. Capitol Records, 2000.

———. "High and Dry." Track 3 on *The Bends*. Capitol Records, 1995.

———. *Kid A*. Capitol Records, 2000.

———. "The National Anthem." Track 3 on *Kid A*. Capitol Records, 2000.

Raffles, Hugh. *Insectopedia*. New York: Pantheon, 2010.

Ragland-Sullivan, Ellie. "The Psychical Nature of Trauma: Freud's Dora, the Young Homosexual Woman, and the *Fort! Da!* Paradigm." *Postmodern Culture* (online) 11, no. 2 (2001).

Reber, Dierdra. *Coming to Our Senses: Affect and an Order of Things for a Global Culture*. New York: Columbia University Press, 2016.

Regalado, Samuel O. *Viva Baseball! Latin Major Leaguers and Their Special Hunger*. Urbana: University of Illinois Press, 1998.

Reichardt, Kelly, dir. *Old Joy*. Kino International, 2006.

Reiner, Rob, dir. *This Is Spinal Tap*. Embassy Pictures, 1984.

———, dir. *When Harry Met Sally . . . .* Columbia Pictures, 1989.

R.E.M. "The Flowers of Guatemala." Track 7 on *Life's Rich Pageant*. I.R.S. Records, 1986.

———. "Losing My Religion." Track 2 on *Out of Time*. Warner Bros. Records, 1991.

———. "Orange Crush." Track 7 on *Green*. Warner Bros. Records, 1988.

———. "Talk about the Passion." Track 4 on *Murmur*. I.R.S. Records, 1983.

Riccio, Anthony V. *The Italian American Experience in New Haven: Images and Oral Histories*. Albany: State University of New York Press, 2006.

Rich, Adrienne. *Of Woman Born: Motherhood as Experience and Institution*. New York: W. W. Norton, 1976.

———. "Why I Refused the National Medal for the Arts." In *Essential Essays: Culture, Politics, and the Art of Poetry*, edited by Sandra M. Gilbert, 319–25. New York: W. W. Norton, 2018 [1997].

Rivers-Moore, Megan. *Gringo Gulch: Sex, Tourism, and Social Mobility in Costa Rica*. Chicago: University of Chicago Press, 2016.

Robbins, Joel. "Beyond the Suffering Subject: Toward an Anthropology of the Good." *Journal of the Royal Anthropological Institute* 19, no. 3 (2013): 447–62.

Robinson, Phil Alden, dir. *Field of Dreams*. Universal Pictures, 1989.

Roediger, David R. *The Wages of Whiteness: Race and the Making of the American Working Class*. London: Verso, 1991.

Rolland, Jacques. "Getting Out of Being by a New Path." In *On Escape: De l'évasion*, by Emmanuel Levinas, translated by Bettina Bergo, 3–48. Stanford, CA: Stanford University Press, 2003 [1997].

The Rolling Stones. "Little T & A." Track 4 on *Tattoo You*. Rolling Stones Records, 1981.

———. "Torn and Frayed." Track 7 on *Exile on Main St*. Rolling Stones Records, 1972.

———. "Tumbling Dice." Track 5 on *Exile on Main St*. Rolling Stones Records, 1972.

Ronell, Avital. *Stupidity*. Urbana: University of Illinois Press, 2002.

———. "Support Our Tropes: Reading Desert Storm." In *Rhetorical Republic: Governing Representations in American Politics*, edited by Frederick M. Dolan and Thomas L. Dumm, 13–37. Amherst: University of Massachusetts Press, 1993.

Rosaldo, Renato. *Culture and Truth: The Remaking of Social Analysis*. Boston: Beacon Press, 1989.

Rostow, W. W. *The Stages of Economic Growth: A Non-Communist Manifesto*. Cambridge: Cambridge University Press, 1960.

Rouleau, Eric. "America's Unyielding Policy toward Iraq." *Foreign Affairs* 74, no. 1 (1995): 59–72.

Rousseau, Jean-Jacques. *Essay on the Origins of Languages and Writings Related to Music*. Vol. 7 of *The Collected Writings of Rousseau*. Edited and translated by John T. Scott. Hanover, NH: University Press of New England, 1998 [1781].

Ruane, Michael E. "A Grisly Photo of a Saigon Execution 50 Years Ago Shocked the World and Helped End the War." *Washington Post,* February 1, 2018.

Russell, Andrew. "Book Review." *Durham Anthropology Journal* 18, no. 1 (2012): 211–13.

Russell, Mark. "Mark Russell." In *Life Interrupted: The Unfinished Monologue,* by Spalding Gray, 180–88. New York: Crown Publishers, 2005.

Russo, Richard. *Straight Man.* New York: Vintage, 1997.

Saks, Gene, dir. *The Odd Couple.* Paramount Pictures, 1968.

Samaras, Nicholas. "Wind Telephone." *Prairie Schooner* 92, no. 1 (2018): 102–3.

Sartre, Jean-Paul. *No Exit.* In *No Exit and Three Other Plays,* translated by Stuart Gilbert, 1–46. New York: Vintage, 1989 [1945].

Saunders, Lesley. "Lesley's Story." In *Hidden Loss: Miscarriage & Ectopic Pregnancy,* 2nd ed., edited by Valerie Hey, Catherine Itzin, Lesley Saunders, and Mary Anne Speakman, 10–14. London: Women's Press, 1996 [1989].

Scarry, Elaine. *The Body in Pain: The Making and Unmaking of the World.* Oxford: Oxford University Press, 1985.

Scheper-Hughes, Nancy. *Death without Weeping: The Violence of Everyday Life in Brazil.* Berkeley: University of California Press, 1992.

———. "Ire in Ireland." *Ethnography* 1, no. 1 (2000): 117–40.

———. "The Primacy of the Ethical: Propositions for a Militant Anthropology." *Current Anthropology* 36, no. 3 (1995): 409–40.

Schiffren, Lisa. "Hey, Flyboy." *Wall Street Journal,* May 9, 2003.

Schine, Cathleen. "Elegy to the Void." *New York Review of Books,* November 24, 2011.

Schirmer, Jennifer G. *The Guatemalan Military Project: A Violence Called Democracy.* Philadelphia: University of Pennsylvania Press, 1998.

Schroeder, Charles. "High TV Demand Delays Mayweather-Pacquiao Fight." *Press of Atlantic City,* May 3, 2015.

Schütz, Alfred, and Thomas Luckmann. *Structures of the Life-World.* Vol. 1. Translated by Richard M. Zaner and H. Tristram Engelhardt Jr. Evanston, IL: Northwestern University Press, 1973.

Scorsese, Martin, dir. *Goodfellas.* Warner Bros., 1990.

———, dir. *Italianamerican.* Janus Films, 1974.

Scott, Tony, dir. *Top Gun.* Paramount Pictures, 1986.

Screaming Trees. "Nearly Lost You." Track 2 on *Sweet Oblivion.* Epic Records, 1992.

Segal, Peter, dir. *Tommy Boy.* Paramount Pictures, 1995.

Seger, Bob, & the Silver Bullet Band. "Against the Wind." Track 6 on *Against the Wind.* Capitol Records, 1980.

Seinfeld. Season 2, episode 6, "The Chinese Restaurant." Directed by Tom Cherones. Aired May 23, 1991, on NBC.

———. Season 9, episode 3, "The Serenity Now." Directed by Andy Ackerman. Aired October 9, 1997, on NBC.

Seneca, Lucius Annaeus. *Letters on Ethics: To Lucilius.* The Complete Works of Lucius Annaeus Seneca. Edited by Elizabeth Asmis, Shadi Bartsch, and Martha C. Nussbaum. Translated by Margaret Graver and A. A. Long. Chicago: University of Chicago Press, 2015 [63–65 CE].

Shah, Hetan. "Global Problems Need Social Science." *Nature* 577, no. 7790 (2020): 295.

Shakespeare, William. *King Henry V.* The Arden Shakespeare. Edited by T. W. Craike. New York: Bloomsbury, 1995 [1599].

Sharff, Jagna Wojcicka. *King Kong on 4th Street: Families and the Violence of Poverty on the Lower East Side.* London: Routledge, 2018 [1998].

Sheekman, Arthur. Introduction to *The Groucho Letters: Letters from and to Groucho Marx,* by Groucho Marx, 7–10. New York: Simon & Schuster, 1967.

Shinebourne, Pnina, and Jonathan A. Smith. "'It Is Just Habitual': An Interpretative Phenomenological Analysis of the Experience of Long-Term Recovery from Addiction." *International Journal of Mental Health and Addiction* 9, no. 3 (2011): 282–95.

The Shirelles. "Will You Love Me Tomorrow." Track 4 on *Tonight's the Night.* Scepter Records, 1960.

Shore, Bradd. *Culture in Mind: Cognition, Culture, and the Problem of Meaning.* Oxford: Oxford University Press, 1996.

Simon & Garfunkel. "The Only Living Boy in New York." Track 8 on *Bridge over Troubled Water.* Columbia Records, 1970.

Simone, Nina. "Sinnerman." Track 9 on *Pastel Blues.* Philips Records, 1965.

Sinatra, Frank. "My Way." Track 6 on *My Way.* Reprise Records, 1969.

Sister Hazel. "All for You." Track 3 on *. . . Somewhere More Familiar.* Universal Records, 1997.

Sloterdijk, Peter. "We're Always Riding down Maternity Drive." In *Selected Exaggerations: Conversations and Interviews, 1993–2012,* edited by Bernhard Klein, interview by Mateo Kries, translated by Karen Margolis, 40–48. Cambridge: Polity, 2016 [2013].

Smashing Pumpkins. *Mellon Collie and the Infinite Sadness.* Virgin Records, 1995.

———. "1979." Track 19 on *Mellon Collie and the Infinite Sadness.* Virgin Records, 1995.

Smith, Kevin, dir. *Mallrats.* Gramercy Pictures, 1995.

Smith, Patti. "Gloria." Track 1 on *Horses.* Arista Records.

The Smiths. "Please Please Please Let Me Get What I Want." Track 16 on *Hatful of Hollow.* Rough Trade Records, 1984.

Snowden, Jonathan. "91 Seconds: Mike Tyson, Michael Spinks and the Knock-out That Shook the World." *Bleacher Report* (online), June 27, 2013.

Soderbergh, Steven, dir. *And Everything Is Going Fine*. IFC Films, 2010.

Solondz, Todd, dir. *Life during Wartime*. IFC Films, 2009.

Soul Asylum. "Runaway Train." Track 3 on *Grave Dancers Union*. Columbia Records, 1992.

South Park. Season 1, episode 8, "Starvin' Marvin." Directed by Trey Parker. Aired November 19, 1997, on Comedy Central.

Spears, Britney. "Oops! . . . I Did It Again." Track 1 on *Oops! . . . I Did It Again*. Jive Records, 2000.

Spivak, Gayatri Chakravorty. "An Interview with Gayatri Chakravorty Spivak." Interview by Sara Danius and Stefan Jonsson. *boundary 2* 20, no. 2 (1993): 24–50.

———. "Questions of Multi-culturalism." In *The Post-Colonial Critic: Interviews, Strategies, Dialogues*, edited by Sarah Harasym, interview by Sneja Gunew, 59–66. London: Routledge, 1990.

Stanley, Phiona. *A Critical Auto/Ethnography of Learning Spanish: Intercultural Competence on the* Gringo *Trail?* London: Routledge, 2017.

Sterritt, David. 1998. "Kerouac, Artaud, and the Baroque Period of the Three Stooges." *Mosaic: An Interdisciplinary Critical Journal* 31, no. 4 (1998): 83–98.

Stevens, Cat. "Where Do the Children Play?" Track 1 on *Tea for the Tillerman*. A&M Records, 1970.

Stevenson, Lisa. "The Psychic Life of Biopolitics: Survival, Cooperation, and Inuit Community." *American Ethnologist* 39, no. 3 (2012): 592–613.

Stewart, Kathleen. "Atmospheric Attunements." *Environment and Planning D: Society and Space* 29, no. 3 (2011): 445–53.

———. "In the World That Affect Proposed." *Cultural Anthropology* 32, no. 2 (2017): 192–98.

———. *Ordinary Affects*. Durham, NC: Duke University Press, 2007.

———. *A Space on the Side of the Road: Cultural Poetics in an "Other" America*. Princeton, NJ: Princeton University Press, 1996.

———. "Worlding Refrains." In *The Affect Theory Reader*, edited by Melissa Gregg and Gregory J. Seigworth, 339–53. Durham, NC: Duke University Press, 2010.

Stewart, Kathleen, and Anya E. Liftig. "Scenes of Life/Kentucky Mountains." *Public Culture* 14, no. 2 (2002): 349–59.

Stiller, Ben, dir. *Reality Bites*. Universal Pictures, 1994.

———, dir. *Zoolander*. Paramount Pictures, 2001.

Stoler, Ann Laura. *Duress: Imperial Durabilities in Our Times*. Durham, NC: Duke University Press, 2016.

Stone Temple Pilots. "Still Remains." Track 5 on *Purple*. Atlantic Records, 1994.

The Strokes. "The Adults Are Talking." Track 1 on *The New Abnormal*. Cult Records and RCA Records, 2020.

———. "Last Nite." Track 7 on *Is This It*. RCA Records, 2001.

———. "You Only Live Once." Track 1 on *First Impressions of Earth*. RCA Records, 2005.

Swift, Taylor. "Fifteen." Track 2 on *Fearless*. Big Machine Records, 2008.

Talking Heads. "Life during Wartime." Track 5 on *Fear of Music*. Sire Records, 1979.

Tamburri, Anthony Julian. "Italian Americans and Television." In *The Routledge History of Italian Americans*, edited by William J. Connell and Stanislao G. Pugliese, 451–63. London: Routledge, 2018.

Tarantino, Quentin, dir. *Pulp Fiction*. Miramax Films, 1994.

Tarasti, Eero. "Existential Semiotics and Cultural Psychology." In *The Oxford Handbook of Culture and Psychology*, edited by Jaan Valsiner, 316–43. Oxford: Oxford University Press, 2012.

Tati, Jacques, dir. *Trafic*. Les Films Corona, 1971.

Taussig, Michael. *Defacement: Public Secrecy and the Labor of the Negative*. Stanford, CA: Stanford University Press, 1999.

———. *My Cocaine Museum*. Chicago: University of Chicago Press, 2004.

Taylor, Frederick Winslow. *Scientific Management, Comprising: Shop Management, The Principles of Scientific Management, Testimony before the Special House Committee*. Edited by Kenneth Thompson. London: Routledge, 2003 [1903–12].

Taylor, Janelle S. "The Story Catches You and You Fall Down: Tragedy, Ethnography, and 'Cultural Competence.'" *Medical Anthropology Quarterly* 17, no. 2 (2003): 159–81.

10,000 Maniacs. "These Are Days." Track 2 on *Our Time in Eden*. Elektra Records, 1992.

Third Eye Blind. "Jumper." Track 4 on *Third Eye Blind*. Elektra Records, 1997.

———. "Semi-Charmed Life." Track 3 on *Third Eye Blind*. Elektra Records, 1997.

Thomas, Kedron. *Regulating Style: Intellectual Property Law and the Business of Fashion in Guatemala*. Berkeley: University of California Press, 2016.

Thompson, E. P. "The Long Revolution (Part I)." *New Left Review*, no. 9 (1961): 24–33.

Thompson, John B. "Editor's Introduction." In *Language and Symbolic Power*, by Pierre Bourdieu, edited by John B. Thompson, translated by Gino Raymond and Matthew Adamson, 1–31. Cambridge, MA: Harvard University Press, 1991.

Traveling Wilburys. "Handle with Care." Track 1 on *Traveling Wilburys Vol. 1.* Warner Bros. Records, 1988.

The Treniers. "Holy Mackerel, Andy!" Track 28 on *This Is It!* Rev-Ola Records, 2008 [1957].

Trouillot, Michel-Rolph. *Global Transformations: Anthropology and the Modern World.* New York: Palgrave Macmillan, 2003.

Trudeau, Justin Thomas. "Stooging the Body, Stooging the Text: Jack Kerouac's *Visions of Cody.*" *Text and Performance Quarterly* 27, no. 4 (2007): 334–50.

Tsing, Anna. "Supply Chains and the Human Condition." *Rethinking Marxism: A Journal of Economics, Culture & Society* 21, no. 2 (2009): 148–76.

Turnbull, Colin. *The Forest People.* New York: Simon & Schuster, 1961.

Turner, Victor. *The Forest of Symbols: Aspects of Ndembu Ritual.* Ithaca, NY: Cornell University Press, 1967.

Ungar, Jay. "Ashokan Farewell." Track 3 on *The Civil War: Original Soundtrack Recording.* Elektra Nonesuch Records, 1990.

US Department of Justice, Civil Rights Division. *The Ferguson Report: Department of Justice Investigation of the Ferguson Police Department.* New York: New Press, 2015.

Vampire Weekend. "Unbearably White." Track 7 on *Father of the Bride.* Columbia Records, 2019.

Van Hollen, Cecilia. "Invoking *Vali:* Painful Technologies of Modern Birth in South India." *Medical Anthropology Quarterly* 17, no. 1 (2003): 49–77.

Van Maanen, John. *Tales of the Field: On Writing Ethnography.* Chicago: University of Chicago Press, 1988.

Van Sant, Gus, dir. *My Own Private Idaho.* Fine Line Features, 1991.

———, dir. *Paranoid Park.* IFC Films, 2007.

Vedder, Eddie. "Setting Forth." Track 1 on *Into the Wild: Music for the Motion Picture.* J Records, 2007.

———. "Society." Track 8 on *Into the Wild: Music for the Motion Picture.* J Records, 2007.

Verhoeven, Paul, dir. *RoboCop.* Orion Pictures, 1987.

The Verve. "Bitter Sweet Symphony." Track 1 on *Urban Hymns.* Hut Records, 1997.

The Verve Pipe. *Villains.* RCA Records, 1996.

The Wachowskis, dirs. *The Matrix.* Warner Bros., 1999.

Walsh, Carl E. "What Caused the 1990–1991 Recession?" *Federal Reserve Bank of San Francisco Economic Review* no. 2 (1993): 33–48.

Watson, Jay. "Guys and Dolls: Exploratory Repetition and Maternal Subjectivity in the Fort/Da Game." *American Imago* 52, no. 4 (1995): 463–503.

Weales, Gerald. "Mailer's *Maidstone.*" *North American Review* 257, no. 2 (1972): 62–64.

Wedge, Chris, dir. *Ice Age.* 20th Century Fox, 2002.

Weissman, Gary E., Raymond J. Morris, Carrie Ng, Anthony S. Pozzessere, Kevin C. Scott, and Marc J. Altshuler. "Global Health at Home: A Student-Run Community Health Initiative for Refugees." *Journal of Health Care for the Poor and Underserved* 23, no. 3 (2012): 942–48.

Welander, Marta, and Leonie Ansems De Vries. "Refugees, Displacement, and the European 'Politics of Exhaustion.'" *openDemocracy* (online), September 30, 2016.

West, Kanye. "All Falls Down." Track 4 on *The College Dropout.* Roc-A-Fella Records, 2004.

Wexler, Haskell, dir. *Medium Cool.* Paramount Pictures, 1969.

Wharton, Edith. *The Age of Innocence.* New York: Scribner, 2020 [1920].

Whiskeytown. "Excuse Me While I Break My Own Heart Tonight." Track 2 on *Strangers Almanac.* Outpost Recordings, 1997.

Whitehead, Alfred North. *Process and Reality: An Essay in Cosmology.* Edited by David R. Griffin and Donald W. Sherburne. New York: Free Press, 1978 [1927–28].

Whitman, Walt. *Leaves of Grass: A Textual Variorum of the Printed Poems.* Vol. 1, *Poems 1855–1856.* The Collected Writings of Walt Whitman. Edited by Sculley Bradley, Harold W. Blodgett, Arthur Golden, and William White. New York: New York University Press, 1980 [1855–56].

Whorf, Benjamin Lee. *Language, Thought, and Reality: Selected Writings of Benjamin Lee Whorf.* Edited by John B. Carroll. Cambridge, MA: MIT Press, 1956.

Williams, Bernard. *Shame and Necessity.* Berkeley: University of California Press, 1993.

Williams, Lucinda. "Are You Alright?" Track 1 on *West.* Lost Highway Records, 2007.

Williams, Raymond. *The Country and the City.* Oxford: Oxford University Press, 1973.

Williamson, Alan. "The Divided Image: The Quest for Identity in the Works of Djuna Barnes." *Critique: Studies in Contemporary Fiction* 7, no. 1 (1964): 58–74.

Wolfe, Tom. *The Right Stuff.* New York: Picador, 1979.

Wolfe, Tom, and E. W. Johnson, eds. *The New Journalism.* New York: Harper & Row, 1973.

Worden, Daniel, and Alex Trimble Young. "On Joan Didion: An Introduction." *a/b: Auto/Biography Studies* 31, no. 3 (2016): 581–86.

World Bank. *Vietnam—Delivering on Its Promise: Development Report 2003.* Washington, DC: World Bank, 2002.

World Party. *Private Revolution*. Chrysalis Records, 1987.

Wright, Steven. "Water." Track 8 on *I Have a Pony*. Pyramids and Ponies Music, 1985.

Wu, Kuang-Ming. *On Metaphoring: A Cultural Hermeneutic*. Leiden, The Netherlands: Brill, 2001.

Yamamuro, Takuya, Kouji Senzaki, Satomi Iwamoto, Yoshimi Nakagawa, Takashi Hayashi, Miyo Hori, Shigeko Sakamoto, Kazuo Murakami, Takashi Shiga, and Osamu Urayama. "Neurogenesis in the Dentate Gyrus of the Rat Hippocampus Enhanced by Tickling Stimulation with Positive Emotion." *Neuroscience Research* 68, no. 4 (2010): 285–89.

Yeats, W. B. "The Land of Heart's Desire." In *The Collected Works of W. B. Yeats*. Vol. 2, *The Plays*, edited by David R. Clark and Rosalind E. Clark, 65–81. New York: Scribner, 2001 [1894].

Yo La Tengo. *I Can Hear the Heart Beating as One*. Matador Records, 1997.

Young, Neil. "Harvest Moon." Track 4 on *Harvest Moon*. Reprise Records, 1992.

———. "Natural Beauty." Track 10 on *Harvest Moon*. Reprise Records, 1992.

———. "The Needle and the Damage Done." Track 9 on *Harvest*. Reprise Records, 1972.

———. *Tonight's the Night*. Reprise Records, 1975.

———. "Unknown Legend." Track 1 on *Harvest Moon*. Reprise Records, 1992.

Young, Neil & Crazy Horse. *Everybody Knows This Is Nowhere*. Reprise Records, 1969.

———. "Pocahontas." Track 4 on *Rust Never Sleeps*. Reprise Records, 1979.

Zaloom, Caitlin. *Indebted: How Families Make College Work at Any Cost*. Princeton, NJ: Princeton University Press, 2019.

Zemeckis, Robert, dir. *Forrest Gump*. Paramount Pictures, 1994.

Zierler, David. *The Invention of Ecocide: Agent Orange, Vietnam, and the Scientists Who Changed the Way We Think about the Environment*. Athens: University of Georgia Press, 2011.

Žižek, Slavoj. *The Puppet and the Dwarf: The Perverse Core of Christianity*. Cambridge, MA: MIT Press, 2003.

———. *The Sublime Object of Ideology*. London: Verso, 1989.

Index

"Autobiography Now" (Gray), 21
"Avant Gardener" (Burnett), 82

Bakhtin, Mikhail M., 100
Band, The, 41
Band of Outsiders (Godard), 104
Bard, Kim A., 221, 222
Barry, Ann Marie Seward, 125
Barth, Fredrik, 174
Barthes, Roland, 223
baseball, 270; author's childhood and, 119–
    20, 163; colonialism/imperialism and,
    256, 257–58; Guatemalan visitors and,
    255–56; pepper game and, 268–69
Baseball (Burns and Novick), 126
basketball, 101
Bataille, Georges, 231, 232, 273
Battle Studies (Mayer), 141
Baudrillard, Jean, 12, 124, 125
Beacon Theatre, 56–57, *57*, 58
Beatles, The, 7, 17, 21, 69, 105, 270, 275
"Beautiful Boy (Darling Boy)" (Lennon and
    Ono), 243
Beauvoir, Simone de, *9*
Beck, 18
Before Sunrise (Linklater and Krizan), 66, 67,
    70, 72, 75, 76, 78, 81, 85, 87, 89
Behar, Ruth, 30, 34, 53, 280, 281
Being and Having (Marcel), 175, 277
Belton, Robert J., 1
"Benediction" (Fitzgerald), 172
Ben Folds Five, 239
Benjamin, Walter, 144, 146–47, 184
Benson, Peter, *8, 119, 159, 248*; "Anthropol-
    ogy in the Clinic," 247; *Broccoli and
    Desire,* 246. *See also Tobacco Capitalism*;
    entries beginning with author
Bento, Berenice, 150
Benveniste, Émile, 273
Bergson, Henri, 187
Berigan, Bunny, 198
Berlant, Lauren, 31; *Cruel Optimism,* 278;
    The Female Complaint, 18; "Genre Flail-
    ing," 16, 101; "Intimacy," 218, 236;
    "Nearly Utopian, Nearly Normal," 250;
    "Slow Death," 154, 183, 184
Bernstein, Robin, 130
Berra, Yogi, 193
Betancourt, Joseph R., 247
"Better Man" (Pearl Jam), 189, 243
Better Than Ezra, 87
Beyoncé, 7. *See also* Carters, The
Beyond the Pleasure Principle (Freud), 101–2

"Beyond the Suffering Subject" (Robbins), 5,
    290
Bhabha, Homi K., 44, 52, 83, 110, 111, 174,
    183, 185, 186, 187
Bible, 77, 118, 242, 285, 286, 288
Biehl, João, 6, 38
Big Lebowski, The (Joel and Ethan Coen),
    188
"Big Toe, The" (Bataille), 231
"Big Yellow Taxi" (Mitchell), 277
biopower, 252
bipolar disorder. *See* mental illness
Bipolar Expeditions (Martin), 14
Birth of the Clinic, The (Foucault), 53
"Bitter Sweet Symphony" (The Verve), 7
"Black Balloon" (Goo Goo Dolls), 233
"Black Exit Interview from Anthropology, A"
    (Mondesire), 278
Black Feminist Anthropology (McClaurin),
    281
Black Lives Matter protests, 19, 112, 259,
    263
Blake, William, 131
Blind Melon, 298
Blink-182, 101
Blue Nights (Didion), 238
board games: adolescence and, 202, 270;
    Monopoly, 117, 118, 150; Stratego, 202–
    3; war in popular culture and, 126, 130
"B.O.B." (Outkast), 116, 173, 278
Body in Pain, The (Scarry), 232
"Bonobo Sex and Society" (de Waal), 193
Borderlands/La Frontera (Anzaldúa), 249
"Bouncing around the Room" (Phish), 212
Bourdieu, Pierre, 5, 75, 263
Bourgois, Philippe, 285
Bowie, David, 174
boxing: cornerman, 268; Pacquiao-May-
    weather fight, 108–12, *109*, 136; Tyson-
    Spinks fight, 116, *117*, 120–22, *121*
"Boys of Summer, The" (Henley), 118
Boyz II Men, 182
"Brass in Pocket" (The Pretenders), 105
Braxton, Toni, 190
Brettell, Caroline B., 25
"Brick" (Ben Folds Five), 239
Broccoli and Desire (Fischer and Benson),
    246
Broken Flowers (Jarmusch), 296
Brown, Michael, 258
Browning, Elizabeth Barrett, 195
Browning, Robert, 242
"Brunch Village" (*Portlandia*), 87

Buckley, Jeff, 1, 299
Buck-Morss, Susan, 17
Burke, Nancy J., 97
Burnett, Courtney, 82
Burns, Ken, 107, 126, 163, 215
Bush, George H. W., 106, 107, 129
Bush, George W., 106, 127–29, 130, 131,
     136; speeches, 128, 129
Bush, Prescott, 107
Butler, Judith, 40, 50, 53, 125, 238, 239,
     249
Byrds, The, 3, 18

Callahan, James E., *155*
Canterbury Tales, The (Chaucer), 137
"Cantinas and Drinkers in Mexico" (Palafox),
     241
Capital (Marx), 11
Cappuccino, Frank, 121, *121*
Caputo, John, 293
Carmichael, Hoagy, 10
"Carry That Weight" (The Beatles), 17
Carter, Jimmy, 118
Carters, The, 7, 14
"Case for Letting Anthropology Burn, The"
     (Jobson), 4
"Case of Mistaken Identity, The" (Ginsberg),
     25
Castañeda, Quetzil E., 280
Castillo Armas, Carlos, 251
@catcontentonly, 86
Celermajer, Danielle, 38
Chaffin, Larry Wayne, 139, *140*, 146
Chakrabarty, Dipesh, 72, 212, 260
"Challengers" (New Pornographers), 10
"Champagne Supernova" (Oasis), 155
Chapman, Tracy, 7
Chaucer, Geoffrey, 137
Childish Gambino, 298
"Chinese Restaurant, The" (*Seinfeld*), 75
Chinoise, La (Godard), 97
Christianity: author's childhood and, 173–
     75; author's relationship with father and,
     118–19; Bible, 77, 118, 242, 285, 286,
     288; hypocrisy and, 285, 288–89; lost
     religion and, 214, 267, 272
Civil War, The (Burns), 126, 215
"Clavado en Un Bar" (Maná), 271
Clifford, James, 250, 281
Clinton, Bill, 131, 260
Clown, The (Mingus), 181
Cocker, Joe, 105
Cocoon (Howard), 182

Cohen, Esther, 223
Coldplay, 7, 10, 192, 272, 299
Cold War, 150, 252
Cole, Nat King, 10
Cole, Teju, 253, 262
colonialism/imperialism: anthropology pro-
     fession and, 247–48, 250–53, 258–60,
     281; baseball and, 256, 257–58; ethno-
     graphic practice and, 12, 13; Guatemala
     and, 250–53, 258–59, 261–62; Manifest
     Destiny, 255–56; Vietnam War and, 148,
     150–52. *See also* decolonization rhetoric
Coming of Age in Samoa (Mead), 193
Coming to Our Senses (Reber), 17
Common Sense (Paine), 150
Communist Manifesto, The (Marx and
     Engels), 67, 75
*Community of Those Who Have Nothing in
     Common, The* (Lingis), 267
"*Comparution, La*/The Compearance"
     (Nancy), 217, 259
Conant, James Bryant, 258
Connecticut. *See* author's Connecticut
     adolescence
Conrad, Joseph, 95
"Constant Craving" (lang), 21
*Contribution to the Critique of Political Econ-
     omy, A* (Marx), 90
"Control and Becoming" (Deleuze), 81
Cooleyhighharmony (Boyz II Men), 182
"Corduroy" (Pearl Jam), 7, 190
Coronil, Fernando, 276
corporate social responsibility, 133–34, 135,
     261–62
Corporeal Generosity (Diprose), 35
Costello, Elvis, 179
Counting Crows, 2, 9, 16, 241
Country and the City, The (Williams), 126
Courteeners, The, 296
"Cradle Song, A" (Blake), 131
Cranberries, The, 191, 228, 298
Crapanzano, Vincent, 34
Creedence Clearwater Revival, 276
Critchley, Simon, 203
critical analysis: anthropology profession
     and, 25, 27, 278–79; Guatemala and,
     250–53, 258; life choices and, 261, 289–
     91, 293–95; neighborhood choice and,
     64–65, 73–76, 84–85, 88–89; tobacco
     book and, 27–28, 29–30, 31, 33, 35, 36,
     37; within academic employment, 78–79,
     81–84, 92–93, 292. *See also* colonialism/
     imperialism

Founded in 1893,
UNIVERSITY OF CALIFORNIA PRESS
publishes bold, progressive books and journals
on topics in the arts, humanities, social sciences,
and natural sciences—with a focus on social
justice issues—that inspire thought and action
among readers worldwide.

The UC PRESS FOUNDATION
raises funds to uphold the press's vital role
as an independent, nonprofit publisher, and
receives philanthropic support from a wide
range of individuals and institutions—and from
committed readers like you. To learn more, visit
ucpress.edu/supportus.